Claire

W9-CLM-105

Dictionary of
World War I

Dictionary of
World War I

NTC *Publishing Group*
Lincolnwood, Illinois USA

Cataloging in Publication Data
is available from the United States Library of Congress

© 1997 by NTC Publishing Group, 4255 West Touhy Avenue,
Lincolnwood (Chicago), Illinois 60646-1975 U.S.A.
Manufactured in the United Kingdom.

Contents

About the author

Ian Vernon Hogg was born in 1926. He enlisted in the Regular Army (Royal Artillery) during WWII and served in Europe and the Far East during the Korean War with various field and Horse Artillery regiments. Qualifying as a gunnery instructor in 1953, Mr Hogg served on the staff of the Royal School of Artillery teaching artillery equipment, ammunition and explosives. A further qualification in electronic warfare and counter–bombardment followed in 1959–60 and he became Warrant Officer in charge of trials 1961–66. Promoted to Master Gunner in 1965, he was posted to the instructional staff at the Royal Military College of Science. Reaching retirement age in 1972, Mr Hogg became a full-time writer specializing in defence journalism. Ian Hogg has written, contributed or edited over 100 books on military subjects and is a contributor to over 25 specialist magazines internationally.

Married with two sons and one daughter, Mr Hogg lives in Worcestershire.

Picture credits
1, 2, 3, 7 courtesy of the author (Ian V Hogg) and 4, 5, 6, 8, 9, 10, 11 courtesy of Topham Picture Source.

Chronologies, tables and maps

World War I

1914 June	Assassination of Archduke Franz Ferdinand of Austria 28 June.
July	German government issued 'blank cheque' to Austria, offering support in war against Serbia. Austrian ultimatum to Serbia. Serbs accepted all but two points. Austria refused to accept compromise and declared war. Russia began mobilization to defend Serbian ally. Germany demanded Russian demobalization.
Aug	Germany declared war on Russia. France mobilized to assist Russian ally. Germans occupied Luxembourg and demanded access to Belgian territory, which was refused. Germany declared war on France and invaded Belgium. Britain declared war on Germany, then on Austria. Dominions within the Empire, including Australia, automatically involved. Battle of Tannenburg between Central Powers and Russians. Russian army encircled.
Sept	British and French troops halted German advance just short of Paris, and drove them back. First battle of the Marne, and of the Aisne. Beginning of trench warfare.
Oct-Nov	First battle of Ypres. Britain declared war on Turkey.
1915 April–May	Gallipoli offensive launched by British and dominion troops against Turkish forces. Second Battle of Ypres. First use of poison gas by Germans. Italy joined war against Austria. German submarine sank ocean liner *Lusitania* 7 May, later helping to bring USA into the war.
Aug-Sept	Warsaw evacuated by the Russians. Battle of Tarnopol. Vilna taken by the Germans. Tsar Nicholas II took supreme control of Russian forces.
1916 Jan	Final evacuation of British and Dominion troops from Gallipoli
Feb	German offensive against Verdun began, with huge losses for little territorial gain
May	Naval battle of Jutland between British and German imperial fleets ended inconclusively, but put a stop to further German naval participation in the war.
June	Russian (Brusilov) offensive against the Ukraine began.
July–Nov	First Battle of the Somme, a sustained Anglo-French offensive which won little territory and lost a huge number of lives.
Aug	Hindenburg and Ludendorff took command of the German armed forces. Romania entered the war against Austria but was rapidly overrun.

Sept	Early tanks used by British on Western Front.
Nov	Nivelle replaced Joffre as commander of French forces. Battle of the Ancre on the Western Front.
Dec	French completed recapture of Verdun fortifications. Austrians occupied Bucharest.
1917 Feb	Germany declared unrestricted submarine warfare. Russian Revolution began and tsarist rule overthrown.
March	British seizure of Baghdad and occupation of Persia.
March–April	Germans retreated to Siegfried Line (Arras–Soissons) on Western Front.
April–May	USA entered the war against Germany. Unsuccessful British and French offensives. Mutinies among French troops. Nivelle replaced by Pétain.
July–Nov	Third Ypres offensive including Battle of Passchendaele.
Sept	Germans occupied Riga.
Oct–Nov	Battle of Caporetto saw Italian troops defeated by Austrians.
Dec	Jerusalem taken by British forces under Allenby.
1918 Jan	US President Woodrow Wilson proclaimed 'Fourteen Points' as a basis for peace settlement.
March	Treaty of Brest–Litovsk with Central Powers ended Russian participation in the war, with substantial concessions of territory and reparations. Second Battle of the Somme began with German spring offensive.
July–Aug	Allied counter-offensive, including tank attack at Amiens, drove Germans back to the Siegfried Line.
Sept	Hindenburg and Ludendorff called for an armistice.
Oct	Armistice offered on the basis of the 'Fourteen Points'. Germany went into exile. Provisional government under social democrat Friedrich Ebert formed. Germany agreed armistice. Fighting on Western Front stopped.
1919 Jan	Peace conference opened at Versailles.
May	Demands presented to Germany.
June	Germany signed peace treaty, followed by other Central Powers; Austria (Treaty of St Germain-en-Laye, Sept), Bulgaria (Neuilly, Nov), Hungary (Trianon, June 1920), and Turkey (Sèvres, Aug 1920).

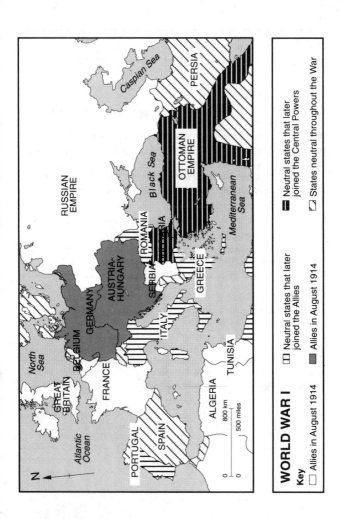

WORLD WAR I
Key

☐ Allies in August 1914

▨ Allies in August 1914

⊡ Neutral states that later joined the Allies

▮ Neutral states that later joined the Central Powers

▨ States neutral throughout the War

A

Aboukir, HMS British armoured cruiser of the Cressy class, built 1898–1901. The Aboukir and its sister ships, ◊HMS Hogue and ◊HMS Cressy were all sunk 22 Sept 1914 by the German submarine U-9 some 30 km/20 mi off the Hook of Holland, with the loss of 25 officers and 535 seamen. It is the only known occasion of three warships being sunk in succession by a single submarine.

Abu Tellul, Battle of engagement between British and Turkish forces, 14 July 1918. The Turkish army had advanced north and east of Jericho, capturing the village of Abu Tellul, but were then halted by British advanced posts. After a counter-attack by the ◊Australian Light Horse the Turkish force was trapped between the British and Australians and defeated. Some 350 prisoners were captured and the village retaken.

Achi Baba barren hill ridge in ◊Gallipoli, about 180 m/600 ft high, which forms a barrier across the western end of the peninsula. It was fortified by the Turkish Army 1915 and the early part of the ◊Dardanelles campaign was dominated by British attempts to take the ridge.

Acre seaport of Palestine, 130 km/80 mi NW of Jerusalem, captured by British and Commonwealth cavalry under General ◊Allenby, 23 Sept 1918.

acrolein gas, used by the French under the code-name 'Papite'. Produced by the dehydration of glycerin, acrolein is a lachrymator and lung irritant, though in heavy concentrations it can be toxic. It was used as a filling for artillery shells and ◊hand grenades but its lack of chemical stability made it difficult to store and it saw relatively little service use.

AEG (*Allgemeine Elektrische Gemeinschaft*). German electrical company which designed the Model G IV twin-engined biplane bombing aircraft. Based on an original design of 1914, the early models were in service from 1915 onward. The design was gradually improved to arrive at the Model G IV of which some 400 were built.

With a crew of three or four men and armed with two machine guns, the G IV could carry 350 kg/770 lb of bombs at 145 kph/90 mph for about 650 km/400 mi. Due to these limitations on its range, the plane was not used against Britain, but it was extensively employed in support of German ground operations against targets in Europe and the Middle East.

Agincourt, HMS British warship, part of the British Grand Fleet, which fought at ◊Jutland. Originally commissioned 1910 from the Tyneside Armstrong shipyard for the Brazilian navy, it was sold shortly after its launch in 1913 to Turkey. As the ship was nearing completion Aug 1914, it was appropriated by the British Admiralty and became HMS Agincourt. By 1918 the Agincourt was obsolescent and armed with 14 12- inch guns which differed from the current standard, and so was scrapped 1921.

F stands for 'Fritz' who flies in the sky,
To bring down the brute we've had many a try,
But the shells we shoot with, all pass him by
And fall in Mesopotamia.
                    Poem in *BEF Times* on ***air defence*** 20 Jan 1917.

---

air defence general term for defence against attack by aircraft and usually divided into two forms, passive and active. ***Passive*** air defence includes such measures as black-outs, air raid shelters, and balloon defences; ***active*** defences include anti-aircraft guns and fighter aircraft.

air raid aerial attack against a ground target, usually dropping bombs from aircraft. Air raids began during World War I, with the advent of military aviation. The first raids were carried out by airships, since only they had the necessary range, but later in the war areoplanes were also used, as their performance improved. Raids were generally against

Air Raids on Britain 1914–18: Casualties and Damage

	raids	bombs	killed	injured
Britain as a whole				
by airship	51	5,806	567	1,358
by aircraft	52	2,772	857	2,058
total	103	8,578	1,414	3,416
Greater London				
by airship	12	746	183	518
by aircraft	19	1,078	687	1,444
total	31	1,624	870	1,880
London as a percentage				
of total figures for Britain	28%	21%	48%	57%

(Comparable figures for air raids on Germany: bombs dropped, 14,208; casualties, 2,589; damage caused, RM24 m/£1.2 m.)

military targets such as railway stations, camps, and supply dumps, but as the war went on there were more attacks against strategic targets such as factories and marshalling yards and against cities.Bombing was generally indiscriminate due to the difficulty of accurately aiming the primitive bombs in use at the time.

There were 103 air raids on Britain 1915–18, of which 51 were carried out by airships, 52 by aircraft. Between them they dropped some 8,578 bombs, killing 1,414 people and injuring another 3,416. About one fourth of these raids were on London, which sustained half the total casualties from air raids; Paris suffered at a comparable rate. Most of the Allied effort was directed against military targets behind the German lines, although the Italians specialized in long-range bombing attacks (see under ◊Caproni).

airship (or *dirigible*) any aircraft that is lighter than air and power-driven, consisting of an elliptical balloon that forms the streamlined envelope or hull and has below it the propulsion system (propellers), steering mechanism, and space for crew, passengers, and/or cargo.

The balloon section is filled with lighter-than-air gas; during World War I this was the easily ignited and highly inflammable hydrogen, although post-war models used helium. The envelope's form is maintained by internal pressure in the nonrigid ('blimp') and semirigid (in which the nose and tail sections have a metal framework connected by a rigid keel) types. The rigid type (such as the German ◊Zeppelin and Schutte-Lanz models) maintains its form using an internal framework. Both Britain and Germany used airships during the war. The British mainly used small machines for naval reconnaisance and patrolling the North Sea. Germany used Schutte-Lanz and Zeppelin machines for similar patrol work and also for long-range bombing attacks against London and other English cities, and Paris and some northern French cities.

Aisne, Battles of three battles between Allied and German forces in France.

The *first battle* took place 14–20 Sept 1914 on a 150 km/100 mi front between Compeigne and Tahure, near Reims. The German forces (1st, 2nd, 3rd, and 4th Armies) had fallen back from the ◊Marne and entrenched north of the river Aisne with a considerable strength of artillery. The Allies launched a frontal attack, crossing the river with great difficulty, and eventually gained the crest of the ridge and the ◊Chemin des Dames which ran along it. A lack of heavy artillery prevented the Allies from making further gains and both sides dug trenches and remained on this line for most of the war.

The *second battle* took place April 16–May 20 1917. General Nivelle planned to throw 27 French divisions against the main German position and so force a decision within 48 hours. The plan was compromised when the Germans captured a copy of Nivelle's orders, and so were able to reinforce both infantry and artillery and prepare a full defence. The French were hampered by snow and rain, overwhelmed by machine gun fire, and forced to advance without support due to the late arrival of their tanks, but nevertheless managed to penetrate some 6 km/4 mi into the German positions before being stopped. French losses came to about 187,000; the Germans lost some 163,000. This heavy casualty rate was one of the factors leading to the mutinies in the French Army the following month.

The *third battle* took place May 27–June 18 1918 and was launched by the German 1st and 7th armies against the British 9th Army Corps and 5th French Army. The German attack broke through and advanced about 16 km/10 mi toward Chateau-Thierry, placing Paris under threat, before their lack of reserves and overstretched supply lines brought them to a halt.

Albatros German fighter aircraft, the DIII model was one of the most significant fighter designs of the war, allowing the German air force to maintain air superiority over the Western Front throughout the first half of 1917. A highly streamlined biplane armed with two machine guns, the DIII could attain a speed of 175 kph/110 mph and was flown by such aces as von ◊Richthofen and ◊Boelke.

The Albatros Aeroplane Factory was founded 1910 at Johannisthal, Berlin. It began by making ◊Taube aircraft, then moved on to its own designs.

Albert, Battle of battle between French and Germans, Sept 20–30 1914, part of the '◊Race to the Sea'. Elements of the 2nd French Army attempted to outflank von Kluck's German forces which were also attempting to make a flanking movement, so leading to a stalemate. This was resolved by the arrival of the German 6th Army under Prince Rupert. The French were forced back but in turn augmented their forces with the 10th French Army under General Maud'huy and outflanking movements began once more, ending in entrenched lines from Albert to Noyon. There was no subsequent major change in these positions until the German retreat of 1917.

Albert I 1875–1934. King of the Belgians 1909–34. He was commander of the Allied army that retook the Belgian coast 1918 and re-entered Brussels in triumph Nov 22.

The younger son of Philip, Count of Flanders, and the nephew of Leopold II, he married Duchess Elisabeth of Bavaria 1900. He was killed while mountaineering in the Ardennes.

Alexeyev Mikhail V 1855–1918. Russian military commander, Chief of Staff 1915–17. The son of a private soldier, he enlisted in the infantry and fought in the Russo-Turkish war of 1877, after which he obtained a place at the Nikolaevsky Military Academy and was commissioned. He served as quartermaster-general in Manchuria during the Russo-Japanese War and became Chief of Staff 3rd Army after the battle of Mukden 1905. In 1914 he was Chief of Staff to General Ivanoff on the SE front, becoming Chief of Staff to the Russian Army in 1915. After the March 1917 revolution he was replaced by General ◊Brusilov, and after the November Revolution, together with other generals, he formed the Volunteer Army to fight Bolshevism. He died of pneumonia on 25 Sept 1918.

Allenby General Henry Hynman 1861–1936. British field marshal, commander of British forces in the Middle East 1917–19. He initially served in France before taking command in the Middle East. His defeat of the Turkish forces at Megiddo in Palestine Sept 1918 was followed almost immediately by the capitulation of Turkey. He became high commissioner in Egypt 1919–35.

Allenstein town in Poland, now known as Olstejn. In 1914 it was in East Prussia and was the headquarters and garrison of the German 2∪th Corps. In Aug 1914 the town was captured by the Russian army but later abandoned during operations leading to the battle of ◊Tannenberg.

Allies in World War I, the 23 countries allied against the ◊Central Powers, including France, Italy, Russia, the UK, Australia and other Commonwealth nations, and, in the latter part of the war, the USA.

Alpini Italian elite mountain troops. They were recruited mainly in the Alpine districts, whence their name and were trained for operations in mountainous country. Formed into 8 special regiments and 38 companies of militia, they used mule transport and were all adept mountaineers and skiers. Among their exploits was the capture, April 1916, of the Adamello Glacier from an Austrian force during a snowstorm at an altitude of over 3,000 m/10,000 ft.

amatol high explosive used by the British and American armies. It is a mixture of TNT and ammonium nitrate, the proportion of the latter varying from 40 to 80 percent of the mixture. Introduced in Britain 1915 to economize on TNT, supplies of which were then limited. It was used as a filling for artillery shells, aerial bombs, mines, and ◊hand grenades, and particular attention had to be paid to waterproofing these munitions, since amatol absorbs atmospheric humidity.

American Expeditionary Force (AEF) US forces sent to fight in Europe after the USA entered the war. On 1 April 1917 the strength of the US Regular Army stood at 5,791 officers and 121,797 enlisted men;

the National Guard had 3,733 officers and 76,713 Guardsmen; while the Army reserve held about 4,000 men of all ranks. Of this total a token force of one division, under General Pershing, was immediately sent to France to form the American Expeditionary Force; eventually some 2,040,000 US troops arrived in France.

By November 1918 the AEF comprised three armies each of three corps, a total of 1,338,000 combat troops. The greater part of this force was infantry, with only small detachments of cavalry being sent to Europe, principally for liaison and remount duties, though a provisional squadron did see some mounted action. A considerable force of artillery was also deployed, but was armed entirely with British or French guns since US production had not made any serious contribution by the time the war ended. A strong tank force was planned but only three battalions, using British and French tanks, saw action.

The US Army Air Corps expanded rapidly, and 45 squadrons were on active service by November 1918 with about 8,000 aircraft of various nationalities. The US Navy was a powerful force which made major contributions to the safety of Atlantic convoys and in 1917 the 4th battleship squadron formed part of the British Grand Fleet.

American Legion organization of American ex-soldiers and sailors who served in the war 1917–19, later expanded to include all US war veterans. It was organized in Paris in 1919 at a meeting of representatives of all the divisions then in France. It was later established in the USA, posts being set up in each state and in some foreign cities. By the end of 1919 over a million members had enrolled, with no distinction made between officers and enlisted men.

Amiens ancient city of NE France at the confluence of the rivers Somme and Avre; capital of the Somme *département*. An important rail junction, it became the hub of military communications in N France during World War I and was awarded the *Croix de Guerre*. It was occupied by the German Army for several days before the battle of the ◊Marne Sept 1914 but thereafter remained in French hands. The ◊German Spring Offensive 1918 brought it within the sound of gunfire and it was in some danger for several weeks, during which the main railway line to Paris was cut. The danger was finally lifted by the Allied counter-offensive Aug 1918.

Amman, operations against British operations against the Turks 1918. In March a British force crossed the Jordan and occupied Es Salt. Using this as a base they then mounted a raid on the suburbs of Amman, blowing up bridges and railway tracks and taking 1,000 prisoners before retiring to Es Salt and then falling back to the Jordan river line. This raid was repeated April 1918, but as the promised Arab support did not appear the offensive did not progress beyond Es Salt, although a further 1,000 prisoners were taken. Amman was later captured by British forces under General ◊Allenby Sept 1918 toward the end of the Palestine campaign.

ammunition general term covering those articles used to charge guns, mortars, and similar ordnance, such as cartridges, shells, fuses, rockets and offensive missiles generally. The First World War saw a considerable increase in the types and varieties of ammunition employed as special projectiles were developed for use against armour, for incendiary purposes against aircraft and airships, for laying smoke screens, and for delivering war gases.

Ancre, Battle of the closing episode of the series of battles in the ◊Somme area 1916–17. In Oct 1916 the British advance on the Somme had left a heavily fortified German salient, containing the village of Beaumont-Hamel, thrusting into the British line on both banks of the river Ancre. The battle began Nov 11 1916 with a one-day artillery bombardment, the infantry attack starting at 0512hrs on 12 Nov. Fighting was heavy, but Beaumont-Hamel was captured by the 51st Highland Division on 13 Nov. By 15 Nov, the British line had been advanced by about a mile, at which point the severe winter weather made the ground impassable, supplying the forward troops became difficult, and fighting impossible. The battle petered out and the line stabilized.

Angels of Mons legendary visions of St. George accompanied by angels, mounted horsemen, medieval cavalry and similar apparitions said to have been seen in the sky by troops during the retreat from ◊Mons 1914. The story can be traced to a work of fiction by Arthur Machen, a journalist, published in the London *Evening News* at the time of the retreat. Soldiers who took part in the retreat asserted that they had seen such apparitions, but this is generally ascribed to fatigue-induced hallucinations.

Anthoine General François Paul 1860–1934. French soldier and commander. Anthoine entered the French Army as an artillery lieutenant and served in Tonkin and China 1884. In 1907 he commanded the 15th Division Artillery and became a member of the French General Staff. He became Chief of Staff to General Castelnau 1914, then commanded the 20th Division at Arras. In 1915 he was given command of the 10th Army Corps operating in the ◊Argonne, and took over the 4th Army 1916. By 1917 he was commanding the 1st Army, and cooperated with the British Army in Flanders, taking part in the Third Battle of Ypres, until the end of the war.

Antwerp port in Belgium on the river Scheldt, capital of the province of Antwerp. In 1914, Antwerp was defended by 30 forts disposed around the city in two rings, reinforced by intermediate works and inundation W of the river. The city was besieged from 27 Sept 1914 until early Oct, starting with a German bombardment of the forts with 42 mm howitzers.

The Belgians prepared to evacuate the city and 9,000 British naval and marine reinforcements arrived 3 Oct 1914 to prolong the defence of the city in order to cover the evacuation. The outer ring of forts was abandoned 6 Oct and the Germans moved their siege artillery closer to the city itself which they began bombarding, as well as reducing the inner ring of forts. The Belgian army began its withdrawal that night, covered by a combined British-Belgian rearguard, which held for three days under intense attack until the last troops withdrew 9 Oct and the city surrendered. This bitter resistance failed to save Antwerp but did delay the German advance so that they were unable to push on though Ypres to the sea where they could have occupied one or more ports on the English Channel. Antwerp remained under German occupation until the end of the war.

ANZAC member of the Australian and New Zealand Army Corps during World War I, particularly one who fought at ◊Gallipoli. The term began as a code name based on the initials of the Corps Jan 1915. It may also be used generally of any Australian or New Zealand soldier, though 'digger' is more usual for Australians and 'Kiwi' for New Zealanders.

Anzac Cove cove on the W coast of the ◊Gallipoli peninsula in Turkey where Australian and New Zealand troops landed 25 April 1915. The name was adopted a few days after the landing. In 1990 it was the site of an international gathering to mark the 75th anniversary of the event.

Aosta Duke Emmanuel Philibert 1869–1931. Italian prince and soldier. Eldest son of Amadeus, King of Spain, and grandson of Victor Emanuel, King of Italy, he entered the Italian Army and rapidly rose to senior rank. In command of the Italian 3rd Army he was largely responsible for the capture of Gorizia from the Austrians Aug 1916 and led an orderly retreat across the Tagliamento river after ◊Caporetto.

Archangel, Expedition to Allied operation in the spring of 1918. It aimed to safeguard the large concentration of military stores which had been sent to Archangel; to safeguard the flank of the ◊Murmansk Expedition; and to stabilize the Eastern Front and make contact with the ◊Czech Legion and the forces of Adm ◊Kolchak.

A mixed force of British, French, and American troops occupied Murmansk July 1918. They were accompanied by a naval squadron which on 1 Aug attacked a Bolshevik force on Modiuga Island some 50 km/30 mi N of Archangel. Air attacks were also made and the island was captured, allowing Allied forces to enter Archangel. A land force then cleared the valleys of the rivers Dvina and Vaga and defeated the Bolshevik forces which had been occupying Archangel. In subsequent months, a local government was formed and formally recognized and several thousand Russians enlisted with the Allied force.

After the Armistice, the Bolsheviks were able to concentrate troops in the area and by early 1919 there seemed little point in holding on to this enclave in a country which had become almost entirely Bolshevik. Archangel was successfully defended until Aug 1919, when withdrawal began, and on 27 Sept the British naval base was closed and the last troops evacuated, having handed their equipment over to White Russian forces.

Archie slang term for anti-aircraft artillery in the British, and later, US forces. It is said to have arisen from the habit of a young British fighter pilot who used the 'punch-line' of a current music-hall chorus whenever a near-miss from an AA shell rocked his aeroplane: 'Archibald, certainly not!'.

Argesul, Battle of the battle fought 30 Nov–3 Dec 1916 on the line of the Argesul river between an attacking joint Austro-German force and Romanian armies attempting to defend Bucharest. The Austrians under FM ◊Mackensen attacked from the south and southwest, while the Germans under General von ◊Falkenhayn attacked from the north and west in a pincer movement.

Romanian resistance was initially strong, but reserves did not arrive due to the treachery of General Sosescu who was later court-martialled and imprisoned. His treachery and the arrival of German reinforcements led to a Romanian collapse, and Bucharest was occupied by German forces on 6 Dec 1916.

Argonne a large forested area of France, NW of Verdun, of considerable strategic importance. A German advance through this area could threaten Verdun, outflank Chalons, and render the French front on the river Meuse untenable. It was thus the scene of constant fighting throughout the war.

In 1914 the right wing of the German Army passed through, but after the Battle of the ◊Marne, fell back again to the area of Varennes. Trenches were dug and apart from local movements the lines remained stable until a German attack June 1915. Savage fighting ensued but what small gains the German made were lost to French counter-attacks and the battle was a stalemate. Throughout 1916–17 minor battles and raids took place but without making any serious change in the lines of battle.

In the autumn of 1918, Marshal Foch determined to clear this area and strike at the Mezieres-Montmedy railway line, the main German line of communication. By this time the area was well defended by the ◊Kriemhild Line, part of the larger ◊Hindenburg Line system of fortifications. Foch was hampered by the fact that his force was mainly made up of 22 inexperienced and poorly trained divisions of US soldiers and by a grave shortage of transport. The US troops were to advance through the Argonne and up the west bank of the Meuse, while General Gouraud's 4th French Army simultaneously advanced west of the Argonne. The initial US attack on 26 Sept was carried out with great dash and overran the German lines, but communication and transport breakdowns caused severe problems: many troops received no food or ammunition for four days and the initial momentum could not be sustained. After solving these problems the advance was resumed 4 Oct, gaining 11 km/ 7 mi, and on 14 Oct the US force broke the Kriemhilde Line at several points. Hard fighting continued until 29 Oct when the German commander finally fell back to the west bank of the Meuse. The attack was resumed 1 Nov 1918 and by 6 Nov Sedan was taken. A further advance began but was ended by the Armistice.

US casualties were 115,519, with 15,599 killed (an unusually low proportion); French casualties were about 7,000; and 17,659 German prisoners and 468 guns were captured.

Ark Royal, HMS British seaplane carrier, mainly used in the ◊Dardanelles campaign. The first ship ever to be built specifically for the purpose of carrying aircraft, the Ark Royal had the engines aft and the waist and forepart were designed for stowage of seaplanes, lifted inboard by cranes.

Armentières town in N France on the Lys River; manufacturing cloth and table linen. It was held by the British in the face of strong German attacks Sept–Oct 1914 and remained in British hands until evacuated 12 April 1918 during the German Spring Offensive – the town was flattened during the German bombardment and rebuilt later. Armentières suffered enormous damage from artillery fire during the war but was a popular rest centre for British troops who commemorated it in the song *Mademoiselle from Armentières*.

Armistice cessation of hostilities while awaiting a peace settlement. 'The Armistice' refers specifically to the end of World War I between Germany and the Allies 11 Nov 1918.

Armistice Day anniversary of the armistice signed 11 Nov 1918, ending World War I. In the US this holiday is now called Veterans' Day; in the UK it is commemorated on the same day as Remembrance Sunday.

Armstrong-Whitworth British armaments firm, formed by the amalgamation of Sir William Armstrong's Elswick Ordnance Company with Sir Joseph Whitworth & Co 1897. During the War the company produced over 13,000 guns, 12,000 gun mountings, 14.5 million shells,

18.5 million fuses, 21 million cartridge cases, 1075 aircraft, 3 airships, and 47 warships.

The Armstrong-Whitworth F.K.8 was a two-seat reconnaissance bomber made to a Dutch design, manufactured 1915–18. The F.K.8 was strong, easy to fly, and could absorb a great deal of damage and yet remain airborne. It was widely used on the Western Front and in the Middle East.

armour (or body protection). Personal armour had been abandoned in the 17th century but was revived due to the demands of trench warfare 1915–16. The steel helmet was adopted by all combatants by mid-1916, and special helmets with face visors, for snipers, were also widely used. Body armour in the form of jerkins covered in small metal plates or steel chain was also worn in particularly vulnerable positions. Steel shields with firing slots were used by snipers in trenches, and portable shields were often carried by bombing parties to protect against close combat.

armoured car vehicles specially protected by armour plate and carrying guns. Development of such vehicles began prior to 1914 and so they were available in numbers from the early stages of the war. They were widely used by the Belgian army during the retreat of 1914 as patrol and rearguard forces, but thereafter saw little use on the Western Front. They were extensively employed in Palestine, Mesopotamia, Egypt, and Russia due to the more fluid nature of operations in these regions.

The Royal Naval Air Service deployed armoured car squadrons in Belgium as a defence for their forward airfields in 1914. One squadron was then sent to Russia where it operated in conjunction with Russian forces until the 1917 revolution. Army squadrons, operated by the Machine Gun Corps, were active in the Middle East.

armoured train railway train protected by armour and usually carrying several guns. Their principal role was to protect vulnerable supply lines by patrolling or escorting supply trains, and they were extensively used by the Russian Army, which had long stretches of railway line liable to attack from roving German cavalry patrols.

Arras, Battle of effective but costly British attack on German forces, April–May 1917. The attack was launched in support of a French offensive, which was only partially successful, on the ◊Siegfried Line. British casualties totalled 84,000; German casualties were 75,000.

Artillery Production 1914–18

	Britain	France	Germany
1914	91	5 per day	100 per month + 20 heavy (Sept)
1915	3,226		120 per month (June)
			270 per month (Aug)
			60 per month (Sept)
1916	4,551	30 per day	480 per month
1917	6,483	36 per day	400 per month (Sept)
1918	10,680	60 per day	
1916	4,551	30 per day	480 per month
1917	6,483	36 per day	400 per month (Sept)
1918	10,680	60 per day	
Totals	**25,031**		

	Italy	Russia	USA
1914		355	
1915		2,065	
1916		8,289	
1917		4,302	
Totals	**11,789**	**15,031**	**3,160**

artillery collective term for military ◊firearms too heavy to be carried. By 1914 artillery had reached a high level of technical efficiency and during the war artillery forces expanded until in many battles there were more artillerymen supporting an attack than troops actually carrying it out.

Distinct types of guns were employed for different purposes; the direct support of front-line troops was largely by field ◊guns and ◊howitzers of 75-105mm calibre. Support for major attacks was provided by heavier weapons of up to about 21cm calibre, which were also used to 'counter-bombard' enemy artillery and engage targets such as supply dumps and communications areas immediately behind the front line. Exceptionally heavy artillery of up to 42cm calibre was used for reducing forts and long-range firing at important targets well behind enemy lines. Heavy guns were also used for coastal defence and by warships, firing armour- piercing projectiles.

The difficulty of moving very heavy guns was overcome by the development of railway-mounted artillery which could then be moved quickly from one part of the front to another. The appearance of military aircraft led to the development of anti-aircraft guns, capable of shooting upwards and equipped with special sights to cater for fast-moving targets. The invention of the tank led to the development of self-propelled guns by the French and the Americans, and of howitzers which could accompany the advancing infantry to give immediate support, though these were rare and were employed only in the last few months of the war.

Artois, Battle of French offensive N of Arras, May–July 1915, intended to hold German forces in France and prevent their movement to the Eastern Front. The 8th and 10th French Armies (under Generals D'Urbal and Maud'huy) were employed, supported by British troops under Sir John French. The main axis of attack was against Lens, a heavily fortified German position. The ground was prepared for the attack by a 1200-gun artillery bombardment and a diversionary attack by the British against ◊Aubers Ridge.

Although the attack was initially successful, with the French capturing two major German positions and so gaining a line from which Vimy Ridge could subsequently be attacked, the German line held and the battle died away into sporadic trench fighting.

The fact that I was exchanging the comparative safety of the front for the probability of being hanged in the streets of London did not worry me.

> *General Ashmore*, on being sent to command the London air defences.

Ashmore General Edward Bailey 1872–1953. British soldier and commander. Ashmore entered the Royal Artillery 1891, serving in South Africa, and then attended the Staff College. He joined the reserve of the Royal Flying Corps and became commander of an RFC brigade in France 1915. In 1917 he returned to England as a major-general to command the air defences of London. In the 1920s he was instrumental in setting up the Royal Observer Corps.

Asiago Plateau, Battles of series of battles between Austrian and Italian forces in the mountainous country N of the Venetian plain and between the Adige and Piave rivers. The action began 10 Nov 1917 with an Austrian attack, capturing the town of Asiago. The Italians fell back to a defensive line against which the Austrians battered for several days before capturing part of the line and some 15,000 prisoners 7 Dec 1917. Thereafter they made small gains before resting on their line while directing their main attack elsewhere. Battle was rejoined 23 Dec 1917 when Austrian troops captured more ground and prisoners. The Italians made a minor attack and regained some ground Jan 1918, after which there was a quiet period until a major Austrian attack in June which included an artillery gas bombardment.

By this time, however, the line had been strengthened by French and British troops, and the Austrians made little impression. An Allied counter-attack on 15–16 June drove the Austrians back with severe losses of prisoners and equipment. This victory led to riots in Austria and a serious attempt at a general strike in Hungary. It also allowed General Foch to use his reserves on the Western Front which he had hitherto held back in case of setbacks on the Italian front. However, the line itself remained stable until a final Allied attack in Oct 1918 which broke the Austrian line and led to a general retreat, ending in a local armistice on 4 Nov 1918.

atrocities term devised by propagandists of both the Allies and Central Powers to cover incidences of brutal and outrageous conduct by their enemy. These ranged from authenticated instances of prisoners and civilian hostages being shot, to fictitious stories of children spitted on German bayonets, Belgian priests poisoning wells, French civilians offering poisoned wine to German troops and wholesale rape by both sides. No evidence was ever forthcoming for the some of the more lurid accusations, but in addition to the genuine cases of individual savagery, there were numerous instances of authorized atrocities such as the burning and destruction of ◊Louvain, ordered by General von Luttwitz as a reprisal against suspected ◊*franc-tireur* activity, and the execution by German troops of 639 civilians in Dinant Aug 1914.

Aubers Ridge, attack on British attack in May 1915 in support of, and as a diversion from, the French attack on Lens in the Battle of ◊Artois. Elements of the British 1st and Indian corps attacked on the right flank, with the British 8th division making the main attack on the left. A 40-minute bombardment began at 0500 hrs 9 May 1915 and at 0525 hrs the British advanced, intending to get close to the German trenches under cover of the artillery. Unfortunately, due to rounds falling short, the British sustained heavy casualties and the troops could not get into place. When the bombardment ceased, the Germans manned their parapets and were able to repulse most of the attack, though in one or two places small British parties reached the German trenches, only to be cut down by enfilade fire. A German counter-bombardment wrecked the British line and prevented reinforcements reaching the front, and by the afternoon the battle had died out. Allied casualties numbered over 6,000 killed and wounded, while German casualties were more than 3,000.

Augustov town in Poland, about 60 km/38 mi N of Bialystok. In Oct 1914 German forces under ◊Hindenburg defeated a Russian reserve army near Lyck (now Elk) which fell back and formed a line at Augustov to fight a delaying rearguard action so that reinforcements could gather in their rear. This completed, the Russians counter-attacked and drove the German forces back, recapturing Augustov by a flanking movement on 3 Dec 1914. German losses were estimated at about 50,000, and the Russians were able to press their advantage and advance into East Prussia.

Australian Imperial Force volunteer military force formed at the outbreak of World War I, the major Australian contribution to the war. It was organized into infantry divisions (eventually five), five light horse divisions, the Australian Flying Corps and the Australian Army Nursing Service. The second AIF was formed 1939–40, with its divisions numbered 6th to 9th to follow those of the first AIF.

Australian Light Horse mounted division, consisting of several brigades, which served in the Middle East in World War I. They served as infantry in the Dardanelles and France, and then reverted to their proper role with the Desert Mounted Corps in Palestine 1917–18.

Austro-Hungarian Army army of the Empire of Austria-Hungary. It was divided into three main components: the *Kaiserlich und Koniglich*, a regular force recruited from Austria and Hungary; the *Kaiserlich-Koniglich* or Austrian *Landwehr*; and the *Koniglich Ungarnische*, or *Honved*, the Hungarian *Landwehr*.

This force was divided into 16 corps each having two infantry divisions, an artillery brigade and a cavalry brigade. The total mobilized strength at the start of the war was about 1,750,000 men, which increased to 2,230,000 by the end of the war. The Austro-Hungarian Navy was principally a coast defence force and conducted limited operations in the Adriatic. The total number of men mobilized during the war was about 7.75 million; total casualties were about 4.5 million. Austria sued for a separate peace on the Italian front and an Armistice was agreed 3 Nov 1918.

autocannon French air defence weapon, consisting of a modified 75mm field gun M1897 fitted to a special high-angle mounting and carried on a De Dion Bouton motor lorry. It became the standard anti-aircraft gun, used for the defence of forward as well as rear areas and cities. A small number were used in London from 1915 and the design was copied in Britain using guns purchased from France.

The main air defence tactic of 1915 was to use motorized guns and turn them out like a fire brigade to chase after the Zeppelins or position themselves in their path. The gradually increasing performance of aircraft soon rendered this tactic obsolete, and the manufacture of motorized guns was abandoned in favour of simpler fixed or towed mountings.

Averescu Aleksandr 1859–1938. Romanian soldier and statesman. Of Bessarabian origin, Averescu enlisted as a trooper in the Russo-Turkish War of 1877, then studied at the Turin military academy and eventually reached the rank of general of division by 1912. He played a considerable role in the defeat of the Austro-German offensive against Moldavia directed by von ◊Mackensen July–Aug 1917.

He acted as foreign minister when Romania was negotiating peace with Germany 1918, and became Minister of the Interior 1919.

Aviatik aircraft Austrian fighter and bomber aircraft. The Aviatik B1 was one of the earliest purpose-built combat aircraft, bulit from Nov 1914 by the *Automobile und Aviatik AG* of Leipzig. In 1915 the Viennese branch of this company produced an improved model, the B2, widely used as a reconnaissance machine in the Eastern Front. At first unarmed, they were eventually fitted with a 7.92mm Schwarzlose machine gun and could carry two bombs. A further development, the B3, had a more powerful engine and carried three bombs but was found to be a poor performer and was dropped. Instead, the B2 was equipped with the better engine and bigger bomb-load and continued in use until the war ended.

Avro aircraft training and combat aircraft manufactured by A.V.Roe & Co. of Manchester. The Avro 504 was designed 1913 and was used widely as both a training machine and later as a combat aircraft; some 8,340 were built before the Armistice. The Avro 504 was the first Allied aircraft to be shot down 22 Aug 1914 and also made the first bombing raid on Germany, the attack on the airship base at Dusseldorf 8 Oct 1914. However, better combat aircraft were developed and the 504 reverted to its initial training role.

It remained in production for the RAF until mid-1933 and continued in use for training purposes until 1940. Large numbers were also built in Russia in the 1920s.

B

Babtie Sir William 1859–1920. British soldier and surgeon. He served in the South African War and won the Victoria Cross at Colenso for tending wounded under fire, then entered the Army Medical Service after qualifying as a surgeon and by 1901 was assistant director-general. In 1914 he became Director Medical Services, India, and in this role was responsible for medical support to operations in Mesopotamia. The organization broke down during the early part of the campaign, and a special commission of enquiry in 1917 did not entirely exonerate him from blame. By the time the commission reported he was Director of Medical Services at the War Office and had been knighted. In 1918 he was promoted to Inspector of Medical Services and created KCB.

Bacon Admiral Sir Reginald Hugh Spencer 1863–1952. British naval commander. He became a lieutenant 1883 and later conducted the first trials of submarines in the Royal Navy. From 1907 he was director of naval ordnance, then resigned to become a director of the Coventry Ordnance Works 1909. He rejoined the service 1914 and went to France as a colonel of the Royal Marines, commanding a battery of 15-inch howitzers manufactured by his company. In 1915 he was appointed vice-admiral in command of the ◊Dover Patrol, a post he held until Jan 1918 when he became controller of the munitions inventions department of the Admiralty. He was knighted 1916.

Baghche town in Armenia on the Baghdad railway between Adana and Aleppo. It was the site of an internment camp for British soldiers captured at the surrender of ◊Kut-al-Imara 1916. The camp was poorly run and conditions were such that many of the men died. The camp medical officer, Assistant-Surgeon Fratel, was subsequently court-martialled in London on charges of treating the prisoners with cruelty. He was sentenced to one year's imprisonment 1918 but was released after the war ended.

Baghdad historic city and capital of Iraq, on the river Tigris. In 1914 it was in ◊Mesopotamia, then part of the Turkish Empire, but was captured by the British under General Maude 11 March 1917. After the recapture of ◊Kut-Al-Imara, the Turkish army retreated up the Tigris followed by a British column and a naval flotilla. In spite of several Turkish attempts to halt their advance, the British were able to force a crossing of the river Diala and the Turks evacuated the city.

Well, if you knows of a better 'ole, go to it.
                    Bruce Bairnsfather, *Fragments from France.*

Bairnsfather (Charles) Bruce 1888–1959. British artist, celebrated for his 'Old Bill' cartoons of World War I. In World War II he was official cartoonist to the US Army in Europe 1942–44.

Baku, expedition to British expedition 1918 to prevent the Germans controlling the Caspian Sea and to protect the oil wells from the Bolsheviks. The collapse of Russia during 1917 revived Turkish dreams of a union of Muslim states, and, cooperating with German forces, they invaded Caucasia in early 1918 at the same time as Bolshevik forces advanced into the area. A British battalion under the command of Maj-Gen ◊Dunsterville left Baghdad in motor vehicles and made contact with anti-Bolshevik Russian forces June 1918. On July 15 the Bolsheviks in Baku were overthrown and the local government requested aid from Dunsterville, who entered the town and strengthened the defences. The British were attacked by overwhelming Turkish forces whereupon local Armenian troops deserted, and the British sustained heavy casualties covering the retreat of Russian and Armenian units. The town was finally evacuated 18 Sept 1918.

The operation was a partial success, in that it deprived the Turks of the use of the bridgehead and oilfields for six weeks and also occupied large numbers of Turkish troops who would otherwise have been free to fight in Palestine and Mesopotamia.

Ball Albert 1896–1917. British fighter pilot and air ace. Born in Nottingham, Ball enlisted at the outbreak of war and was commissioned into the Sherwood Foresters. He then transferred to the Royal Flying Corps where he became an outstanding fighter pilot until he took off on patrol on 7 May 1917 and was never seen again. He was awarded the MC, DSO and Bar, and, posthumously, the Victoria Cross. At the time of his death he had attained the rank of captain and was credited with over 40 enemy aircraft shot down.

balloon lighter-than-air craft that consists of a gasbag filled with gas lighter than the surrounding air and an attached basket, or gondola, for carrying passengers and/or instruments.

Balloons were used for observation purposes during the war by most combatants, being flown on cables behind the front line so as to give artillery spotters an elevated viewpoint. They were frequently attacked by gunfire and aircraft and the observers were issued with parachutes for such emergencies. They were also used as a form of passive air defence, flown on cables above London and other cities and joined by 'aprons' of steel cable, so as to form a barrier, forcing bombing aircraft to fly at altitudes which made bomb-aiming difficult and also made them an easier target for artillery.

Baltic Sea, operations in the In Aug 1914 light German cruisers and destroyers shelled Libau (now Liepaja, Latvia) and other points on the Russian coast, but were driven off by a superior Russian force; one German ship, the Magdeburg, was driven ashore. Her crew attempted to blow her up but the Russians were able to board the remains and found the German Naval Codes, which they took to England, allowing the Allies to read the German Navy codes for most of the war. From this time onward there was a constant low-key battle between German and Russian naval forces. In mid-1915 British submarines began operating in the Baltic, maintaining a tight blockade of the N German coastline, sinking numerous supply ships and several warships. The German Navy remained quiet during 1916, and there was little action. However, with the collapse of discipline in the Russian Navy during the turmoil of 1917 and in the absence of any British force, which had been withdrawn to fight the Battle of the Atlantic, the Germans re-emerged and more or less did as they pleased, attacking the Gulf of Riga.

barrage linear concentration of artillery fire used to interpose a screen of bursting shells between attacking and defending troops. When fired by a defending force to prevent an attack reaching its lines, a barrage may be a simple line of fire in front of a position or shaped so as to surround the position – a 'box' barrage. Fired to assist an attack, a barrage may be stationary, to prevent reinforcements reaching the threatened area, or moving, to act as a continuous screen ahead of the advancing force. Normally using high explosive shells, World War One barrages often included gas and shrapnel projectiles so as to present a more complex threat to the target.

Battenberg (Mountbatten) Prince Louis Alexander 1854–1921. British admiral. A member of a British family of German extraction, Battenberg joined the Royal Navy and became an admiral. In 1914 he was First Sea Lord but was forced to retire due to anti-German public feeling. He was created Marquess of Milford Haven 1917 and in the same year changed the family name to Mountbatten.

Battye grenade simple ◊hand grenade issued to British troops 1915. It consisted of a cast-iron cylinder with an open end, filled with Ammonal and closed with a wooden plug. A hole bored through the plug allowed the insertion of a length of time fuse and a detonator. At the outer end of the time fuse was a percussion cap which, when struck, ignited the fuse to give a delay of about four seconds before the grenade exploded.

Bapaume, Battle of second phase of the British offensive of Aug 1918, the Battle of Bapaume was very similar to the ◊Somme (1916), starting from more or less the same positions and following the same general plan. The operation was carried out by the 3rd and 4th British Armies, a total of 23 divisions, commanded by Gens Byng and Rawlinson respectively, opposed by German forces consisting of 35 under-strength divisions under von Hutier and Marwitz, directed by Ludendorff. Supported by tanks and artillery, the British attack began 21 Aug 1918, broke through the German lines and crossed the river Ancre 22 Aug. The Germans abandoned Albert after a flank attack, and on 23 Aug a massed Allied attack on a front 53 km/33 mi long drove the German line back until the Allied forces held the Arras-Bapaume road, so flanking the Thiepval Ridge position.

At 1 a.m. on 24 Aug the British mounted a concentric attack on the Thiepval position, taking it with immense German losses in prisoners and equipment. The advance continued, British troops taking Bapaume and Combles and French troops taking Noyon and Nesle. On 30 Aug, the 2nd Australian Division attacked a very strong German position at Mont St Quentin, finally taking it 1 Sept and thus removing the principal German strongpoint. This allowed other Australian units to take Peronne, and this phase of the operation closed 2 Sept, having pushed the German line back some 8 km/5 mi and captured 34,250 prisoners and 270 guns.

Bayer, Farbenfabrik German chemical and pharmaceutical company, the largest chemical multinational in Europe, founded 1863. The company was founded by industrialist Friedrich Bayer (1825–1880), initially to manufacture dyestuffs, and during 1914–18 was the principal German manufacturer of explosives and poison gas.

bayonet short sword attached to the muzzle of a firearm. The bayonet was placed inside the barrel of the muzzle-loading muskets of the late 17th century. The *sock* or ring bayonet, invented 1700, allowed a weapon to be fired without interruption, leading to the demise of the pike.

During World War I, the French used a long needle bayonet, the British a sword bayonet, while the Germans adopted a 'pioneer' bayonet with the rear edge formed into a saw. Although the 'Spirit of the Bayonet' was fostered by instructors, it was little used in real life. Of the 13,691 men of the American Expeditionary Force killed in the war, only 5 died from bayonet wounds, and comparable figures can be shown for all combatants.

BBC lachrymatory (tear) gas; see ◊bromo-benzyl-cyanide.

B.E. ('Bleriot Experimental'). The first British military aircraft ever designed. The design was improved into the B.E.2 and three squadrons of the Royal Flying Corps were equipped with them 1913. They were sound and reliable reconnaissance and bombing aircraft, able to carry up to 45 kg/20 lb of bombs and fly at 110 kph/70 mph, but they lacked manoeuvrability and were easily defeated by more advanced fighters so that they were gradually relegated to training roles. The design was developed 1911–12 by Geoffrey ◊de Havilland and FM Green at the Royal Aircraft Factory, Farnborough and over 3,500 were built by 22 manufacturers.

Beatty Admiral David 1871–1936. British admiral, he joined the navy 1888. Beatty commanded the cruiser squadron 1912–16 and bore the brunt of the Battle of Jutland. In 1916 he became commander of the fleet, and in 1918 received the surrender of the German fleet.

Beaumont-Hamel French village in the *département* of Somme, 10 km/6 mi N of Albert. Under German occupation, it resisted capture by the British in the Battle of the ◊Somme, July 1916. In the Battle of the ◊Ancre, later in 1916, it was severely bombarded by British artillery and captured by the Royal Naval Division and other units, under the command of Lt-Col R C Freyberg, who was awarded the Victoria Cross for his leadership. It was the scene of fierce fighting during the German Spring Offensive 1918.

Becker gun German aircraft gun, developed 1916. It was an automatic weapon firing a small high explosive shell (19 mm calibre) at about 300 rounds per minute. Development continued throughout the war, though weapons were produced for service use at various times. Some were fitted into Gotha bombers for self-defence, while an estimated 130 were issued to German ground air defence units. Records show that 392 guns were confiscated and scrapped by the Allied Disarmament Commission after the war. After the war the design was sold to a Swiss company and formed the basis of the later, and more famous, Oerlikon cannon.

Beersheba, Battle of battle between British and Turkish armies, 31 Oct 1917. Beersheba formed the left anchor of a Turkish defensive line extending some 50 km/30 mi to Gaza and General Allenby planned to attack this flank, which was only protected by empty desert. An attack on 27 Oct against Gaza fixed Turkish attention on the other end of the line and on 31 Oct a night attack was made against Beersheba. Two divisions mounted a frontal attack, while a mounted force mainly composed of ANZAC troops moved across the desert to make another attack from the flank. The frontal attack succeeded in taking both lines of defence, while the 4th Australian Light Horse made a cavalry charge from the flank and captured Beersheba. About 2,000 Turkish troops were taken prisoner.

Belleau Wood battle between Germans and Americans June 1918. After their success at Chateau-Thierry, the Americans then attacked German positions in Belleau Wood 6 June 1918. The initial German posts were driven back, but strong German defences then turned the battle into a tree-by-tree advance by the US Marine Brigade. The Marines spent almost three weeks clearing the wood, every yard of which was bitterly contested. The last German positions were taken 12 June, but sporadic fighting continued until 25 June before the wood could be considered secured.

Benet-Mercie gun modified version of the French-Hotchkiss light machine gun adopted by the US Army 1909. Just over 1,000 were made by Springfield Arsenal under license and they were used in the 1916 expedition to Mexico. The first units of the American Expeditionary Force were armed with them, but after a short period they were withdrawn and replaced by ◊Hotchkiss and Lewis guns, since the Benet-Mercie design proved less resistant to trench conditions and demanded a supply of spares only obtainable from the USA. It was relegated to use as a training gun and made obsolete as soon as the war ended.

benzyl bromide lachrymatory (tear) gas introduced by the Germans at Verdun March 1915 as 'T-Stoff'. It was then adopted by the French who called it 'Cyclite'. It is a powerful eye irritant, and high concentrations produce irritation of the nose and throat. However, its prime component was toluene, more urgently needed for the manufacture of explosives, and since other substances of greater power were later discovered, benzyl bromide was not used for very long.

Berchtold Count Leopold Anthony Johann von 1863–1942. Austrian diplomat and foreign minister of Austria-Hungary 1912–15. After various diplomatic posts in London, Paris, and St Petersburg, he was minister for foreign affairs during the diplomatic exchanges of July–Aug 1914. Regarded as one of the principal authors of the war, he was dismissed 1915 and replaced by Count Burian von Rajecz.

Bergmann musquete common wartime name for the Machine Pistol 18, designed by Hugo Schmeisser, manufactured by Th. Bergmann &

Co, and first issued to the German Army in 1916. A simple automatic weapon with a short barrel and wooden stock, it fired the standard 9mm pistol cartridge at 400 rounds per minute. The first issues were for trench defence, but the adoption of the infiltration tactic by General von Hutier led to the weapon being issued to 'Storm Troops' since it provided the ideal combination of firepower and portability demanded in this role. It was, in fact, the ancestor of every submachine gun invented since then.

Bergmann machine guns series of machine guns manufactured by *Th. Bergmann* of Berlin and designed by Louis Schmeisser. The first patents were taken out in 1902 but the gun was only adopted by the German Army 1910. A water-cooled, belt-fed weapon of 7.92mm calibre mounted on a tripod, it fired at a rate of about 550 rounds per minute. In 1915 the design was modified by removing the water jacket and generally making the weapon lighter, thus providing the German infantry with a more portable weapon with a faster rate of fire.

The design was quite advanced for its time, with such features as an aluminium-link belt and quick-change barrel, but the gun was never produced in great numbers, since the Army preferred, in time of war, to stick with the standard Maxim with which it was familiar.

Beseler General Hans von 1850–1921. German soldier. Beseler entered the German Army in a pioneer battalion 1868, by 1904 was Chief of the Pioneer Corps, and became general of Infantry 1907. In 1915 he commanded the force attacking Antwerp, which he captured 9 Oct. He was then moved to the Eastern Front where he was in command of the siege artillery, and in 1915 was appointed governor of Warsaw and then governor-general of Poland.

Béthune French town in the *département* of Pas-de-Calais, located at the junction of two canals in a rich coal-mining area. During the war it was the principal railhead for Allied forces N of the River Lys, communicating with the Channel ports. In Jan 1915 the Germans launched a strong attack on the Allied line protecting Béthune but were beaten off with heavy casualties. An even greater effort was made April 1918, during the general German assault on the Ypres salient. The town was almost lost, only being saved by a flanking movement by a British force. The attempt continued for most of April before finally dying out, during which time the town was severely damaged by artillery fire.

Big Bertha name commonly applied to many large-calibre German guns but which strictly refers only to one, the 42cm Krupp howitzer L/14, used to reduce the fortress of Liège and other strongpoints 1914. The name came from Bertha Krupp von Bohlen und Halbach, wife of Gustav Krupp, manufacturer of the gun. Four such howitzers were made. Each was dismantled into its component parts and drawn on trailers by Daimler Benz tractors, being assembled at the firing point by a portable crane. The shell weighed 820 kg/1800 lbs and the maximum range was 9,370 m/10,250 yds. The four weapons were used until the end of the battle of ◊Verdun, then withdrawn and scrapped since by then they were out-ranged by most Allied heavy artillery.

Bingham Captain Edward Barry Stuart, RN 1881–1939. British sailor, son of Lord Clanmorris. He entered the Royal Navy 1895 and commanded HMS Invincible during the Battle of the ◊Falkland Islands Dec 1914. He commanded a division of destroyers at the Battle of Jutland and was awarded the Victoria Cross for taking his destroyer HMS Nestor to within 2,750 m/3,000 yds of the German battle fleet in order to launch torpedoes. This inevitably attracted German gunfire and Nestor was sunk, Stuart being captured; he remained in a prisoner-of-war camp until after the Armistice By the time of his retirement 1932 he had been promoted to rear admiral.

Birch General Sir James Frederick Noel 1865–1939. British soldier. Commissioned into the Royal Artillery 1885, he served in Ashanti and South Africa. During the war he acted as artillery adviser to the commander in chief in France and was promoted to lieutenant-general. He became director-general of the Territorial Army 1921 and later master-general of the Ordnance.

Birdwood General Sir William Riddell 1865–1951. British soldier. Joined the Scots Fusiliers 1883, transferred to the Bengal Lancers 1886, and saw active service in several Indian campaigns. Severely wounded in the South African War he returned to India as a member of Kitchener's staff and was appointed quartermaster general 1912. In 1914 he was selected to command the Australian Corps, which he led in Gallipoli, assuming command there when General Hamilton retired. After Gallipoli he continued to command the Australians in France until Aug 1918 when he took command of the 5th British Army until the war ended.

Birmingham, HMS British light cruiser of the 'Chatham' class. On 9 Aug 1915 the Birmingham sank the German submarine U 15, the first German submarine sunk during the war. Later took part in the battles of Heligoland and Jutland.

Bishop William Avery (Billy) 1884–1956. Canadian air ace. He shot down over 70 enemy aircraft in World War I, and was awarded the Victoria Cross 1917.

Blackburn (the Blackburn Aeroplane and Motor Car Company of Leeds, Hull, and London). British aircraft manufacturer, their principal wartime machine was the Blackburn Kangaroo, a twin-engined biplane used by the Royal Naval Air Service for anti-submarine operations in the North Sea.

Black Sea, Operations in the naval operations by Allied and Central Powers' fleets. The operations commenced 29 Oct 1914 with a combined German–Turkish bombardment of the Russian port of Odessa, sinking three Russian ships. On 18 Nov a Russian battleship squadron met the German battle-cruisers Goeben and Breslau, severely damaging the former. Raiding operations were then conducted by both sides, with little strategic value; minefields were laid and claimed minor victims, torpedo-boats and gunboats sank merchant ships, and coastal towns were shelled, until the Russian revolution paralysed the Russian fleet in 1917. In 1918 most of the Russian ships were captured by the Germans or Turks and the German Army occupied Russian naval bases. Allied warships entered the Black Sea after the surrender of Turkey and a British force remained in the area throughout 1919, assisting Denikin to repel the Bolshevik forces, but the British withdrew 1920.

Blighty popular name for England among British troops in World War I. From the Hindi 'bilati' – 'foreign'. The term was also used to describe serious but non-fatal wounds requiring hospitalization in Britain; e.g., 'He caught a Blighty one'.

blockade cutting-off a place with hostile forces by land, sea, or air so as to prevent any movement to or fro, in order to compel a surrender without attack or to achieve some other political aim.

During World War I, Germany attempted to blockade Britain with intensive submarine warfare, and Britain attempted to blockade Germany. No nation has the right to declare a blockade unless it has the power to enforce it, according to international law. The Declaration of London 1909 laid down that a blockade must not be extended beyond the coasts and ports belonging to or occupied by an enemy.

Blue Cross gas German term identifying respiratory irritant gases, from the mark painted on the shells. The group consisted of diphenylchlorarsine, diphenylcyanarsine, and ethylcarbazol, although the latter was little used.

Boelke Captain Oskar 1889–1916. One of the foremost German fighter pilots, by 1916 he had more enemy aircraft to his credit than any other German flier and received the '*Order pour le Merite*'. On 19 Oct 1916, by which time he was credited with 40 victories, he collided with another German aircraft during a dogfight with a British unit. His aircraft was damaged and he was killed on crash-landing behind the German lines.

Bojna Field Marshal Borovic von 1862–1929. Austrian soldier. During the war he commanded the 3rd Austrian Army operating in the Central Carpathians during 1915. He took part in General Mackensen's offensive in Galicia but was then transferred to the Italian front. By 1917 he commanded all Austrian forces on the Isonzo and later on the Lower Piave. In Jan 1918 he succeeded Archduke Eugene as commander in chief of all Austrian armies and was promoted to field marshal Feb 1918. In June he commanded the attack against the Italian army on the Piave with some success but was then defeated Oct–Nov 1918. After the Armistice he resigned and vanished into obscurity.

Bojovich Field Marshal Peter 1858–1936. Serbian soldier. He joined the Serbian artillery 1876, later transferred to the cavalry, and saw action in the Serbo-Turkish and Serbo-Bulgarian wars. A general by 1912, he commanded the Serbian First Army in the Balkan Wars of 1912. He continued in this command during the war, and played a leading part in the defeat of the Austrian attacks 1914–15. In 1916 he led the First Army in operations leading to the capture of Monastir by the Allies. Promoted to Field Marshal Sept 1918, he then commanded

Serbian forces during the offensive which led to the collapse of
Bulgaria.

Bolimov, Battle of battle between German and Russian forces, forming part of the third German attack on Warsaw, Feb 1915. This was the
first battle in which gas was tactically employed, the German artillery
firing several thousand shells filled with Ɖxylyl bromide, a lachrymatory gas. However, as the weather was extremely cold and the liquid
failed to vaporize, it had no effect whatever on the Russian defenders.
The Russians did discover that gas had been used, and took steps to
issue rudimentary masks to their troops thereafter. They also alerted
Britain and France to the attempt, but since it was not immediately followed up, the incident was forgotten and thus the use of gas at Ypres
came as a surprise.

Bolo Paul (Pasha) (d. 1918). French traitor. Bolo was born in Réunion,
went to France as a boy and then appears to have lived as a confidence
trickster for most of his life. In Feb 1915 he gained the confidence of
the Khedive of Egypt and proposed that money might be obtained from
Germany to promote a campaign in the press for peace in France. In
1915 and 1916 he travelled between the United States and Europe, and
it was later discovered that he had received some £300,000 from
German sources. Arrested in Paris Sept 1917 he was tried on a charge
of obtaining money from an enemy in order to create a pacifist movement in France. He was sentenced to death and shot at the Fort of
Vincennes on 17 April 1918.

bomb container filled with explosive or chemical material and generally used in warfare. Any object designed to cause damage by
explosion can be called a bomb (car bombs, letter bombs), but in a war
context the term is usually taken to mean aerial bombs.

Aerial bombing started in World War I, one of the earliest attacks
being that by a Royal Naval Air Service squadron based at Dunkirk
against the German airship base at Dusseldorf on 8 Oct 1914. Two 20
lb bombs were dropped, destroying a shed and the Zeppelin Z-9 which
was inside. The German air force carried out 103 raids on Britain, dropping 273 tons/269 tonnes of bombs, killing 670, and wounding 1,960
people. Bombing raids were also carried out by British, French, and
Italian aircraft, principally against military targets.

Bourlon Wood wood 5 km/3 mi W of Cambrai, carefully organized by the Germans as a defensive position, forming an outpost of the Hindenburg Line, which was the subject of British operations Nov 1917–Sept 1918. In the *First Battle of Cambrai*, 20 Nov 1917, British tanks reached the edge of the wood but by that time the infantry were too worn out to act in support. On 23 Nov the wood was cleared by a force of tanks aided by infantry of the 40th Division but they were driven out the following day by a German counter-attack. The wood was finally captured 27 Sept 1918 by the Canadian Corps aided by the 7th Tank battalion in an attack from both sides of the wood. The Canadians took some 10,000 prisoners and 200 guns.

Boy-Ed Captain Karl 1872–1943. German sailor. Boy-Ed entered the German Navy as a youth and came to the notice of Admiral von ◊Tirpitz, for whom he then directed propaganda aimed at enlarging the German Navy. Reaching the rank of captain he went to Washington as German naval attaché 1911, and after the outbreak of the war in 1914 directed a network of spies and saboteurs active in the USA. His activities became so blatant that President Wilson demanded his recall to Germany early in 1917. Upon his return he became director of the press section of the German Naval headquarters.

Breguet French two-seat biplane used as a day bomber. The Breguet XIV was a most advanced machine, being the first to be constructed largely of the then-new light alloy Duralumin. Powered by a 500-hp Renault engine it had a maximum speed of 180 kph/112 mph, a ceiling of 5,550 m/18,250 ft, and a range of 700 km/435 mi. The armament was generally a single Vickers machine gun firing forward and twin Lewis machine guns fired by the observer, in addition to racks for up to 32 10-kg bombs. The first machine flew Nov 1916, and before the war ended it saw service with 71 French squadrons on the Western Front plus several more in the Middle East and Balkans, and was also employed by the American and Belgian air forces.

The Breguet XIV remained in use until 1930, with numerous improvements, and in total over 8,370 were built. Many were adapted for use as seaplanes and commercial transports.

Brest-Litovsk, Capture of German victory over the Russians, Aug 1915. After the German capture of Warsaw the Russian forces fell back slowly, harried by German thrusts from several directions. Eventually the fortress of Brest-Litovsk was isolated by the forces of Mackensen in the east and Gallwitz in the north. Siege artillery was deployed, but the Russian High Command decided not to hold the position and on 16 Aug gave orders to evacuate the civil population. As the German forces closed in from the west and south, the Russians withdrew and abandoned the fortress 25 Aug 1915. All its guns and most of its stores were successfully removed before the German occupation.

Brest-Litovsk, Treaty of bilateral treaty signed 3 March 1918 between Russia and Germany, Austria-Hungary, and their allies. Under its terms, Russia agreed to recognize the independence of Georgia, Ukraine, Poland, and the Baltic States, and to pay heavy compensation. Under the Nov 1918 Armistice, it was annulled, since Russia was one of the winning allies.

Bristol (the British & Colonial Aircraft Company of Bristol). British aircraft manufacturer. The *Bristol Scout*, a single-seat biplane, was developed before the war and adopted 1914 as a reconnaissance machine. By 1916 they were armed with the first synchronized machine guns used by the Allies, and frequently carried bombs or incendiary darts. They saw service on all fronts and were also flown by the Royal Naval Air Service from the aircraft carrier HMS Vindex at Gallipoli.

The *Bristol Fighter* appeared 1916. This was a two-seater biplane with a single machine gun firing forward and twin Lewis guns for the observer. With a 275 hp Rolls-Royce Falcon engine it could reach 200 kph/125 mph, was highly manoeuvrable, and could dive faster than any other contemporary machine. It was built under license in the USA and over 5,500 were eventually made, seeing service with 14 air forces in addition to the British. The last service machine, in New Zealand, was withdrawn 1938.

British Army In 1914 the British Army was a volunteer force, backed by Territorial and Reserve forces. The strength of the Regular Army stood at 253,540 officers and men split into 31 regiments of cavalry, 157 infantry battalions, 169 field artillery batteries, 98 garrison artillery companies, and various supporting troops. Enlistment continued on a voluntary basis, with the Territorial and reserve forces being embodied within the Regular Army, until conscription was introduced 1916. Up to Feb 1916 some 2,630,000 men had enlisted, and from then on some 2,339,000 were conscripted. In Nov 1918 the Army's strength stood at some 3,563,466 officers and men.

British Commonwealth Forces general term for troops raised by British colonies and dependencies. Among these were Australian (340,000), Canadian (600,000), Indian (1.3 million), South African (375,000), and New Zealand (124,000) troops, and there were also smaller contingents from the smaller colonies. During the war, they were more generally known as 'Empire' troops. They were usually remarked upon for being of superior physical standards to the British conscript of the period and their wartime record was uniformly impressive.

British Expeditionary Force (BEF). Name given to the initial British force sent to France in 1914. It consisted of five infantry and one cavalry division, numbering about 100,000 men. A sixth infantry division joined this force in September. The term 'BEF' continued to be commonly applied to the British forces operating in France and Flanders, but it was no longer strictly correct. The expression was revived 1939 for the similar British force sent to France in World War II.

British Legion federation of ex- servicemen's organizations, formed 1 July 1921, incorporating the Officers' Association, Comrades of the Great War, National Association of Discharged Soldiers and Sailors, and the National Federation of Discharged and Demobilised Soldiers and Sailors. Its objects were to 'unite all those who served in the Great War in the army, navy, air force or auxiliary forces', to safeguard their interests, and the interests of the dependents of the fallen. In later years, its charter expanded to also include all ex-members of British forces who fought in later wars.

bromacetone lachrymatory (tear) gas, one of the most effective developed during the war. First used by the Germans under the name 'B-Stoff', it was then adopted by the French as 'Martonite' and the British and American forces as 'BA'. The most widely used tear gas, it has been estimated that over 1,000 tons were fired off in projectiles alone. It produces intolerable irritation of the eyes in concentrations of 0.01 mg/l and in heavy concentrations can be lethal. The liquid produces extremely painful blisters on the skin. It was used by the Germans in artillery shells and mortar bombs for some months during 1916, and by the British for a similar period, but was abandoned since it demanded acetone, which was required for other purposes considered more vital. The French and American armies mixed it with chloracetone and continued to use it throughout the war.

bromo-benzyl-cyanide (BBC) powerful lachrymatory (tear) gas introduced by the French as 'Camite' July 1918 and simultaneously adopted by the Americans as their standard lachrymatory gas. With an odour of spoiled fruit, BBC produces a burning sensation in the nose and throat, together with a severe headache. It is effective at very low concentrations, and at higher concentrations prolonged exposure could be fatal, though a toxic concentration cannot be reached in practice due to its low volatility.

Brooke Rupert (Chawner) 1887–1915. English soldier and poet. He was commissioned as an officer in the Royal Naval Division 1914. After fighting at Antwerp, he sailed for the Dardanelles, but died of blood-poisoning on the Greek island of Skyros, where he is buried. He stands as a symbol of the World War I 'lost generation'. His five war sonnets, the best known of which is 'The Patriot', were published posthumously. Other notable works include 'Grantchester' and 'The Great Lover'.

If I should die, think only this of me … That there's some corner of a foreign field/ That is forever England.
                                    Rupert Brooke 'The Soldier' 1915

Browning automatic rifle American light machine gun designed by John M. Browning of the USA and adopted by the US Army 1917. It was intended for use in a newly-developed French tactic, 'marching fire' in which advancing troops fired from the waist during their assault on enemy trenches, but this was soon found to be an impractical technique and the BAR became a conventional light machine gun supporting the infantry. It used a 20-shot magazine and fired at 500 rounds per minute. It was adopted after the war by the Belgian, Polish, and other armies, and remained in use with the US Army until the early 1950s.

Browning machine gun A water-cooled, tripod-mounted, belt-fed medium machine gun of 30-in calibre developed by John M Browning and adopted by the US Army 1917. Resembling the Vickers and Maxim guns, it was operated by recoil force and fired at about 500 rounds per minute. Over 68,000 were made before the war ended.

The original design was modified to an air-cooled version and extensively used as an aircraft and tank machine gun after the war. A •50-in calibre version was also developed as an anti-aircraft weapon 1919 and later saw extensive use as an infantry support and tank weapon. It is still in use today in virtually every country of the world.

Bruchmuller General Georg 1853–1928. German soldier. Recalled from the Reserve 1914, he became a lieutenant-colonel on the General Staff concerned with artillery. He first came into prominence when he used artillery to break up a Russian attack in the vicinity of Lake Naroch. Instead of doctrinaire fixed barrages, Bruchmuller employed his artillery in a flexible manner, switching from target to target and using a mixture of explosive, smoke, and gas ammunition to confound the attack and paralyse the attacking forces.

In 1917 he was on the staff of General von Hutier for the attack on Riga where his inspired handling of artillery again broke the Russian defenders and allowed Riga to be taken in a day. Together with von Hutier he was transferred to the Western Front late 1917 and planned the artillery support for the German Spring Offensive which, again, was highly successful. His innovative tactics earned him the nickname 'Durch-Bruchmuller', a play on *durchbruch* ('breakthrough'), among German soldiers.

Brusilov General Alexei 1853–1926. Russian general, military leader in World War I who achieved major successes against the Austro-Hungarian forces in 1916. He was commander of the Red Army 1920, which drove the Poles to within a few miles of Warsaw before being repulsed by them.

Brusilov Offensive attack by Russian forces June 1916 against the southern sector of the Eastern Front in order to relieve pressure on the Western and Italian fronts by drawing German forces east. Brusilov commanded the Russian 7th, 8th, 9th, and 11th Armies, advancing on a line from the Pripet Marshes to the Romanian border. The Austro-Hungarian Fourth Army was almost totally destroyed, and the Austro-German 'Southern Army' was forced to retreat due to this collapse. The attack achieved its purpose, since Hindenburg had to withdraw troops from many areas, including Italy, to bolster the defences in Galicia and Bukovina. Although an Austro-Hungarian counter-attack checked the Russian advance north, Brusilov pushed forward in the south as far as the Carpathian mountains before his attack came to a halt due to exhaustion of his troops, poor supply and lack of support from other Russian forces.

The offensive had far-reaching effects: it cost the Russians almost one million casualties, which demoralised the Russian forces and so aided the revolutionary cause; it brought Romania into the war on the Allied side, resulting in the eventual conquest of Romania by German forces; and the decimation of Austro-Hungarian forces made the German Army the dominant partner among the Central Powers thereafter.

Bulgaria Bulgaria began the war with a policy of neutrality, but, in order to take Macedonia which they had failed to achieve during the Balkan War 1912, the Bulgarians invaded Serbia Oct 1915 in a joint operation with an Austro-German assault. As a result the Allies declared war on Bulgaria and sent forces to ◊Salonika. Having gained Macedonia, the Bulgarians were inclined to rest on their achievement and did little 1916–17. However during that time conditions became harsh domestically, with food stocks being stripped to supply Germany and Austria and by late 1917 the Bulgarian people wanted to withdraw from the war. In March 1918 German supplies, upon which the Bulgarian army depended, ceased; attempts to form a pro-Allied government failed, and the subsequent collapse of the Bulgarian army on the Macedonian front led to a request for Armistice, which was signed 30 Sept 1918.

Bullecourt French village in the *département* of Pas-de-Calais. It formed part of the ◊Hindenburg Line for most of the war but was attacked by British and Australian troops of the 5th Army April 1917, and they eventually captured it 17 May. It was re-taken by the Germans March 1918 after heavy fighting in the spring offensive. The Germans held Bullecourt until it was briefly captured by Canadian troops 30 Aug, only for the Germans to re-take and immediately lose it again, after which it remained in Allied hands.

Bulow Field Marshal Karl von 1846–1921. German soldier. He entered the Guards Regiment 1864 and served as a captain on the staff during the Franco-Prussian war 1870–71. In 1914 he commanded the German 2nd Army and invaded Belgium, taking Namur and Charleroi, then advanced into France past the river Marne. Heavily defeated in the Battle of the Marne, 8–10 Sept 1914, his forces retreated to a line on the Aisne river. Shortly afterward he mounted an abortive attack on Reims and was then transferred to the Northern Command, where his task was purely defensive, and was promoted to field marshal Jan 1915. He suffered a heart attack March 1915, was relieved from active duty, and was retired 1916.

Byng General Julian Hedworth George 1862–1935. British general, he commanded the 3rd Cavalry Division 1914, the Cavalry Corps 1915, the 9th Army Corps at the Dardanelles, Turkey, and the Canadian Army Corps 1916–17 in France, where, after a victory at Vimy Ridge, he took command of the Third Army.

On Nov 20–Dec 7 1917 he led the successful tank attack on Cambrai. He was made a baron 1919, served as governor-general of Canada 1921–26, then became a viscount 1926, and was made a field marshal 1932.

C

Cadorna Count Luigi 1850–1928. Italian soldier, entered the Italian Army 1868. In 1914 he became chief of the general staff and upon Italy's entry into the war 1915 became commander in chief. He held this post until after the battle of Caporetto, when he was relieved by General Diaz. He then represented Italy in the military council at Versailles and was retired Sept 1919.

Cambrai, Battles of two battles in World War I at Cambrai in NE France.

First Battle 20–27 Nov 1917. The first battle in which tanks were used in large numbers, and in which the usual preliminary artillery bombardment was not employed. The British attacked with 330 tanks and 2 infantry corps, accompanied by a specific rather than general artillery bombardment of German defensive positions by 1,000 guns. Considerable gains were made, with 10,500 prisoners and 142 guns taken, but the tank force suffered heavy losses and the infantry were exhausted. Together with the lack of fresh troops in reserve, the German counter-attack could not be resisted, so that by 27 Nov the British were back almost where they had started and the battle was broken off.

Second Battle 26 Sept–5 Oct 1918. In 1918 Cambrai was protected by the formidable ◊Hindenburg Line and was attacked as part of the British general advance. Specially lengthened Mark V tanks, which could span the broad trenches of the Line, were used. Preceded by a strong artillery barrage, the attack broke through the Line, eventually making a 65 km/40 mi gap and Cambrai was captured on 5 Oct 1918.

Cameroons, Conquest of Allied operation in W Africa, 1915–16. At the outbreak of war, elements of the British Nigerian Frontier Force crossed into Cameroon, then a German protectorate, but were driven back. Shortly after, a British force with naval support landed at Douala and moved inland. By the spring of 1915 the Germans had lost most of their outposts, railway lines, and administrative stations but they continued to mount remarkably strong counter-attacks in all areas, slowing the Allied advance which was also hindered by sickness. The final effort of the campaign began Nov 1915, by which time the Allied force had been augmented by Belgian and Indian troops. The last of the German forces were finally defeated Jan 1916. In 1919 the colony was divided, four-fifths going to France (now Cameroun) with the northern fifth becoming part of Nigeria.

camouflage disguising a piece of military equipment (such as a building, ship, or aircraft) or a military position so that it will blend into its background. Three elements – shine, shape, and shadow – combine to identify an object, and camouflage is the art of so altering these features as to make the object difficult to identify. The most common technique is to use disruptive pattern painting, destroying shine and creating false shadows; this works effectively on ships, buildings, aircraft, and vehicles. Concealment of field works such as trenches and gunpits, ammunition dumps and supply points, was usually achieved by stretching netting, laced with coloured cloth, straw, branches, and other material, over the object to be concealed so that it would blend into the local terrain. Once a site is camouflaged it then becomes necessary to maintain the pretence – by, for example, changing greenery regularly – and also enforce discipline on any troops in the area so that a carefully-camouflaged spot is not revealed by tracks and footpaths leading to it.

Caporetto, Battle of joint German-Austrian victory over the Italian Army, Oct–Nov 1917. At the end of Sept 1917 the Italian offensive against the Austrians ended in the Isonzo area, but during Oct the Austrians were joined by substantial German reinforcements. The Italians were expecting an attack from the north but a massive German force was assembled in great secrecy at the southern end of the Italian front and on 24 Oct, after a heavy artillery bombardment, General von Bulow broke through the Italian lines west of the Isonzo and headed for Caporetto. Heavy fighting continued throughout the following day, with delays in sending reserves weakening Italian resistance. As the

Germans penetrated deeper, so the flanks of the remaining Italian line were threatened and had to fall back. By 26 Oct Caporetto had fallen and masses of Italian troops were in headlong retreat. Eventually General Cadorna authorized a full retreat, which continued some 95 km/60 mi to the line of the river Piave before the Italian defence could be stabilized.

The sudden collapse of the Italians took von Bulow by surprise and he was unable to bring up reserves or take advantage of the situation. As it was, the Austro-German forces merely moved slowly forward in the wake of the Italians, taking Gorizia, Cividale, and Udine as they did so. Von Bulow's forces crossed the river Tagliamento, the advanced Italian line, 3 Nov 1917 and broke through Italian outposts but their advance was halted by the Piave line.

Caproni (Societa de Ing. Caproni). Italian aircraft manufacturer which had already developed a tri-motor heavy biplane bomber 1913 when most countries were still thinking of the aeroplane as a possible reconnaissance machine. The design was gradually improved, and the Ca 33 of 1916 became the most common type, some 269 being built. With three 150hp engines it could carry up to 700 kg/320 lb of bombs at 150 kph/94 mph to a range of 450 km/280 mi. These machines were in constant use in long-range bombing attacks against the Austro-Hungarian lines and strategic targets such as the Austrian naval bases of Pola and Trieste.

Carpenter Captain Alfred Francis, RN 1881–1955. British sailor. Carpenter entered the Royal Navy 1907 and was promoted to commander 1915. He commanded HMS Vindictive in the attack on ◊Zeebrugge April 1918, for which he received the Victoria Cross. He was then promoted to captain and appointed to the Naval Intelligence Department.

Carso, Battles of the The Carso is a limestone plateau lying N of the Adriatic, formerly part of the Austro-Hungarian empire and, after 1919, part of Yugoslavia. It was the scene of four major battles 1916–17 between Italian forces under General Cadorna, pressing an attempt to seize Trieste, and Austrian forces trying to stop them.

The *first battle* took place Sept 1916 and resulted in the Italians gaining some ground before being stopped by a concentration of Austrian heavy artillery and bad weather.

The *second battle* occurred Oct 1916, when Cadorna resumed his attack and made a steady advance, repulsed Austrian counter-attacks, and established a new line before the onset of a severe winter stopped further movement.

The *third battle* broke out May 1917 when the Italians drove the Austrians from their trench lines from Kostanjevica to the Adriatic shore. After a further advance, they were brought to a standstill by a shortage of ammunition. The Austrians, on the other hand, were well stocked due to the collapse of the Russian front, and after a powerful bombardment, they counter-attacked 1 June 1917. They met with only limited success and the battle died out. Cadorna had gained a great deal of territory, 16,500 prisoners and a quantity of guns and stores.

The *fourth battle* took place Sept 1917: the Italians had been gradually creeping forward throughout the summer and were preparing a major attack on San Gabriele, but the Austrians discovered this and mounted a spoiling attack 4 Sept. The battle lines swayed back and forth but eventually the Austrians prevailed and drove the Italian forces out of their forward positions to a second, rearward, line where the battle died out and the Italians consolidated their position.

case shot non-explosive artillery projectile consisting of a sheet-metal canister filled with lead or cast-iron balls. On being fired from a gun the canister is split by the force of the propellant explosion and the balls and canister fragments are ejected from the gun muzzle in the manner of a shotgun charge. Devastating at close range against troops, it had fallen into disuse in the mid-19th century but was revived by the British as a loading for the 6-pounder guns used in early tanks. It was used primarily as an anti-personnel weapon for clearing trenches as the tank passed along them.

Castelnau General Marie-Joseph Edouard de Curieres de 1851–1944. French soldier. He entered the army 1870 and fought in the Franco-Prussian war. By 1906 he was a brigadier-general, and he was placed in command of the French Second Army 1914. While in command of the Army Group Centre he directed the Champagne offensive in the autumn of 1915. He then became Chief of Staff under Marshal Joffre and was responsible for the defence of Verdun. Late in 1915 he went to Salonika but returned and resumed his position at Verdun where he was responsible for the decision to appoint General Petain to oversee the defence. When Joffre was removed, Castelnau was considered as his replacement but his religious beliefs were unpopular and he was temporarily relieved of active duty. Returning 1918, he took command of the Eastern Army Group and directed the campaign into Lorraine. He was preparing to besiege Metz and march on the Rhine when the Armistice was signed. He was elected to the Chamber of Deputies 1919. One of the finest French commanders, it was unfortunate that his religion and politics were, even in war, enough to bar him from the highest command.

Causes of Casualties

Cause of wound	wounded but survived	died of wounds	total	Percentage of total hospital admissions attributable to this type of wound
air attacks	170	28	198	0.08 %
artillery (fragments)	18,261	1,778	20,039	8.94 %
artillery (shrapnel)	31,802	1,985	33,787	15.08 %
bayonets	369	5	374	0.16 %
gas	69,331	1,221	70,552	31.49%
grenades	824	56	880	0.4 %
machine gun	67,409	7,474	74,883	33.42 %
pistol shot	229	13	242	0.1 %
rifle fire	19,459	961	20,420	9.12 %
swords	9	3	12	0.006 %
miscellaneous	2,535	167	2,702	1.205 %

*includes casualties sustained in falls, crushed in trenches, trapped in buildings, etc. These figures relate to US casualties actually admitted to hospital and so do not take into account those cases that never made it that far, such as deaths on the battlefield. This gives rise to some discrepancies, such as the figure given for gas casualties which is slightly lower than the figure given for total US casualties from gas attacks in the separate table on the subject. However, due to the comparatively short period of US involvement in the war and their well-organized record-keeping, these are probably the most accurate figures available for any of the combatants and so provide a valuable insight into the overall picture. For example, gas turns out not to be the mass killer it is generally assumed to be, but nonetheless it was highly effective in causing casualties. Similarly, although artillery fire killed far more on the battlefield itself, rifle and machine gun fire accounted for far more hospital cases.

Casualties from Gas 1915–18

	Total casualties	Deaths
Austria-Hungary	100,000	3,000
British Empire	188,706	8,109
France	190,000	8,000
Germany	200,000	9,000
Italy	60,000	4,627
Russia	419,340	56,000
USA	72,807	1,462
British Empire	188,706	8,109
France	190,000	8,000
Germany	200,000	9,000
Italy	60,000	4,627
Russia	419,340	56,000
USA	72,807	1,462
Others	10,000	1,000

Air Raid Casualties and Damage 1914–18

	Casualties	Damage	Bombs dropped
Britain	4,830	£2,962,111	8,575
Germany	2,589	RM24 m (= £1.2 m)	14,208

casualties *Military:* the final number of deaths and injuries due to the war will never be known, since record-keeping in the midst of a battle can never be relied upon, and even records conscientiously kept can be easily destroyed or lost in a subsequent action. The best available figures, collated from a variety of authoritative sources, are as follows:

Country	Dead	Wounded	Missing	Total
Australia	58,150	152,170	–	210,320
Austria-Hungary	922,000	3,600,000	855,283	5,377,283
Belgium	102,000	450,000	–	552,000
Britain	658,700	2,032,150	359,150	3,050,000
Canada	56,500	149,700	–	206,200
France	1,359,000	4,200,000	361,650	5,920,650
Germany	1,600,000	4,065,000	103,000	5,768,000
India	43,200	65,175	5,875	114,250
Italy	465,560	959,100	–	1,424,660
New Zealand	16,130	40,750	–	56,880
Russia	1,700,000	5,000,000	–	6,700,000

Turkey	250,000	400,000	–	650,000
USA	58,480	189,955	14,290	262,725
Grand Totals:	7,289,720	21,304,000	1,699,248	30,292,968

civilian: it is impossible to arrive at even approximate figures for civilian casualties due to the war. Attribution of civilian deaths in wartime is always difficult as a connection between the war and any particular death may not be readily made. During World War I, in the confused conditions of Central Europe, ravaged by the oscillations of armies, the fate of many civilians will never be known.

I have many times asked myself whether there can be more potent advocates of peace...than this massed multitude of silent witnesses to the desolation of war.
> King George V on the massive *casualties*, while viewing war cemeteries in Flanders, 1922.

Caudron (Caudron Freres of Issy-les-Moulineaux). French aircraft manufacturer. The Caudron G3 was developed 1914 and was one of the first French military aircraft, being used as a reconnaissance bomber. A peculiar machine, it had a short body with two seats and a rotary engine, biplane wings, and an openwork frame extending rearward to carry the tail. However, it was reliable and easy to fly and hence was used in large numbers by the French, Belgian, British, Italian, and Russian forces and later as a trainer by the US Army air service. It was also built under license in Britain and Russia. The later G4 (1915) was of similar design but had two engines and could carry up to 100 kg/ of bombs.

cavalry Mounted troops formed a large part of all 1914 armies, since they constituted the mobile and shock force and the reconnaissance element of an army, as well as the arm best able to exploit a victory. In conditions of open warfare they occasionally performed well, as in the activities of German cavalry in France and Belgium during 1914 and British cavalry in Palestine and Mesopotamia 1917–18, but in the trench warfare phase they were of little use.

The prime tactical aim of most attacks was to drive a hole through the opposing line, through which the cavalry could then pour to expand behind the enemy lines and create havoc. This never actually happened, since the intense artillery preparation and the use of trenches, wire, and other obstacles all conspired to make the movement of cavalry in the front line virtually impossible, even if it was possible to breach enemy lines, which was rare. Moreover the vulnerability of the horse in the face of machine gun and artillery fire made cavalry operations especially risky. A considerable number of cavalry eventually fought dismounted as infantry in most armies.

Cavan Frederick Rudolph Lambart, 10th Earl of. British soldier, he started his career in the Grenadier Guards and served in South Africa. He took command of the Guards Division 1915, then of 14th Corps, taking them to Italy 1917. In 1918 he became commander in chief British Troops Italy with the rank of general, a post he held until the end of the war.

Cavell Nurse Edith 1865–1915. British matron of a Red Cross hospital in Brussels, who helped Allied soldiers escape to the Dutch frontier. She was court-martialled by the Germans and condemned to death.

Standing as I do, in the view of God and eternity I realize that patriotism is not enough. I must have no hatred or bitterness towards anyone.

> *Edith Cavell* to chaplain before her
> execution by a firing squad 12 Oct 1915

---

censorship control by state or other authority of the dissemination of information. In 1914–18 this meant overseeing newspapers and magazines to ensure that information of value to the enemy was not published, monitoring outgoing mail to foreign countries and soldiers' mail to their families for the same purpose, and monitoring incoming foreign mail to extract any information about enemy movements, equipment, or morale. This latter also included monitoring correspondence to and from prisoners of war in case coded information was included. All the combatant countries employed censorship in varying degrees of strictness.

Central Powers Germany and her allies, Austria-Hungary, Turkey, and Bulgaria. The name derived from the geographical position of the Germans and Austrians in Central Europe. Italy had also been allied to Germany and Austria-Hungary under the Triple Alliance 1882 but when war broke out, Italy initially remained neutral before leaving the alliance to join the ◊Allies.

Champagne, Battles of two battles 1914–15 between German and French armies on the Eastern Front.

First Battle: Dec 1914–March 1915. This was a battle of attrition in which General Joffre hoped to engage as many Germans as possible in order to wear them down and also allow the Russians on the Eastern Front to obtain some successes. Both sides were entrenched and the battle was simply a series of limited attacks and counter-attacks at intervals throughout the winter. Artillery support was, for the period, enormous; over 100,000 shells were fired by the French in one 24-hour period in February. At the end of the battle, the French had advanced 450 m/500 yds.

Second Battle: Sept–Oct 1915. This, too, was designed to relieve pressure on the Russians by drawing German troops away from the Eastern Front. The initial French assault gained 4 km/2.5 mi to the north in the first day, but the units in the south of the line were less effective, allowing the Germans to withdraw troops to reinforce their northern defences. They held the French advance long enough for reserve troops to be brought from other parts of the front. When the French resumed their attack 26 Sept the German forces drove them back, and a third French attempt on 4 Oct was also stopped. The battle died away at the end of Oct 1915 without further gains. The French army lost 120,000 killed or taken prisoner, and 260,000 wounded, while the German dead were estimated at 140,000.

Channel Ferry train ferry across the English Channel constructed early 1918 for the rapid movement of vehicles, tanks, guns, and train-loads of stores. Four services were run: from Richborough to Calais or Dunkirk and from Southampton to Dieppe or Cherbourg. Roll-on/roll-off ships were used to carry both rail and road vehicles: the record time for unloading one ship, reloading it, and casting off again was 19 minutes.

Charleroi, Battle of battle between French and German forces 21–24 Aug 1914. The poorly equipped and organized 5th French Army, which had concentrated around Charleroi on mobilization, was the main French force involved. In addition there were some 25,000 Belgian troops at Namur and about 30,000 French reservists at Maubeuge in the process of being clothed and equipped. Three German armies, the 1st (under von Kluck), the 2nd (under von Bulow), and the 3rd (under Hausen) were all moving in the direction of Charleroi and the French were in danger of being encircled and destroyed. The French commander, General Lanrezac, was ordered to take the offensive but, appreciating that he would walk into a German trap, stood fast, waiting for the Germans to cross the Sambre, when he could attack them in strength. Unfortunately his Corps commanders ignored his orders and made independent attacks. However, the German operations were equally badly co-ordinated, so that the French were able to fall back in good order, though this exposed the flank of the British Army and led to the retreat from ◊Mons. This fighting retreat by the British and French held up the German advance and gave time for the French to rally troops ready to fight the battle of the ◊Marne.

Lanrezac was severely criticized at the time, but when the full picture was understood it was realized that his actions had saved the 5th French Army from total destruction and bought sufficient time to prepare a counter-blow.

Chateau-Thierry, Battle of American victory, May–June 1918. During the German attack on the Marne, the 2nd US division and additional infantry regiments relieved French troops and immediately counter-attacked the Germans N of Chateau-Thierry. Due to the destruction of a bridge behind them, the US troops were unable to retire when ordered to withdraw and fought their way down the Marne valley to the next bridge, where they then crossed; they had been in action continuously for 72 hours. They then prevented the Germans from crossing, after which the battle died away for a few days. It was revived by the action at ◊Belleau Wood 6 June 1918.

chemical warfare use in war of gaseous, liquid, or solid substances intended to have a toxic effect on humans, animals, or plants. Together with biological warfare, it was banned by the Geneva Protocol 1925.

Chemical agents are classified according to their effect and their persistence. The classes by effect are: Nerve, Toxic, Lung Injurant, Lachrymatory (tear gas), Vesicants (blister gas) and Sternutators (sneeze or irritant gas). They may be persistent – the liquid remains in an active condition on dry ground for over one hour – or non-persistent – the gas or liquid vaporizes or becomes inert in less than one hour.

Gas was first used by the Germans as a substitute for explosives in artillery shells, the first major attempt being at ◊Bolimov Feb 1915. This was unsuccessful and chlorine released from storage cylinders to drift over enemy trenches with the wind was then used with considerable success at Ypres April 1915. As defensive measures such as gas masks were evolved, so different agents were introduced to circumvent these defences and different methods of delivery developed. Over 3,000 chemical agents were investigated for possible use during the war but of these only about 30 were found suitable for actual use in the field. The principal gases used 1915–18 were ◊chlorine and ◊phosgene (lung injurants), ◊mustard gas (vesicant), ◊diphenylchlorarsine (sternutator) and ◊ethyliodoacetate (lachrymatory).

chemin des dames road in the *département* of Aisne, France, from Craonne to Malmaison across the crest of the Craonne plateau. Its possession was fiercely contested throughout the war.

After their defeat on the Marne Sept 1914, the Germans occupied the area and it was the scene of intermittent fighting thereafter. In April 1917 General Nivelle decided on an offensive to capture the road, the plateau, and the Aisne valley beyond. After a prolonged and fierce battle the French finally captured the road and plateau by the beginning of Nov 1917. During the German Spring Offensive 1918 the French were driven from their position and the road passed back into German hands. Finally, in the Allied advance Sept 1918 the road was retaken by General Mangin's 10th French Army.

Chetwode Sir Philip Walhouse 1869–1950. British soldier. Chetwode entered the 19th Hussars 1889, and served in Burma and South Africa. In 1914 he commanded the 5th cavalry brigade in action against the Germans before Mons. In 1916 he went to Egypt to assume command of the desert mounted column of the Egyptian expeditionary force, which he led in the early campaigns in Palestine.

Allenby based his plans during the conquest of Palestine largely on Chetwode's experience and advice. He was promoted to lieutenant-general 1919.

chlorine the first gas to be used effectively in war, being employed by the Germans against British and French positions near Ypres on 22 April 1915. On this occasion 165 tonnes/168 tons of chlorine gas were released from 5,730 cylinders in the German lines to drift across the Allied positions on a 6 km/4 mi front. Some 15,000 casualties were caused, 5,000 of which proved fatal. Chlorine remained the principal cloud gas used by both sides during the war; initially, when no effective masks existed, it was highly effective and caused thousands of casualties, but as gas-masks were perfected its effectiveness was greatly reduced. Thereafter, it was mixed with other gases, such as ◊phosgene and ◊chloropicrin, and continued to be used in this way for the rest of the war.

chloropicrin lung-injurant war gas first employed by Russia against the Germans Aug 1916 and subsequently used by all combatants. Also called 'Nitrochloroform', it was used both in artillery and mortar projectiles and as a cloud gas. The British also mixed it with chlorine as 'Yellow Star' gas, released from cylinders in cloud attacks.

Chloropicrin is a lethal compound which also acts as a lachrymator (tear gas). It could penetrate the canisters of all gas-masks to cause nausea, vomiting, colic, and other ill- effects which would cause troops to remove their masks, leaving them vulnerable to lethal concentrations of other gases, such as ◊phosgene, fired simultaneously. In time, gas-masks were made impervious to it, and this, coupled with its persistence, which limited its tactical use, led to its eventual abandonment.

Christmas truce unofficial cessation of hostilities between British and German troops in the front lines on Christmas Day 1914. Quite spontaneously, soldiers of both sides emerged from their trenches and fraternized in 'No Man's Land', exchanging food and drinks, playing football and singing carols. They then returned to their trenches but no shots were exchanged for the rest of the day.

Churchill Winston (Leonard Spencer) 1874–1965. British Conservative politician, prime minister 1940–45 and 1951–55. In

Parliament from 1900, as a Liberal until 1923, he held a number of ministerial offices. As 1st Lord of the Admiralty 1915, he took responsibility for the ill-fated plan to attack the Dardanelles in order to remove Turkey from the war and open up a supply route to Russia. Hence he is often blamed for the Gallipoli debacle involving Anzac troops. In 1915 a coalition government was formed and Churchill was relegated to the Chancellorship of the Duchy of Lancaster. He resigned office and in 1915–16 served in the trenches in France, but then resumed his parliamentary duties and was minister of munitions under Lloyd George 1917, when he was concerned with the development of the tank.

The British people have taken for themselves this motto –
'Business carried on as usual during alterations on the map of Europe'.
> Winston *Churchill*, speech at the Guildhall 9 Nov 1914.

After the Armistice he was secretary for war 1919–21 and then as colonial secretary played a leading part in the establishment of the Irish Free State.

Clemenceau Georges 1841–1929. French politician and journalist, prime minister 1906–09 and 1917–20. After World War I he presided over the peace conference in Paris that drew up the Treaty of ◊Versailles, but failed to secure the Rhine as a frontier for France.

It is easier to make war than to make peace.
> Georges *Clemenceau*, speech at Verdun 20 July 1919.

Clemenceau was mayor of Montmartre, Paris, in the war of 1870, and was elected a member of the National Assembly at Bordeaux 1871. He was elected a deputy 1876 after the formation of the Third Republic. An extreme radical, he soon earned the nickname of 'the Tiger' on account of his ferocious attacks on politicians whom he disliked. He lost his seat 1893 and spent the next 10 years in journalism. In 1902 he was elected senator for the Var, became minister for the interior 1906 and shortly afterwards prime minister, and was soon one of the most powerful politicians in France. When he became prime minister for the second time 1917, he made the decisive appointment of Marshal ◊Foch as supreme commander.

Conrad Count Franz von Hotzendorf 1852–1925. Austrian soldier. Appointed Chief of Staff 1906, he was largely responsible for modernizing and re-organizing the Austro-Hungarian army. Believing in an aggressive policy towards Italy and Serbia, he supported the diplomatic moves which set the war in motion. Although a good organizer and strategist his performance in the field was poor and his successes were largely due to German support. Created field-marshal 1916 his failures against ◊Brusilov led to German assumption of command of the combined Austro-German forces and he was relieved of his post March 1917. He continued to serve as commander in the southern Tyrol area, but without notable success and was eventually dismissed July 1918.

conscientious objectors those refusing military service under conscription upon grounds of conscience or religious belief. Such objections were considered by tribunals and some objectors were given total exemption; others were directed to other work of national importance or were placed in non-combatant corps. Those who refused these alternatives were usually imprisoned or drafted into military service where, if they persisted in refusal, were court-martialled and imprisoned. In Britain, objectors were disenfranchised for five years after the war unless they had performed some work of national importance.

conscription legislation for all able-bodied male citizens (and female in some countries, such as Israel) to serve with the armed forces. It originated in France 1792, and in the 19th and 20th centuries became the established practice in almost all European states. Modern conscription systems often permit alternative national service for conscientious objectors. In the USA a Selective Service Act was passed 1917. In Britain conscription was introduced for single men between 18 and 41 in March 1916 and for married men two months later, but was abolished after the Armistice.

convoy system grouping of ships to sail together under naval escort in wartime. In World War I navy escort vessels were at first used only to accompany troop ships, but the convoy system was adopted for merchant shipping when the unrestricted German submarine campaign began 1917.

Coronel, Battle of naval engagement between British and German forces 1 Nov 1914. At the outbreak of war the German naval squadron on the China station under Admiral von ◊Spee began commerce raiding in the W Pacific ocean. In Oct 1914 a small British squadron under Admiral Sir Christopher Cradock (1862–1914), sent in search of von Spee, encountered the Germans off Coronel, on the coast of Chile. Cradock was outgunned and outnumbered and was completely defeated, losing two cruisers and 1,500 men. He was lost along with his flagship.

Courland, Campaign in clashes between German and Russian forces, April–May 1915. The Germans crossed the Niemen river in three dispersed columns advancing toward Shavli (now Siauliai). Having captured Shavli they moved on to Libau (now Liepaja) but were met by a strong Russian force which threw them back. A fourth column, moving along the coast, took Libau 8 May, but a flanking movement by Bavarian cavalry to attack the main railway from Petrograd was routed by Russian cavalry. This caused the German line to fall back, pursued by the Russians who gained another victory before the Germans finally stabilized their line, though they retained their hold on Libau. The German advance was resumed in July, when they were able to drive the Russians back 80 km/50 mi in 3 days. By 1 Aug they had captured Mitau (now Jelgava) and the Russians then fell back toward Dvinsk (now Daugavpils), leaving the whole area in German hands.

Cowans Sir John Steven 1862–1921. British soldier. Joined the Rifle Brigade 1882. In 1906 Cowans went to India and commanded a brigade there 1908–10. He was director-general of Territorial Forces in Britain 1910–12, and became quartermaster-general and member of the Army Council 1912, posts he held throughout the war. Knighted 1913, he retired 1919.

Cressy, HMS British armoured cruiser of the Cressy class, built 1898–1901. The Cressy and its sister ships, ◊HMS Hogue and ◊HMS

Aboukir were all sunk 22 Sept 1914 by the German submarine U-9 some 30 km/20 mi off the Hook of Holland, with the loss of 25 officers and 535 seamen. It is the only known occasion of three warships being sunk in succession by a single submarine.

cryptography construction and use of secret codes and similar methods of communication. The breaking and decipherment of such codes is known as 'cryptanalysis'.

The codes used during 1914–18 varied in complexity; those dealing with strategic and diplomatic affairs were the most difficult to construct or break, while those dealing with simple tactical movements needed only be difficult enough to preserve their secrets until the particular situation was over. Codes were changed frequently in order to forestall their being broken, and all combatants employed special staffs to intercept and, where possible, decipher enemy messages. Notable successes in this field include the seizure of German naval code-books from the warship ◊Magdeburg and the decipherment of the ◊Zimmerman Telegram.

Ctesiphon, Battle of battle between British and Turkish forces, 22 Nov 1915. After the British capture of Kut the Turks retreated up the Tigris river towards Baghdad, entrenching at Ctesiphon, some 40 km/25 mi from the city. A force of about 9,000 men under General Townshend attacked 22 Nov 1915 and after a severe fight took the trench line. Short of ammunition, they withdrew to the captured trenches overnight but next day were forced back by the Turks and retreated to Kut with 1,600 prisoners. British losses during the battle and retreat were 4,567 men, over half Townshend's force.

Currie Sir Arthur William 1875–1933. Canadian soldier. A member of the militia, in 1914 he was a lieutenant-colonel and led a Canadian brigade in the Second battle of ◊Ypres 1915. Promoted to leading a division, in 1917 be succeeded General Byng as commander of the Canadian Corps. He forced the ◊Quéant Switch line and captured Cambrai 1918. Knighted 1917, he was the first Canadian officer to reach the rank of general. In 1920 he became principal of McGill University, Montreal.

cyanogen bromide tear gas introduced by the Austrians Sept 1916 and later adopted by the British and Italian armies. Its prime effect is lachrymatory and irritant, becoming lethal at higher concentrations. However it is highly corrosive and decomposes in contact with metal, and is also unstable in storage, losing its effect and becoming inert. Hence its use as a war gas was short, and it was soon replaced by more stable compositions.

cyanogen chloride toxic nerve gas introduced by the French Oct 1916 to replace hydrocyanic acid. It acts on the nerve centres, particularly those controlling breathing, causing rapid paralysis and death. At low concentrations it acts as a tear gas and lung irritant and prolonged exposure at these concentrations can be lethal due to lung damage.

D

Damascus capital of Syria, on the river Barada, SE of Beirut. Reputedly the oldest continuously inhabited city in the world, Damascus was an ancient city even in Old Testament times.

During World War I, it was taken from the Turks by the British with Arab aid Oct 1918. It became the capital of French-mandated Syria 1920, under the Emir Faisal (1885– 1933) who was crowned King Faisal I of Syria there March 1920.

Dankl Victor 1854–1941. Austrian soldier. Dankl joined the Austro-Hungarian cavalry 1874 and became general of cavalry 1912. In 1914 he took command of the 1st Austrian Army which invaded SE Poland Aug 1914 and was heavily defeated by the Russians in the battles of ◊Rava Russka. After operations against Ivangorod July–Aug 1915, he was transferred to the Italian front and from then until the Austrian defeat was commander in chief of Austrian troops in N Italy.

d'Annunzio Gabriele 1863–1938. Italian poet, novelist, and play-wright who was active during 1915 in turning public opinion to the side of the Allies. He joined the air service and flew many bombing missions, losing an eye as a result of an accident. He led a flight of eight Italian aircraft dropping leaflets over Vienna Aug 1918.

Following the end of the war, d'Annunzio was dissatisfied with delays by the Versailles Conference in deciding the future of Fiume, and in 1919 led an expedition of volunteers to capture it. He then took the port of Zara in Dalmatia, which he held until 1921, becoming a national hero, and was created Prince of Montenevoso 1924. Influenced by Nietzsche's writings, he later became an ardent exponent of fascism.

Dardanelles, attacks on the the Dardanelles is a narrow channel between Asiatic and European Turkey, forming a passage between the Mediterranean and the Sea Of Marmora and thence to the Black Sea.

◊Churchill first suggested attacking the Dardanelles in order to defend Egypt at the War Cabinet 25 Nov 1914. On 2 Jan 1915 the Russian government asked for some military diversion to relieve pressure on the Eastern Front, but ◊Kitchener said he had no troops available. Therefore a naval attack was mounted 19 Feb 1915 by eight warships, which fired at the various coastal defence batteries and put landing parties ashore to wreck some of the forts. On 18 March an attempt was made to run warships through the channel but four were lost to gunfire and mines and others damaged. The Allies lost some 750 sailors while the Turks lost less than 200 men.

After this debacle the idea of a purely naval attack was given up, and instead planning began for a military action against the ◊Gallipoli peninsula. The only real effect of the naval attack was to alert the Turkish army so that they had time to reinforce and fortify the area before the Gallipoli landings.

Dardanelles Commission Royal Commission appointed in Britain to enquire into the failure of the Dardanelles and Gallipoli expeditions. The Commission interviewed many witnesses 1916 and presented its final report 1919. It concluded that planning had been poor, difficulties under-estimated, delays by the government after the first attack had wasted precious time, that there had been insufficient artillery and ammunition, and that there had been personality clashes among the commanders. Various people were mildly censured, but no careers were affected.

Debeney General Marie-Eugene 1864–1943. French soldier. After education at St Cyr, he entered the army as a lieutenant of Chasseurs 1886. In 1914 he was sub-Chief of Staff of the 1st French Army. He subsequently commanded the 33rd and 32nd Corps and the 7th Army 1916, and was appointed to command the 1st Army Dec 1917. He defended Amiens March–April 1918, and captured Montdidier and carried his line forward to the river Somme Aug 1918. He was appointed commandant of St Cyr military academy June 1919.

Degoutte General Jean Marie Joseph 1866–1938. French soldier. Entered the French army as a volunteer, and was commissioned into the 4th Zouaves 1890. After extensive service in the French colonies during 1914, he became Chief of Staff of the 4th army corps. Promoted to brigadier-general March 1916, he commanded the Moroccan Division and became general of division March 1918. In June 1918 he commanded the 6th Army at ◊Chateau-Thierry and at the second battle of the ◊Marne, and played a considerable part in the liberation of Belgium. He became commander in chief of the Allied Armies of Occupation in Germany 1920.

Deguise General Victor 1855–. Belgian soldier. Entered the Belgian army as a lieutenant of engineers 1877 and was appointed professor of fortification at the military academy 1888. Later served as commandant of engineers at Brussels 1909–11, and was then promoted to director of fortifications for the 3rd Military District. In 1914 he was military governor of ◊Antwerp and directed the defence of that city until it fell. Together with many of his troops his escape route led into Holland, where he was interned for the rest of the war.

De Havilland Geoffrey 1882–1965. British aircraft designer who designed and whose company produced the Moth biplane, the Mosquito fighter-bomber of World War II, and the postwar Comet, the world's first jet-driven airliner to enter commercial service.

The principal De Havilland aircraft produced in World War I were the DH2, a pusher biplane (with the engine behind the pilot so that the propeller pushed rather than pulled the machine) very similar to the ◊FE2, the DH4, a more conventional two-seater biplane used as a bomber, and the DH9 twin-engined biplane heavy bomber.

Deimling Field Marshal Berthold Karl Adolf von 1853–1934. German soldier. Entered the German army 1871, trained for the General Staff and served in ◊German Southwest Africa 1904–07, then returned to Germany to command an infantry brigade. He was prominent in the early stages of the battle for ◊Verdun, was promoted to Field-Marshal, and was in command of the German troops in the Somme area from Nov 1916.

Denikin Anton Ivanovich 1872–1947. Russian soldier. Entered the army 1887 and distinguished himself in the Russo-Japanese War 1904–05. During the Great War he was promoted to general but did not come into prominence until after the March Revolution, when he became chief of staff to General ◊Alexeyev May 1917. In Sept 1917 he became commander in chief of the Russian Southwest Armies but after the November Revolution he withdrew his forces to Rostov-on-Don and organized a volunteer army of 60,000 Whites (loyalists) under Alexeyev. After Alexeyev's death in 1918 he took command and had several military successes, but in 1919, just as he was preparing to join with the forces of ◊Kolchak, he was routed and escaped to England. He wrote a history of the Revolution and the Civil War.

De Robeck Admiral Sir John Michael 1862–1928. British sailor. Son of the 4th Baron de Robeck of Naas, Ireland, a Swedish title. He joined the Royal Navy 1875 and by 1911 was a rear-admiral. In 1914 he was admiral of patrols, and in 1915 was appointed commander of the force sent to assist the landing at ◊Gallipoli, directing operations off the coast until the evacuation 1916. In 1919 he became commander in chief in the Mediterranean and high commissioner at Constantinople. Knighted 1916, he was made a baron 1919, and full admiral 1920.

destroyer small, fast warship, originally termed 'torpedo-boat destroyer' and designed by Britain to counter the large flotillas built by the French and Russian navies in the late 19th century. It proved so effective that torpedo-boats were more or less abandoned in the early 1900s, but the rise of the submarine found a new task for the 'destroyer', as it now became. They proved invaluable as anti-submarine vessels in both World War I and World War II.

Deventer Sir Jacob Louis 1874–1922. South African soldier. Originally a farmer, he became second-in-command to General Smuts in the Boer invasion of Cape Colony. When rebellion broke out in South Africa 1914, he was in command of a force which prevented the rebels capturing Upington. He became commander in chief East Africa May 1917 and held that post until the colony was captured. He was knighted 1917 and made honorary lieutenant-general 1919.

Diaz General Armando 1861–1928. Italian soldier. Educated in the military academy of Turin, he entered the army 1881 and saw active service in Abyssinia 1896. In 1915 he was a junior major-general and commanded the 23rd Corps in the battles of the ◊Carso 1916. After the battle of ◊Caporetto he replaced General ◊Cadorna as commander in chief Nov 1917 and held the Austro-Hungarian advance on the line of the Piave. In June 1918 he beat off a strong attack, and severely defeated the Austrians along their whole line Oct–Nov 1918. He became inspector-general of the Italian Army 1919.

digger familiar name for Australian soldiers. Originally used between themselves and derived from the argot of the Australian goldfields, it was picked up by British soldiers and gradually spread into common use.

dimethyl sulphate war gas, used by the Germans (as 'D-Stoff') and the French (as 'Rationite'), it is a combination lachrymatory, toxic, and vesicant substance. A powerful irritant in low concentrations it is fatal in higher concentrations and long exposure, and it also has a peculiar caustic action on the skin. It decomposes readily in the presence of moisture, even damp air, and so has very short persistence – hence it was little used.

diphenylchlorarsine war gas, developed by the Germans and introduced simultaneously with ◊mustard gas as the agent to be used on offensive operations, since mustard was too persistent to be used against areas toward which German troops were advancing. Known to the Germans as 'Clark 1' it was specifically aimed at penetrating Allied gasmasks, by distributing the substance as a fine dust which could not be neutralized by the chemicals or stopped by the coarse filters in the masks. Inhaling the dust causes nausea, vomiting, headaches, and chest pains. It is rarely lethal and then only in extremely high concentrations rarely achieved in field conditions.

Clark 1 was the greatest German technical error in the chemical warfare field, as they fired it in shells which pulverized on landing and liberated the dust and due to the design of the shells much of the dust was too large to penetrate gasmasks. Allied experimenters discovered that if the substance was vaporized by heat, it was dispersed as a fine mist or smoke with molecular particles which were far more effective. In this condition it was easier to achieve a lethal result, and the Allies were preparing a suitable design of smoke generator when the war ended.

Dixmude Belgian town in province of West Flanders, on the River Yser 12 miles N of Ypres. In late 1914 the town changed hands several times before finally being held by the Germans, but the resistance there, particularly by a force of French Marines, effectively halted the German drive to Dunkirk and allowed the French armies of the North to prepare for the battle of the ◊Yser. The town was nearly recaptured during the battle of ◊Ypres 1915, but remained in German hands until taken by the Belgian Army 29 Sept 1918, by which time the civilian population had fallen from 4,000 to 450. The town was awarded the *Croix de Guerre* by President Poincaré of France 1920.

Doberitz village near Potsdam, Germany. In 1914 a prisoner-of-war camp was established there on an old Prussian Army exercise ground, in which British, French, and Russian prisoners were confined. Conditions in the early days were notoriously bad, largely due to the unexpected number of prisoners taken in the first weeks of the war, but in 1915 permanent huts were erected and conditions improved.

Dogger Bank, Battle of the Dogger Bank is an extensive sandbank in the middle of the North Sea, site of a naval engagement between British and German forces 24 Jan 1915. A German force of 4 battle-cruisers, 4 light cruisers, and 22 destroyers left Germany to attack the English coast. By coincidence, the British Grand Fleet of 6 battle-cruisers, 8 light cruisers, and 28 destroyers left Scapa Flow on the same day to carry out a sweep of the North Sea. The two forces met at 7.20 a.m. 24 Jan. The British put on speed to overhaul the German line, the first shots were fired at about 9 a.m., and the two fleets exchanged shots for about three hours. The German battle-cruiser Blucher was sunk by gun and torpedo fire, while the British flagship Lion was hit in the engine-room and stopped. Admiral ◊Beatty transferred his flag to a destroyer, but when the German fleet approached Heligoland the British disengaged due to the danger of attack by submarines and minefields. British casualties amounted to 6 killed and 22 wounded; German casualties came to about 1,000 killed and 300 wounded. Several ships on both sides were damaged.

Doiran-Struma Front, Campaign on the Graeco-British operations against Bulgarian forces on the Greece–Bulgaria border in Salonika, 1918. Apart from a minor Bulgarian attack 1917 this front had lain dormant until the British attacked a Bulgarian salient thrusting toward Greece Sept 1918. This led to more fighting and eventually the British and Greek forces launched a heavy attack enveloping Lake Doiran and capturing the town. At about the same time the French launched an attack on another part of the front, so the British attack was renewed in order to prevent the Bulgarians reinforcing the areas threatened by the French. Both attacks moved forward with success, crossing the Bulgarian border and reaching Petric 30 Sept 1918 when Bulgaria surrendered and the advance stopped.

Dolomites, Campaign in the Fighting between Austrian and Italian forces, 1915. The Dolomite mountain range became an almost continuous front throughout the war, from Cortino d'Ampezzo in the west to the Predil Pass on the east. The ◊Trentino front lay to the west and the ◊Isonzo Front to the south.

When the Italians entered the war 1915 they made a general advance into the mountains, trying to cut off strategic Austrian railway links on the northern side. Fighting in extremely difficult conditions, and making full use of their elite ◊Alpini troops, the Italians made considerable gains and fended off strong Austrian attacks. However they were never able to break through the Austrian defences to reach the railway lines and the whole front eventually settled down to a static line.

DORA in the UK, acronym for the *D*efence *o*f the *R*ealm *A*cts, passed Nov 1914 and March 1915, which conferred extraordinary powers on the government for the duration of the war. Their general tenor was to prevent communication with the enemy, prevent spreading of false reports, and secure the safety of the armed forces, but beneath that lay a multitude of regulations and orders affecting the entire population.

Among other things, the regulations permitted the commandeering of buildings for military use or even their demolition where they might interfere with defensive measures; ordered lights to be obscured or extinguished during air raids; prohibited melting down gold coins for ornamental purposes; controlled the opening and closing of public houses, the sale of liquor near dockyards or barracks, and eventually the supply of food to public restaurants. Most of these regulations were repealed as soon as the war ended, but many were not, notably the restrictions on the sale of liquor, some of which remained in force until the 1980s.

Douaumont French village in the *département* of the Meuse, near which is a fort of the same name. The fort became one of the principal points of battle during the attack on ◊Verdun, and was captured by the Germans Feb 1916. The village itself was taken by the Germans March 1916 and subsequently changed hands several times before being finally retaken by the French along with the fort Oct 1916.

doughboy nickname for a US infantry soldier in the two world wars, especially World War I. One possible derivation of the name is from the large buttons on the uniforms of the soldiers of the US Civil War, which were so called.

Dover Patrol sub-unit of the British Navy based at Dover and Dunkirk throughout the war. Its primary task was to close the English Channel to German ships and escort Allied ships safely through the area. It also mounted fighting patrols against the German-held channel coast and German coastal craft, made two daring raids against ◊Ostend and ◊Zeebrugge. The Royal Naval Air Service unit attached to the patrol made frequent bombing attacks against Zeebrugge, Ostend, Bruges, and other targets. A naval siege gun force, operating a number of heavy gun ◊monitors, acted as heavy artillery support for the left flank of the Allied armies in France. Throughout the war a total of 125,100 supply ships passed through the area controlled by the patrol, of which only 73 were sunk.

Dragomirov Vladimir (b. 1862). Russian soldier. He first became prominent commanding a regiment in Galicia and Volhynia 1916, where he was wounded. He took command of the armies of the Northern Front May 1917, and succeeded ◊Denikin as commander of the Southwestern Front Sept 1917. He became premier of an anti-Bolshevik government Nov 1918 and was president of Denikin's military council and military governor of Kiev Oct 1919. He vanished after the Polish capture of Kiev 1920.

Dreadnought class of battleships built for the British navy after 1905 and far superior in speed and armaments to any other vessel of the time. The first modern battleship, the Dreadnought remained the basis of battleship design for more than 50 years. The first of the class was launched 1906, with armaments consisting entirely of big guns.

The German Nassau class was begun 1907, and by 1914 the USA, France, Japan, and Austria-Hungary all had battleships of a similar class to the Dreadnought. German plans to build similar craft led to the naval race that contributed to Anglo-German antagonism and the origins of World War I.

Drina, Battle of the battle between Austrian and Serbian forces, Sept 1914. Fighting broke out when the Austrians crossed the river Drina to invade Serbia 8 Sept. In the north the Serbs were gathered in strength and repulsed the attack, but in the south the Austrians had more success and made a considerable advance. On 14 Sept the Serbs counter-attacked and after hard fighting drove the Austrians back to the river Drina, whereupon both sides, exhausted, dug in and the battle died off.

Dubail Augustin Yvon Edmond 1851–1934. French soldier. Dubail joined the French army as a lieutenant of infantry 1870 and served in the Franco-Prussian War. He later became Chief of Staff of the Algerian command and colonel of the 1st Zouave Regiment. At the outbreak of war he was Chief of Staff of the French Army and member of the military council. He was given command of the 1st French Army operating in Alsace and Lorraine, successfully defended Nancy, and then held the German attack on the Heights of the Meuse. He was appointed military governor of Paris April 1916 and remained in that post for the rest of the war.

Dubois Pierre Joseph Louis Alfred 1852–1924. French soldier. He joined the French Army as a lieutenant of Dragoons 1874, and served in Algeria and Tunisia. He became commander of the 9th French Army Corps 1913 and in 1914 was engaged in the defence of Nancy under General ◊Castelnau. He then took the corps to Belgium where more heavy fighting ensued. He took command of the 6th Army 1915 and in 1916 was placed in command at ◊Verdun. He was placed on the reserve 1917.

dug-out term coined in the war for any underground shelter for troops. Dug-outs were generally excavated close to the trench line to provide places for troops to rest, sleep, or eat in some degree of safety and comfort. The term was also used to refer to elderly officers and men who had retired from military service prior to the war but who volunteered to serve again in administrative and training posts.

Dunajetz, Battles of battles between Austro-German and Russian forces, 1915. A large German force was assembled around Cracow April 1915 for an intended attack on Galicia. The Russians held a line on the Dunajetz river with about 4 corps against the Germans' 12 until a strong Austrian attack in the Gorltz area in early May broke through the Russian lines on a 16 km/10 mi front. While the Russians were attempting to stem this breach, the force on the Dunajetz river attacked, intending to break through in the direction of Tarnow. They had little success, failing to cross the river, until the Russian collapse in the south worsened and the Russian forces in the north were forced to fall back to avoid exposing their flank. The advance continued on the entire front, the Russians fighting every inch of the way but by 11 May they had been driven back to a line on the San river, where they were finally able to consolidate and stop the German drive. The Germans captured upwards of 100,000 prisoners during their advance but were unable to bring the Russians to a decisive battle and destroy them.

Dunnite high explosive used in American service. Named after Major Dunn, its developer, and also called 'Explosive D', it was made of ammonium picrate powder. Relatively insensitive, it was widely used in armour-piercing shells for naval use and coastal defence, since it withstood the shock of impact against armour without detonating, allowing the shell to pierce the armour before the fuse initiated the explosive.

Dunsterforce British military force led by General Dunsterville to ◊Baku, consisting of about 750 motor vehicles and a battalion of infantry. It left Baghdad 27 Jan 1918 and drove 700 miles via Kormanshah to link up with White Russian forces near Tehran 1 June 1918, from where the combined force advanced to Baku.

Dunsterville General Lionel Charles 1865–1946. British soldier. He joined the infantry 1884 then transferred to the Indian Army with whom he served on the Northwest Frontier, in Waziristan, and in China. After various posts in India, he went to Mesopotamia 1918 and commanded the expedition to ◊Baku. He was promoted to major-general 1918.

He was a schoolmate of Rudyard Kipling, who used him as the model for 'Stalky', the hero of his book *Stalky & Co*.

Dvina, Battles of the inconclusive series of engagements between German and Russian forces, 1915–16. The river Dvina formed a natural barrier before Riga and the first battle, Aug–Sept 1915, swayed back and forth across the river but died away with both contestants in their original positions. The second battle flared intermittently Jan–Aug 1916 as a series of attacks by German forces under Hindenburg were repulsed by the Russians under Kuropatkin. Before either side could gain an advantage, the Galician front flared up and both commanders turned to that, leaving the forces on the Dvina more or less where they had been in 1915.

Dvinsk, Battles for Russian town, now Latvian and known as Daugafpils. As a result of the first battles for the ◊Dvina, German forces crossed the river and advanced on Dvinsk, a strategic rail and road junction. The Germans mounted three successive attacks, each in increasing strength, but all were driven back by the Russian defenders.

The second battle began 19 Jan 1916 and lasted for most of the year in a series of attacks and counter-attacks. However, the success of the ◊Brusilov Offensive in Galicia diverted the attention of the commanders and the Dvina front settled into trench warfare. The front remained in that state until the collapse of the Russian armies 1917.

E

E-Class submarines British submarine class begun 1911, some 23 boats being built. The E11 and E14 entered the Sea of Marmora 1915 beneath Turkish minefields and sank several Turkish and German ships, while the E15 was sunk attempting to run through the Dardanelles April 1915.

Eagle Hut, The American YMCA centre opened for US troops in London, 3 Sept 1917. The centre was staffed by over 800 voluntary workers and provided beds and meals for visiting troops as well as entertainment and sight-seeing trips. It remained open until 25 Aug 1919.

East Africa, Campaign in war began in this German colony (later Tanganyika, now Tanzania) on 13 Aug 1914 when a British warship bombarded Dar-es-Salaam, destroying the radio station and floating dock and rendering the port temporarily useless. On land, the British made a number of battalion-strength attacks across the border from Uganda and Rhodesia. Various small gains were made but they were all beaten back by German forces, who then turned to making raids against British posts across the borders. Eventually, it was realised that a more serious effort had to be made and General ◊Smuts arrived in Mombasa Feb 1916 with some 30,000 South African troops to reinforce the British and take command.

Smuts attacked with two divisions, one feinting to confuse the defences, and by April he had driven back the Germans and set up his command at Moshi. Operations re-started April 1916, with three divisions, plus British and Belgian troops attacking from the Belgian Congo and Rhodesia. The Germans under General ◊Lettow-Vorbeck, fought well but were outnumbered, and when, the main railway line was cut in several places July 1916, the German forces were fragmented and Smuts was able to deal with them individually. However, the difficult country made progress slow and it was not until 14 Nov 1918 that resistance was finally overcome and Lettow-Vorbeck surrendered.

Eastern Front battlefront between Russia and Germany/Austria-Hungary. In 1914 it was effectively the E Prussia/Russia, Germany/Poland, Galicia/Poland and Galicia/Russia borders, which then ran roughly (in present-day terms) from Kaliningrad in Russia via Bialystok, southwesterly to Torun in Poland, south to Katowice, east to Lvov and south-easterly to the mouth of the River Danube.

Eichhorn Field Marshal M Hermann von 1848–1918. German soldier. Eichhorn joined the Prussian Army 1866, served in the Franco-Prussian war 1871, and attained the rank of General 1912. In 1914 he was one of Hindenburg's commanders, operating on the Eastern Front. Given command of the 10th German Army he captured Kovno Aug 1915 and Vilna in the following month, resulting in his promotion to field-marshal. He remained on the Eastern Front and was military commander in the Ukraine 1918, acting as virtual dictator of the country. His oppressive regime made him unpopular with the local population and he was murdered by Ukrainian activists in Kiev, Oct 1918.

Einem General Rothmaier Karl von 1853– 1934. German soldier. He joined the Prussian cavalry 1870, became Chief of Staff of an army corps 1898, and was promoted to lieutenant-general and became Prussian minister of war 1903. By 1910, he commanded the 7th Army Corps and held various staff positions during the war. He was given command of the 3rd German Army July 1918 and mounted the unsuccessful attack on the French near Reims.

Emden German warship. A light cruiser of 3,500 tonnes/3,600 tons displacement and armed with 10 105mm guns, the Emden was mainly used as a 'commerce raider' in the Indian and Pacific oceans, sinking several merchant ships. Her captain, von Müller, became renowned for his humanity in providing for the safety and survival of the crews of the ships he sank. The Emden was eventually caught by the Australian ship HMAS Sydney at Cocos Island, driven ashore on North Keeling Island

and then destroyed by shellfire 9 Nov 1914. Although 230 of her crew were lost, Capt von Muller was among the survivors.

Enfield M1917 rifle US Service rifle. Made to a British design, the Enfield Pattern 1914, it was manufactured in the USA to British contract in British .303 inch calibre 1914–16. When the USA entered the war, production of their standard Springfield rifle was insufficient for the expansion of the army, and the Enfield design was re-engineered to the US .300 inch calibre and manufactured as the Model 1917. Three factories, operated by Remington and Winchester under the supervision of General J T Thompson, manufactured a total of 2,193,429 rifles by the end of 1918.

Enver Pasha 1879–1922. Turkish soldier and politician. He entered the army 1898, became active in the 'Young Turk' movement 1905, and in 1908 joined the revolutionaries who captured Monastir and proclaimed a new constitution. He was then appointed military attaché to Berlin, but returned to Salonika 1909 when the Turkish counter-revolution began and assisted in the overthrow of Abdul Hamid. He was active in organizing the Arabs of Tripoli in the Tripoli War against Italy 1911, and in the Second Balkan War he recaptured Adrianople from the Bulgarians 1913. By that time he had been appointed minister of war, with the rank of Pasha and married a princess. His pro-German influence was a major factor in the Turkish decision to align with Germany against the Allies. His attempts at military command during the war were invariably failures. After the Turkish surrender he fled to the Caucasus, from where he urged resistance to the terms of the Peace Treaty. Having no success in returning to power in Turkey he joined a group of anti-Bolsheviks in Uzbekistan and was killed leading them in a skirmish.

Epehy, Battle of battle between British and German forces, 12–25 Sept 1918, as the British attacked outposts and advanced positions of the ◊Hindenburg Line, which the Germans had fallen back on following the battles of ◊Bapaume and ◊Arras. The objective consisted of a fortified zone some 5 km/3 mi deep and almost 32 km/20 mi long, together with various subsidiary trenches and strongpoints. British troops of the 3rd and 4th Army (under Generals ◊Byng and ◊Rawlinson

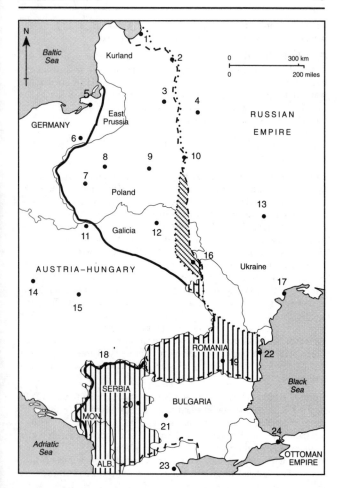

THE EASTERN FRONT 1914–17

Key

—— Maximum Russian advance and Austrian front against Serbia 1914

– – · Front line June 1916

···· Armistice line Dec. 5 1917

▨ Russian gains in Brusilov offensive June 4 – Aug. 10 1916

▥ Central Powers conquests: Serbia, Montenegro and Albania Dec. 1915 – Jan. 1916, and Romania Sept. – Dec. 1916

Cities/towns

1	Riga	13	Kiev
2	Daugavpils	14	Vienna
3	Vilna	15	Budapest
4	Minsk	16	Czernowitz
5	Königsberg	17	Odessa
6	Tannenberg	18	Belgrade
7	Lodz	19	Bucharest
8	Warsaw	20	Nish
9	Brest Litovsk	21	Sofia
10	Pinsk	22	Constanza
11	Cracow	23	Salonika
12	Lemberg	24	Constantinople

respectively) and French troops of the 1st Army (under General Debeney) attacked elements of the 2nd and 18th German armies. Fighting was fierce, in difficult country, and was broken into a series of battles against limited objectives. By 25 Sept the entire area was in Allied hands; 11,750 prisoners and 100 guns had been captured, but British casualties totalled 72,000.

Erzerum, capture of Russian success against the Turks, 16 Feb 1916. The Russians under General ◊Yudenich had advanced from the Caucasus Mountains into Armenia, forcing the Turks to retreat before them and take up positions on a strongly fortified ridge in front of Erzerum. On Jan 26 1916 the Russians split into two wings and moved to outflank the Turkish position; the Turks fell back and lost various fortified positions. The Turkish defence collapsed 15 Feb 1916 and Yudenich entered Erzerum the next day.

The capture was a remarkable feat of arms, conducted in severe winter conditions, in mountainous country, and against well-prepared fortifications. The Russians captured 13,000 prisoners, 300 guns, huge quantities of ammunition and stores, and the Turkish loss was estimated at 60,000 killed and wounded. The town remained in Russian hands until re-occupied by the Turks 11 March 1918.

Essen Admiral Peter von 1860–1915. Russian sailor. Essen commanded the Vladivostok Fleet in the Russo-Japanese War 1905, and played an important part in the subsequent re-organization of the Russian Navy. In Aug 1914, as commander of the Baltic Fleet, he disguised several of his ships as German, sailed out of Libau harbour and engaged the German fleet in the Gulf of Finland, destroying the cruiser ◊Magdeburg and damaging another warship. Stricken by illness, he died in Reval 20 May 1915.

Etaples fishing port and seaside resort on the Canche estuary, in the Pas de Calais *département*, France. During World War I it was a British base and hospital centre. There were also extensive training grounds, convalescent depots, motor vehicle repair facilities, and a large military cemetery which eventually contained some 12,000 graves.

ethyldichlorarsine chemical agent; non-persistent lung injurant. Introduced by the German army March 1918 for use in preparatory bombardments and support for infantry attacks. Short exposure brings about immediate irritation of the respiratory passages, but longer exposure can be lethal. In addition to the pulmonary effects, the arsenic component is absorbed rapidly and leads to systemic poisoning. Long exposure also burns the skin, so that the gas is a complex of lung injurant, toxic, and vesicant effects. It was used in mixtures with the equally toxic dichlormethyl ether in artillery shells.

Evans Commander Edward Ratcliffe 1881–1957. British sailor. Evans joined the Royal Navy 1897 and was second-in-command of the Antarctic Expedition of 1909. After the death of Capt Scott 1913 he led the expedition safely home. A commander RN in 1914, he commanded HMS Broke in the Dover Patrol. On 20 April 1917, in company with HMS Swift, he engaged six German destroyers in darkness off the Dutch coast, sinking one by ramming and another after a hand-to-hand fight on the Broke's deck. A third was also sunk and the remainder driven off. Promoted to captain and awarded the DSO, he was thereafter known as 'Evans of the Broke'.

Evert General Alex Emolaevitch 1857–1920. Russian soldier. Evert joined the army 1874 and served in the Russo-Turkish and Russo-Japanese wars. In 1914 he took command of the Russian forces in S Poland, with which he defeated the Austrian Army Aug–Sept 1914. He commanded the central group of armies 1915–16 and conducted the retreat from the Niemen with great skill. He resigned his command March 1917.

F

F-Boats group of British flying-boats developed by the Felixstowe experimental seaplane station of the Royal Naval Air Service. A numbered series, the F2, F2a, F3, and F5 were built in some numbers and were used for anti-submarine patrolling in the waters around Britain. All were large biplane machines powered by twin Rolls-Royce engines from 250 to 375 hp, had a crew of five, and carried machine guns and a large load of bombs.

Fairey aircraft British aircraft manufactured by the Fairey Aviation Company of Hayes, whose principal product was seaplanes for the Royal Naval Air Service. The Fairey IIIA was a two-man reconnaissance machine, and the larger three-man Campania was the first aircraft designed to be operated from an aircraft carrier, the name being taken from that of the ship. It was fitted with floats but used a wheeled trolley to take off from the deck, landing in the sea and being hoisted inboard. These machines were widely used around Britain and in N Russia.

Falkenhayn Erich von 1861–1922. German soldier. Falkenhayn entered the army 1880 and later attended the War Academy and joined the General Staff. He served on the expedition to China 1900 and by 1912 was Chief of Staff of the 4th Army Corps. In 1913 he became minister of war, but became chief of the General Staff Sept 1914 and remained in this post until he was removed by the Kaiser Aug 1916 due to the failure of the German attacks on Verdun. In Sept 1916 he was appointed commander in chief of the 9th Army on the Eastern Front, and after clearing the Romanians from the area north of the Transylvanian Alps he crossed the mountains and subjugated Romania. He handed over his command to ◊Mackensen 1917, returned to Germany, and then went to the Middle East to direct Turkish operations against the British in Mesopotamia and Palestine. He was unsuccessful and so was recalled March 1918 and given command of the 10th Army in Lithuania. He retired 1919. Considered by many to be the German Army's finest strategist, Falkenhayn was less successful as a field commander.

Falkland Islands, Battle of naval engagement between British and German forces, 8 Dec 1914. After the defeat at Coronel, Admiral ◊Fisher sent a powerful fleet of two battle-cruisers, five other cruisers, and two armed ships into the South Atlantic. They arrived in the Falkland Islands 7 Dec 1914 and began coaling. The old battleship Canopus, armed with 12-inch guns, was already in the area, acting as a floating defence battery for the islands. The German commander Admiral ◊von Spee knew nothing of this force and had sailed around Cape Horn intending to bombard the Falklands in passing before proceeding around the Cape of Good Hope to arouse the disaffected Boers of South Africa. Von Spee approached the Falklands early on the morning of 8 Dec and sent the Gneisenau to bombard the islands, but she was fired at by the Canopus; believing this fire to come from coastal defence guns of unknown strength the ship turned away. Von Spee then saw, over the masking shoreline, the tripod masts of the British battle-cruisers and realised he had sailed into a trap. His fleet set off eastward at full speed but the British force under Admiral ◊Sturdee had already raised steam and rapidly overhauled them. Battle opened at 12.51 p.m.; at 4.17 p.m. the Scharnhorst sank from the effects of British gunfire, and at 5.55 p.m., severely damaged, the Gneisenau was scuttled in deep water, taking over 800 of her crew with her. Two other German ships were sunk; one escaped but was later caught and sunk. Von Spee's squadron was thus entirely destroyed with a loss of 2100 men. The British lost no ships, though some damage was done, and suffered only 5 men killed and 16 wounded.

Farman French aircraft built by the brothers Henry and Maurice Farman. Henry was an early aviator, designing his own machine 1908 and setting several records; Maurice began making aircraft 1911 and in 1912 the two combined. Their most enduring product in the war years was the MF7 Longhorn, so-called because of two large curved members which extended in front of the fuselage and carried a forward elevator. Used by almost all Allied air services as a training machine, it was a biplane with a short fuselage section having the cockpit in front and engine at the rear; the rudder and tail unit were carried on open-work struts. The MF11 Shorthorn dispensed with the forward elevator and was used as a fighter and bomber by British and French forces until mid-1915.

fascine bundle of wood, generally chestnut fence paling about ten feet long and four to six feet in diameter, tightly wrapped and carried on the top of a tank. On arrival at a trench too wide to be crossed unaided, the fascine was released to fall into the trench and the tank then dropped into the trench, landed on the fascine, and clambered out the other side. Where trenches were very wide or deep, several tanks would drop fascines and then all would cross at the same spot.

Fayolle General Marie Emile 1852–1928. French soldier. Fayolle joined the army as a lieutenant of artillery 1877 and served in North Africa. He became an instructor at the Ecole Supérieure de Guerre and was promoted to general 1910. In 1914 he was a brigade, divisional, and corps commander in rapid succession and, replacing ◊Castelnau, he commanded the 1st and 6th Armies in the Somme 1916. In 1917 he took command of the Army of the Centre, fighting the Aisne battles, and became commander in chief of French forces in Italy Oct 1917. Returning to France 1918 he was given command of the reserve army, and after the Armistice commanded the French Army of Occupation in Germany.

FE aircraft British aircraft built by the Royal Aircraft Establishment, Farnborough. The initials stood for 'Farman Experimental', since it was a pusher biplane (with the engine behind the pilot so that the propeller pushed rather than pulled the machine) and Farman is generally credited with being the originator of this type. The short fuselage carried the observer and pilot at the front and a 120hp or 160hp engine at the rear, while the tail unit was carried on an openwork frame. Capable of about 130 kph/80 mph, it was originally used as a fighter until its performance was outstripped by other designs, after which it remained in use for the rest of the war as a night bomber.

Festubert, Battle of battle between British and German forces, May 1915. In order to assist the French, who were attacking in Artois and

Arras, the British 1st Army was ordered to make an attack against the Aubers Ridge. A short bombardment on 9 May did little or no damage to the German trenches and the British assault was repulsed with over 12,000 casualties. The attack was repeated on 15 May after a much longer artillery bombardment and broke through the German lines in two places. In spite of a counter-attack, these two inroads were linked up and a gain of about half a mile was eventually made before the battle died out and fresh trench lines were dug. Total British losses amounted to 3,620 dead, 17,484 wounded, and 4,321 missing.

Fisher Admiral John Arbuthnot, 1st Baron Fisher 1841–1920. British admiral, First Sea Lord 1904–10, when he carried out many radical reforms and innovations, including the introduction of the ◊Dreadnought battleship. Fisher joined the navy 1854, served in the Crimean War 1855 and the China War 1859–60, and then held various commands before becoming First Sea Lord. He returned to the post 1914, but resigned the following year after disagreeing with Winston Churchill over sending more ships to the ◊Dardanelles.

flamethrower weapon emitting a stream of burning liquid which can be directed against troops or strongpoints. Introduced by the German army during the Battle of Hooge, 30 July 1915, the weapon consisted of a back-pack with a reservoir of compressed nitrogen and a tank containing about 10 l/18 pts of 'flame liquid', usually a mixture of coal tar and benzine. A hose ran from the fuel tank to a nozzle, on which was an ignition device. On pressing the trigger, gas forced the liquid through the nozzle and at the same time the ignition device fired the liquid. The gas pressure was sufficient to give the flaming liquid a range of about 45 m/50 yds.

The principle was adopted by the British, French, and US armies. A terrifying weapon, its operator was usually a marked man, and when assaulting a strongpoint with a flamethrower it was necessary to provide a protection squad for the operator.

Flanders, Battle of collective term for the series of actions which constituted the British advance in Belgium and N France, Sept–Nov 1918, more usually divided into the battles of the ◊Yser and ◊Ypres. The overall plan conceived by General ◊Haig was to develop a series of attacks along the entire length of the British front from Dixmude to the

Ypres salient. To do this a massive army group was assembled, consisting of the Belgian Army with three divisions on the Allied left; the French 6th Army with four divisions in the centre; and the British 2nd Army plus the 2nd and 19th Corps, on the right. The group was under overall direction of the Belgian King ◊Albert, and his chief of staff was General ◊Degoutte of the French army.

The attack began 28 Sept 1918 with no preliminary bombardment but with a creeping barrage covering the assault. By 1 Oct the Allies had gained eight miles of ground and all the German defensive lines had been taken. Between 1–14 Oct another British corps was brought in, communications were reorganized, supplies dumped, and preparations made for the next attack, which began 14 Oct. By 17 Oct Ostend had been cleared of Germans and on 19 Oct Bruges was liberated. The advance reached Dutch frontier 20 Oct and the pressure turned eastward to push the Germans back into Germany. By 11 Nov the Allies had reached a line running from the Dutch frontier at Terneuzen, to Ghent, along the Scheldt river to Ath and thence to St Ghislain where the line linked up with Haig's main group of armies.

Foch Marshal Ferdinand 1851–1929. French soldier. Foch enlisted as a private soldier when the Franco-Prussian War broke out 1870 but returned to civil life for a few months and then entered the artillery school and was commissioned as a second lieutenant 1874. He attended the Ecole de Guerre 1885 and was appointed to the staff of a division and then to the general staff 1894. In the following year he became a professor of military history, strategy, and applied tactics at the Ecole Supérieure de Guerre. In 1901 he took command of a regiment and progressed from colonel to brigadier-general on the general staff 1907, then returned to be commandant of the Ecole Supérieure where he was a great influence on the French officer corps. both from his lectures on stretegy and tactics and from his careful attention to the training of young officers. In 1911 he returned to general duties and by 1914 was commanding the 20th Army Corps at Nancy.

He was appointed to command 9th Army 28 Aug 1914 and fought the Battle of the ◊Marne with great success. After this ◊Joffre appointed him assistant commander of the French Forces of the North; he took full command Jan 1915 and commanded the French right wing during the battle of the ◊Somme 1916. Later in that year he reached the official age limit and was removed from active service, being side-lined into various administrative and consultative posts. His retirement was partly due to political infighting; Foch was a protegé of Joffre, and when Joffre fell from favour, Foch was bound to suffer. He was recalled by ◊Pétain to serve as Chief of the General Staff, and after the Italian defeat at ◊Caporetto 1917 he had the task of co-ordinating Allied support for Italy. This led to his appointement as co-ordinator of Anglo-French forces in France, and in April 1918 he became the Allied commander in chief, later extended to cover the Italian front as well. He launched the Allied counter-offensive of July that brought about the negotiation of an armistice to end the war, and was elected Marshal of France 6 Aug 1918.

Fokker German aircraft. Anthony Fokker was a Dutchman who began designing aircraft 1912 and settled in Germany. His first machine, the EIII, was a monoplane in which he introduced the synchronized machine gun, firing between the propeller blades. Some 300 were built and shot down over 1,000 Allied aircraft. His DR 1 triplane was another famous fighter, used by the ◊Richthofen Circus; it was a highly manoeuvrable machine which caused great damage among Allied aircraft. His final wartime design was the D VII, a powerful biplane which appeared early 1918 and is generally considered to be one of the great combat aircraft of all time. This, too, was used by Richthofen's squadron, and about 1,000 are believed to have been built.

'My centre is giving way; my right is in retreat; situation
excellent, I shall attack!'
   Ferdinand Foch, at a staff meeting during the battle of the Marne.

Fonck René 1896–1953. French fighter ace. He took up flying 1912 and on the outbreak of war became a military pilot in the observation service. He then transferred to the fighter service and shot down his first German aircraft 6 Aug 1916. On 9 May 1918, over Montdidier, he shot down six German machines in one dogfight. By the end of the war he had claimed 75 enemy aircraft and was the highest-scoring French ace.

He was awarded the British MC and DCM, as well as many French honours.

Fourteen Points the terms proposed by President Wilson of the USA in his address to Congress 8 Jan 1918, as a basis for the settlement of World War I. Wilson was obliged to compromise on many of the points in light of secret agreements concluded by several of the Allies. The Germans, having agreed to the armistice largely on the basis of the Fourteen Points, felt betrayed by subsequent decisions imposed upon them by the Treaty of ◊Versailles.

1. Open covenants of peace, openly arrived at

2. Freedom of navigation upon the seas in peace or war

3. The removal of all economic barriers and the establishment of an equality of trade conditions among all nations

4. Adequate safeguards given and taken that national armaments will be reduced to the lowest point consistent with domestic safety

5. A free, open-minded and impartial adjustment of all colonial claims, based on the principle that the interests of the populations concerned have equal weight with the equitable claims of the government whose title is to be determined

6. The evacuation of all Russian territory

7. Belgium must be evacuated and restored

8. All French territory should be freed and the invaded portions restored, and the loss of Alsace-Lorraine in 1871 righted

9. Readjustment of the frontiers of Italy should be effected along clearly recognizable lines of nationality

10. The peoples of Austria-Hungary should be accorded the freest opportunity of autonomous development

11. Romania, Serbia, and Montenegro should be evacuated; occupied territory restored; and the relations of the several Balkan states to one another determined by friendly counsel along lines of allegiance and nationality

12. The Turkish portions of the Ottoman empire should be assured secure sovereignty, but the other nationalities now under Turkish rule should be assured an undoubted security of life and unmolested opportunity of autonomous development

13. An independent Polish state should be erected, including territories inhabited by indisputably Polish populations, which should be assured a free and secure access to the sea

14. A general association of nations must be formed under specific covenants for the purpose of affording mutual guarantees of political independence and territorial integrity to great and small states alike

franc-tireur (lit., free-shooter.) civilian who, contrary to the rules of war, takes up arms in a private capacity against the enemy. The name comes from the Franco-Prussian War when French patriots in German-occupied France took pot shots at German soldiers as opportunity presented itself.

Franchet d'Esperey Louis 1856–1942. French soldier. Educated at St Cyr, he joined the army 1876, serving in North Africa and China. In 1914 he commanded the 1st Army corps at Lille and then took command of the 5th Army Aug 1914. He fought in the first battle of the ◊Marne, then held the Aisne bridgeheads. In April 1916 he was placed in command of the Armies of Eastern France, and of the Armies of the North Jan 1917. He remained in this post until June 1918 when he was appointed supreme commander of the Allied armies in the East, receiving the surrender of Bulgaria Sept 1918. He then commanded the Allied forces in Turkey until 1920 and was created Marshal of France 1921.

Franz Ferdinand 1863–1914. Archduke of Austria. He became heir to his uncle, Emperor Franz Joseph, 1884 but while visiting Sarajevo 28 June 1914, he and his wife were assassinated by a Serbian nationalist. Austria used the episode to make unreasonable demands on Serbia that ultimately precipitated World War I.

French Army the French Army of 1914 was a conscript force guided by a regular cadre of volunteer soldiers. Its strength 4 Aug 1914 was 823,000 and 2,887,000 reservists were mobilized within 14 days. Eventually some 8,317,000 French troops were to serve during the war, 475,000 from the French colonies, and the total mobilized strength on 11 Nov 1918 was 5,075,000.

In 1914 the army had 173 infantry regiments, 91 cavalry regiments,

62 field artillery regiments, 30 horse artillery batteries, and 134 medium, heavy, and seige batteries of artillery, plus engineers, supply, and other supporting troops.

French General John Denton Pinkston 1852–1925. British field marshal. In the second South African War 1899–1902, he relieved Kimberley and took Bloemfontein; in World War I he was commander in chief of the British Expeditionary Force in France 1914–15; he resigned after being criticized as indecisive and became commander in chief home forces.

It is a solemn thought that at my signal all these fine young fellows go to their death.

Field Marshal John French quoted in Brett,
Journals and Letters of Reginald, Viscount Esher

Freyberg Brigadier-General Bernard Cyril 1889–1963. British soldier. He enlisted in the New Zealand Territorial Army 1912 and on the outbreak of war returned to England and joined the Royal Naval Division, serving at Antwerp, in the Dardanelles, and then in France. He was awarded the Victoria Cross for his leadership on the river Ancre Nov 1916, where he led the attack on Beaucourt. When the war ended, he was a brigadier-general with the 29th Division. He remained in the army and won more honours during World War II.

Freytag-Loringhoven Baron Alexander von 1849–1926. German soldier. Entered the Prussian Army 1868 and served in the Franco-Prussian War 1870–71. Appointed quartermaster-general on the staff of ◊Falkenhayn 1915, in late 1916 he became deputy chief of the General Staff, in which post he remained for the rest of the war. In 1917 he published a book, *Deductions from the World War*, which plainly explained why German would fail to win World War I and laid out the strategy by which Germany would win the 'next world war'.

Friedrichshafen town of Württemburg, Germany, on Lake Constance. It was the site of the principal Zeppelin factory and depot during the war, and was bombed several times by Allied aircraft 1914–15.

G

Gaba Tepe, landing at Australian operation at ◊Gallipoli. On 24 April 1915 the ◊ANZAC corps landed at 'Z Beach', about 3 km/2 mi N of the hill known as Gaba Tepe. The first wave drove the Turks from the immediate area of the beach, allowing further Anzac troops to land. This force then moved through broken country until it established a line anchored on Gabe Tepe. The Turkish force, about 20,000 strong, attacked this line but were beaten back by the entrenched Anzacs, supported by naval gunfire. The position was entrenched, ammunition and supplies were landed, and the Anzac force was reinforced by the Royal Naval Division. Reinforcements were landed 6 Aug and, in conjunction with an attack at the southern tip of the peninsula, the beach-head was enlarged, but no further progress was made and the surviving force was evacuated from Suvla Bay 20 Dec 1915.

Galicia, Battles in during the war Galicia was the largest province of Austria; today it covers most of the Slovak Republic and parts of Poland and Russia north and east of the Carpathian mountains. At the end of 1915 the Russians began an offensive towards Czernowitz (now Cernovcy) in order to forestall a possible Austro-German move against Romania and to further their own plan of an advance toward the Caucasus. At the same time ◊Brusilov began an offensive in the area of the Pripet Marshes, capturing Chartoryisk (Cartorijsk) and drawing off Austro-German forces from Galicia. The southern offensive made good progress and captured a bridgehead over the river Dniestr at Uscieczko (Kostrizevka) 9 Feb 1916. Having gained this they drew their trench lines and there was little change until the start of the ◊Brusilov Offensive June 1916.

Gallieni General Joseph Simon 1849–1916 ('The Saviour of Paris'). French soldier. Gallieni joined the French army 1870 as a lieutenant of marines and served in the Franco-Prussian War, the Sudan, and Indo-China (now Vietnam). As governor of Madagascar 1896–1905, he organized the island as a French colony. In 1909 he became a member of the Conseil Superior de Guerre and on the outbreak of war was appointed military governor of Paris. He brought the city's fortifications to a state of readiness and rendered considerable assistance to the French 6th Army operating outside Paris. His nickname came from his plans prior to the Battle of the ◊Marne which helped shape the course of the battle, and his rallying of all the Parisian taxi-cabs to take reinforcements to the front became a legend. He became minister of war Oct 1915 but resigned due to ill-health and died 27 May 1916. He was posthumously awarded the distinction of Marshal of France 1921.

The Gallipoli Campaign

1915

Feb 19	First Allied naval bombardment
Feb 25	Second Allied naval bombardment
March 18	Allied naval attempt to force The Narrows
Apr 25	Allied landings at Helles and Anzac
Apr 28 – June 4	First, Second and Third Battles of Krithia
Aug 6	Allied landings at Suvla Bay
Dec 19–20	Allied evacuation of Anzac and Suvla

1916

Jan 8	Allied evacuation of Helles

Gallipoli port in European Turkey, giving its name to the peninsula (ancient name ***Chersonesus***) on which it stands. In World War I, at the instigation of Winston Churchill, an unsuccessful attempt was made Feb 1915–Jan 1916 by Allied troops to force their way through the Dardanelles and link up with Russia. The campaign was fought mainly by Australian and New Zealand (◊ANZAC) forces, who suffered heavy losses. An estimated 36,000 Commonwealth troops died during the nine-month campaign.

I asked him about the landing at Gallipoli, but he could tell me nothing about it. All he knew was that he had jumped out of a bloody boat in the dark and before he had walked five bloody yards he had a bloody bullet in his foot and he had been pushed back to Alexandria almost before he bloody well knew he had left it.

Compton Mackenzie on *Gallipoli*, in *Gallipoli Memories*.

Gallwitz General Max von 1852–1932. German soldier. Gallwitz joined the German Army as a lieutenant of artillery 1872 and was attached to the General Staff 1883–85. By 1901 he commanded an artillery brigade and was promoted to general and appointed inspector general of field artillery 1911. He was one of ◊Hindenburg's generals in the battles for the ◊Masurian Lakes 1915, forcing a crossing of the river Narev and acting as part of the pressure which drove the Russians to evacuate Warsaw Aug 1915. Later that year he commanded one of ◊Mackensen's armies in the conquest of Serbia.

In 1916, he was in Galicia fending off the ◊Brusilov Offensive, and by the end of the year he was commanding an army on the ◊Somme. After the Somme he commanded the 4th Army in the ◊Verdun zone but was defeated Sept 1917 and relieved of his command. Soon reinstated, he commanded an Army Group on the Western Front until the war ended. Although never famous, Gallwitz was a highly competent tactician and, apart from his defeat at Verdun, rarely put a foot wrong on the battlefield.

Garros Roland 1888–1918. French aviator. Initially a music student, he was soon attracted to aviation and obtained his pilot's certificate 1910. He held several records 1911–12 and made his name with a 800 km/500 mi flight across the Mediterranean from St Raphael to Bizerta. At the outbreak of war he joined the Stork Squadron and was promoted to flight-lieutenant. He had some success as a fighter pilot but crash-landed in enemy territory April 1915 and was taken prisoner. He escaped Feb 1918 and returned to France, rejoined the air service and scored several more victories before being shot down and killed 5 Oct 1918.

Garros was the first pilot to fire machine guns through the propeller blades, giving him a considerable advantage over his enemies. He had sheets of steel attached to the propeller blades so that bullets would be deflected if they hit, but a sufficient number passed between the blades to be effective. When shot down in 1915 the Germans discovered this and developed a more reliable system of synchronizing the discharge of the bullets with the passage of the blades (see ◊Fokker).

gas cloud method of dispersing a chemical agent by simply releasing it from storage cylinders and allowing it to drift in the wind across an enemy position. First used by the Germans at Ypres 1915, it was subsequently used by all combatants, but was a more effective weapon in British and French hands since the prevailing wind in Flanders was from west to east, and thus the Allies were able to mount more and better cloud attacks than the Germans.

In half an hour nothing is left and we take off our helmets, sniffing the morning air dubiously. But all we smell is the old mixture – corpses and chloride of lime.
Ian Hay on *gas masks* in *The First Hundred Thousand*

---

gas mask face mask designed to filter out or neutralize chemical agents from the air inhaled by the wearer. Early masks, produced hurriedly in the wake of the first attacks, were simply cotton pads soaked in various chemicals to protect against ◊chlorine gas. Then came the 'gas helmet', a flannel bag soaked in chemicals and with a celluloid window in the front. Breathing drew air through the saturated flannel, neutralizing the gas, and exhaled air was expelled through the bottom of the bag suspended around the man's neck. Various improved helmet designs appeared but eventually the moulded face mask with goggles and either a self-contained canister or a canister in a haversack, connected to the mask by a flexible pipe, became standard. The canister system allowed for replacement of the protecting chemicals and filters as they became clogged or inert, and also allowed improved canisters to be fitted as new gases appeared and demanded new counter-measures.

gas shell artillery projectile carrying a chemical agent. Early designs used an ordinary high explosive shell with a lead cylinder containing the liquid gas buried centrally in the explosive so that it would be shattered and thus disperse the gas. This was gradually replaced by shells in which the explosive was placed in a central cylinder and the remaining space filled with the liquid, so that the explosion was sufficient to break open the shell and release the gas but not so violent as to disintegrate the liquid before the gas could be generated. This design also permitted larger quantities of gas to be loaded into each shell.

Gaza, Battles of battles between British and Turkish forces, March–April 1917. During the invasion of Palestine, a British force under General Sir Charles Dobell advanced along the coast from Rafa and mounted an attack on Gaza 26 March 1917. The attack was three-pronged: an infantry division attacked from the south while Anzac forces and cavalry attacked from the east and north. The attack was at first partially successful, and Anzac troops entered the town. However the Turks put up a strong defence, the British force had no water for its horses, Turkish reinforcements were coming up in rear of the enveloping British forces, and General Dobell had to withdraw. On 17 April he made a second attack, but in the interval Gaza had been heavily reinforced and fortified, and in spite of support from tanks the British were beaten off with losses of about 7,000 troops. When night fell the battle was broken off and was not renewed the next day. General Dobell was relieved of his command as a result of the failure. Gaza was finally taken 7 Nov 1917, following the battle of ◊Beersheba also known as the third battle of Gaza.

German Spring Offensive Germany's final offensive on the Western Front.The collapse of Russia allowed Germany to bring all her best troops from the Eastern Front to reinforce the Western Front, giving them a strength of about 1,600,000 men and 16,000 guns against an Allied strength of 1,400,000 men and 16,400 guns. The Germans made a concerted effort to conclude the war before the arrival of US troops, launching the *Second Battle of the Somme* 21 March–3 April 1918 (codenamed 'Michael'). They attacked the weak British sector between Cambrai and the Oise river, held by the 5th Army and drove the British back a considerable distance. They launched a second attack on the

Armentières front 9 April ('Georgette'), overwhelming the Portuguese Corps and driving a deep wedge into the British front, capturing the Messines Ridge. On 27 May a third attack ('Blücher') was launched against four weak British and four tired French divisions on the Aisne, between Soissons and Reims, which reached the Marne in the region of Chateau-Thierry. The Germans extended this front and came to within 72 km/45 mi of Paris.

The German Spring Offensive 1918

March 21 – Apr 5	Offensive on the Somme (Operation Michael)
Apr 9–29	Offensive on the Lys (Operation Georgette)
May 27 – June 17	Offensive on the Aisne (Operation Blücher–Yorck)
June 9–13	Montdidier–Noyon offensive (Operation Gneisenau)
July 15–19	Offensive on the Marne (Operation Marne–Reims)
July 18	Opening of Allied counter-offensive

By this time, however, their troops were beginning to flag, and a barrage of mustard gas, the first time the French had used it, halted a further attack 12–13 June ('Gnieisenau'). The Germans paused to consolidate their gains and were then further delayed by bad weather, so it was not until 15 July that Ludendorff launched 35 divisions across the Marne to envelop Reims; his attack was held and driven back in the *Second Battle of the ◊Marne*. During this time Foch had been preparing a large French-US force, well supported by tanks, for the Allied counter-attack which began May 1918 in the ◊Chateau-Thierry area. The assault was successful and marked the end of the German campaign and the commencement of the Allied advances which ended the war.

Gillain General Cyriaque Cyprien 1857–1931. Belgian soldier. Gillain enlisted as a private 1875, attended the Military Academy 1878, and was commissioned into the cavalry 1880. He served in the Congo, and became colonel of the 4th Lancers 1913. When war broke out he was commanding this unit then took command of the 1st Cavalry Brigade Oct 1914, and took part in the battle of the ◊Yser. In 1915 he was promoted to major-general and in 1917 to lieutenant-general, being given command of the 5th Division. He became Chief of Staff April 1918 and his victory in the battle of Thourout-Thielt in Oct was instrumental in clearing the Belgian coast of all German forces.

Givenchy, Battle of battle between British and German forces, 16–22 Dec 1914. In early Dec 1914 an Allied force was opposing strong German defences around Givenchy, a French village in the Pas-de-Calais. In order to relieve pressure on the French, then fighting at Arras, orders were given to attack and thus pin down the Germans so that they could not reinforce Arras. Indian troops of the Lahore division attacked 19 Dec and captured two lines of German trenches but were then driven out by a fierce counter-attack. On 20 Dec the Germans, strongly reinforced, mounted a sudden attack against the Indian trenches which were inundated due to rain, and broke through to occupy part of the village. Two British battalions in reserve were called up and recaptured the village in the evening. The battle continued and several salients were driven into the British line, until General ◊Haig brought up reinforcements from the 1st Army 21 Dec, relieved the Indian division, and forced the Germans back to their original line. The battle died out the following day with all participants back where they had started, at a cost of about 4,000 British and 2,000 German casualties.

Goeben German battle-cruiser. Built 1911, the Goeben had 22,640 tons displacement, could steam at 28 knots, and was equipped with a 10-inch armour belt, eight 14-inch guns, and twelve 6-inch guns. At the outbreak of war she was in the Aegean Sea with the Breslau, an armoured cruiser. They were found off Messina by the British Mediterranean fleet 6 Aug 1914 but escaped through the Dardanelles. After this the Goeben led the Turkish fleet in the Sea of Marmora and the Black Sea. On 20 January 1918, again acting jointly with the Breslau, she passed through the Dardanelles and attacked British ships near Mudros. Both German ships were herded into a minefield where the Breslau was sunk and the Goeben severely damaged and run ashore. While there she was bombed by British aircraft but the crew managed to make repairs and limp back through the Dardanelles once more. Back in the Black Sea she resumed her duties with the Turkish fleet but accidentally ran into a Turkish minefield and sustained more damage. When the Allied fleets entered the Black Sea after the Armistice they found the Goeben awaiting repair at Ismid.

Goltz Colmar, Freiherr von der 1843–1916. German soldier. Goltz joined the Prussian army as a lieutenant 1861 and served on the staff of Prince Frederick during the Franco-Prussian war 1870–71, after which he served with the General Staff in Berlin. In 1883 he was attached to the Turkish Army with the rank of Pasha, and re-organized it along German lines. In 1908 he was promoted to field-marshal and led a military mission to Turkey where he became involved with the 'Young Turks' political movement. At the outbreak of war he accompanied the German Army into Belgium to become governor-general, first of Brussels and then of Belgium. He returned to Turkey 1915 and commanded a Turkish Army during the ◊Gallipoli campaign. He then directed Turkish operations in the Middle East but on 19 April 1916 died of spotted fever at his headquarters.

Gommecourt French village in the *département* of Pas-de-Calais, between Albert and Arras. It was held and fortified by the Germans 1914–17. During the battle of the ◊Somme, Gommecourt was a major British objective but was never taken, a failure that had significant effects on the course of the battle. It was finally abandoned by the Germans in their withdrawal to the ◊Hindenburg Line Sept 1917. Several British war cemeteries were established in the area.

Gorizia, capture of Italian victory over Austrian forces, Aug 1916. The town of Gorizia was then part of the Austro-Hungarian empire and its position made it a strategic obstacle since it closed the road to Trieste, a prime Italian objective. The Italian offensive on the ◊Isonzo of 1915 made little headway but Italian forces were able to drive out the Austrians Aug 1916 after an intense artillery bombardment and, after a three-day battle, occupied the town. This enabled them to outflank other Austrian positions holding up the general advance. The Italians held Gorizia until the Austro-German offensive of autumn 1917 forced them to withdraw on 28 Oct. They eventually recovered it in late 1918 and it became part of Italy after the war.

Gorlice Polish town, about 40 km/25 mi S of Tarnow on the edge of the Carpathians, it became a focal point in the struggles between Russian and Austro-German forces in the various battles in ◊Galicia. Gorlice was occupied by the Russians Dec 1914–May 1915 and was then occupied by the Germans before being the centre of struggles once again 1916. Also called Gorlitza or Gorlitze in contemporary reports, it should not be confused with Gorlitz in Silesia.

Gotha bomber German aircraft manufactured by the *Gothaer Wagenfabrik*. A large twin-engined biplane bomber, it was the principal strategic bomber of the German air force, used in raids over Britain and France from 1917 onwards. Early models (G1 and G2) were used on the Balkan and Eastern Fronts as tactical bombers but they were unreliable. The G3 was an improvement but was almost immediately superseded by the G4 which became the standard heavy bomber. The G4 had a maximum speed of about 145 kph/90 mph and could carry 500 kg/1100 lbs of bombs to a range of about 800 km/500 mi. The G5 was a slightly improved model, but performance remained about the same.

Gough General Sir Hubert de la Poer 1870–1963. British soldier. Gough joined the 16th Lancers 1889 and then served in India and South Africa. At the outbreak of war he commanded the 3rd Cavalry Brigade in France, later took command of a division, and took over 1st Corps July 1915. He was given command of the 5th Army July 1916, leading it through the ◊Somme. In 1917 his army was involved in the Third battle of ◊Ypres and his tactics were criticized for causing excessive casualties. In 1918 the main weight of the German attack fell on the 5th Army and, unable to hold the line, Gough fell back to take up a shorter and more easily defended line. His action was held responsible for the German success and he was relieved of his command. However, subsequent examination of the battle showed that this was the only sensible course that could have been taken in the circumstances. He became head of a military mission to the Baltic States 1919.

Green cross gas German term identifying 'severely harmful' gases, from the mark painted on the shells. Principally lung injurants, the group included ◊chlorine, ◊phosgene, diphosgene, and ◊chloropicrin.

Green Cross Society British corps of women motor drivers, officially known as the Women's Reserve Ambulance but named from their green uniforms, established June 1915. Using their own, or corps', vehicles they collected wounded soldiers from the main London railway stations and took them to various hospitals in the suburbs. They were also trained in first aid and ambulance duties. The corps also included several hundred part-time workers who staffed canteens, acted as guides for wounded soldiers, and rendered first aid during air raids. A company was sent as ambulance drivers to Romania and Russia.

grenade, hand see ◊hand grenade.

grenade, rifle see ◊rifle grenade.

Guise, Battle of (also called the Battle of St Quentin) battle between French and German forces 29–30 Aug 1914. The retreating 5th French Army under ◊Lanrezac had fallen back to Guise when it was ordered to attack St Quentin some 25 km/15 mi away, in order to relieve pressure on the British at ◊Mons and buy time for the 6th French Army to assemble near Paris. The attack was mounted, but the force's open flanks were immediately threatened by German attacks, forcing Lanrezac to abandon the St Quentin objective and Lanrezac concentrate instead on a frontal holding battle against whatever forces the Germans sent. He met and drove back an attack from von ◊Bulow's army, but the danger of his flank being turned by von ◊Kluck's forces was such that he could not pursue his victory. He had no choice but to break off and re-start his retreat. Nevertheless, his action caused some 6,000 German casualties and upset the German plans.

gun tank British tank designed to carry a 60-pounder (5-inch) gun across broken ground. It resembled the regular tanks of the period but the rear of the body was a flat platform on to which the gun could be hauled. The gun's wheels were removed and it was clamped to the platform. Once the gun had been taken to its position the wheels were replaced and it was then used in the normal way. The idea worked but was cumbersome, and it was found that an ordinary ◊Holt tractor could tow the gun across mud faster than the gun tank could carry it. Gun tanks were withdrawn and converted into store-carrying tanks for supplying front line troops with ammunition under fire.

H

Haber Fritz 1868–1934. German chemist who made many important discoveries with scientific and commercial applications, partly overshadowed by his involvement in the German chemical warfare programme during World War I.

Haber was director of the Kaiser Wilhelm Institute for Physical Chemistry at Dahlem, Berlin, 1914–33. At the outbreak of war, the German Army asked the Institute to investigate substitutes for explosive in shells, and poison gas was suggested. Haber, after watching early trials with gas shells, proposed releasing gas from cylinders and thereafter became one of the principals in the German chemical warfare effort. Haber's involvement in chemical warfare led to protests against his Nobel prize in 1918.

If I were fierce and bald and short of breath,
I'd live with scarlet majors at the Base,
And speed glum heroes up the line to death.

Siegfried Sassoon's caustic comment
on *General Haig* in *Base Details*.

Haig Douglas 1861–1928. British army officer, commander in chief 1915–17. Haig commanded the 1st Army Corps 1914–15, and the 1st Army 1915 until he succeeded Sir John French as commander in chief the same year. He then loyally supported the French marshal Foch in his appointment as supreme commander of the Allied armies. Haig's Somme offensive in France in the summer of 1916 made considerable advances, but only at enormous cost to human life, and his Passchendale offensive in Belgium July–Nov 1917 achieved little at a similar loss, although he was promoted to field marshal the same year.

He supported Foch in his victorious 1918 offensive, and it was Haig's foresight that persuaded Foch to extend his attack north, so breaking the Hindenburg Line.

Following the war, he was awarded the Order of Merit, an earldom, and £100,000 1919, and became first president of the ◊British Legion 1921. Although a national hero at the time of his funeral, Haig's reputation subsequently suffered after ◊Lloyd George's memoirs depicted him as treating soldiers' lives with disdain, while remaining far from battle himself.

D. is a very weak-minded fellow I am afraid, and, like the feather pillow, bears the marks of the last person who has sat on him!
General Haig the 17th Earl of Derby in
letter to Lady Haig 14 Jan 1918.

Halberstadt German aircraft, made by the Halberstadt Flugzeugwerk and several other firms under license. The 'C' models were two-seat biplane reconnaissance machines, sturdy and reliable, which were also used for ground attacks during the battles of Somme and Cambrai. The 'D' model was a single-seat fighter which, though highly agile, had insufficient speed to match the Allied fighters on the Western Front and was more usually found in the minor theatres of war.

Hall Admiral Sir William Reginald 1871–1943. British sailor. Joined the Royal Navy 1883, promoted to commander 1898, inspecting captain of mechanical training 1906–07, and assistant controller to the Navy 1911–13. In Oct 1914 he was appointed director of Naval Intelligence and founded 'Room 40', the naval cryptanalysis office which successfully broke German naval codes and was responsible for decoding the ◊Zimmerman Letter. Knighted 1918, he resigned 1919 and became the Conservative Member of Parliament for West Derby, Liverpool.

Halsey Admiral Sir Lionel 1872–1949. British sailor. Halsey joined the Royal Navy as a cadet 1885, was promoted to lieutenant 1893, served in the South African War, became a commander 1901, and was promoted to captain 1905. He commanded HMS New Zealand in the battles of ◊Heligoland Bight Aug 1914 and ◊Dogger Bank Jan 1915. He was on ◊Jellicoe's staff on HMS Iron Duke at ◊Jutland, was promoted to rear-admiral and became Third Sea Lord 1917, and commander in chief of the Australian Navy Oct 1918. He was knighted 1918.

Hamel, Capture of operation, July 1918. On 4 July 1918 the 33rd Illinois National Guard Division decided to celebrate Independence Day by attacking Hamel Wood, near Corbie on the Somme. In co-operation with some Australian troops, and after a severe artillery preparation, the combined force advanced under cover of tanks on a 6 km/4 mi front, the US forces concentrating on Hamel. The joint force advanced 2.5 km/1.5 mi, Hamel and Vaire woods were taken, and 1,500 prisoners, 20 mortars, and 100 machine guns were captured.

Hamilton Sir Ian Standish Monteith 1853–1947. British soldier. Hamilton joined the Gordon Highlanders 1873 and served in the various colonial wars across the Empire throughout the 1880s. Promoted to colonel 1891, he served in South Africa 1899–1902, some of the time as Chief of Staff to ◊Kitchener. He attended the Russo-Japanese War as a military representative of the Indian Army. In 1910 he was adjutant-general, and 1910–15 commander in chief, Mediterranean forces. He was promoted to full general 1915 and was given command of the forces in Gallipoli. Although he did his best he was removed Oct 1915 and was given no further command during the war. He retired shortly after.

hand grenade small missile, containing an explosive or other charge, thrown by hand. Grenades were known in the 15th century, but were obsolete by the 19th, only being revived in the Russo-Japanese War 1905. They were revived once more when trench warfare began, first as locally-manufactured missiles – empty cans filled with gunpowder and stones, with a primitive fuse – and then as an official, properly-designed weapon.

Hand grenades were generally fitted with some sort of time fuse burning for about four seconds: a sufficient amount of time for the grenade to reach the target but not enough for the enemy to pick it up and throw it back. Many experimental designs appeared, but the three standard patterns which survived the war were the British ◊Mills bomb and the French 'pineapple' grenade, both ball-like objects easily thrown, and the German stick grenade which carried the metal canister of explosive on the end of a wooden handle. A trained man could accurately throw an average grenade about 30–35 m/35–40 yds. In addition to explosive anti-personnel grenades, smoke and gas grenades were used, principally for trench clearing and raiding.

Handley Page British aircraft manufactured by Frederick Handley ◊Page. He opened the first aircraft factory in the world 1909 and in 1914 began work on the first large bombing aircraft, the O/100. A twin-engined biplane, 46 were taken by the Royal Naval Air Service and put into service Sept 1916. Better engines were used to produce an improved model, 550 of which were built in Britain and a further 100 in the USA. Handley Page then designed the O/400, the first British four-engined aircraft and the first strategic bomber. Three were in service by time of the Armistice, and more were built after, seeing service on the Northwest Frontier of India in the 1920s. The O/400 had a top speed of 156 kph/97 mph and could carry sixteen 112-lb bombs to a range of 1050 km/650 mi.

Hannover aircraft German fighter aircraft made by the Hannoverische Wagenfabrik 1917. A two-seater biplane, the Hannover CLII, was also used for ground attack and as an escort for bombers. A small aircraft, it was highly manoeuvrable and over 400 were put into service on the Western Front. An improved model, the CLIII, was built in small numbers, and, improved further as the CLIIIA, it became a major part of the German Air Force, over 550 being built in 1917–18.

Hansa-Brandenburg aircraft German seaplanes built by the Hansa und Brandenburgische Flugzeugwerke, which were the most popular float-planes with the Germany Navy. The KDW was a small single-seater biplane converted from a land plane and used to patrol the Baltic, North Sea, and Mediterranean coasts. The W.12 was designed as a float-plane and introduced the upswept rear fuselage and upside-down tail configuration which was unique to the company. About 150 of these were built and they saw extensive service on the N German and Belgian coasts, one of them shooting down the British airship C27.

With the W.29 the company pioneered a monoplane design which proved itself as a useful fighter; an enlarged version, the W.33, appeared 1918. They continued in use after the war, and the chief designer, Ernst Heinkel, become famous as a manufacturer of warplanes during World War II.

Harington General Sir Charles 1872–1940. British soldier. Harington joined the King's Regiment 1892, served on the staff during the South African War, as an instructor at the Royal Military College, and then on intelligence duties at the War Office. In 1911–13 he was brigade major at Aldershot, and in the early part of the war was a brigadier-general on the staff of and then Chief of Staff to General ◊Plumer. When Plumer went to Italy 1917, Harington accompanied him and became chief of the General Staff, British Forces Italy. In 1918 he was appointed Deputy Chief, Imperial General Staff, War Office. He became general officer commanding the army of the Black Sea, replacing General ◊Milne, 1920. Knighted 1919, he was promoted to lieutenant-general 1920.

Hartlepools, bombardment of German attack on the N Yorks coast, specifically the seaports of Hartlepool, West Hartlepool, Whitby, and Scarborough 16 Dec 1914. Carried out by a German battle-cruiser squadron under the command of Admiral ◊Hipper, the bombardment began at 8.15 a.m. and continued until 8.50 a.m. The Germans fired 1,150 shells were fired, killing 137 people and wounding 592. The two coastal defence batteries at Hartlepool – Heugh Battery which had two 6-inch guns and Lighthouse Battery which had one 6-inch gun – fired 143 shells at the German ships, damaging three. The SMS Blucher had two of her gun batteries put out of action and sustained severe damage to her bridge. Two British destroyers, Patrol and Forward, and the submarine C9 attempted to attack the German ships but were beaten off by their superior armament. A number of seamen were killed and wounded, as were several Territorial gunners in the coastal batteries.

Heligoland island in the North Sea, about 70 km/45 mi from the mouth of the Elbe. Britain ceded it to Germany 1890 in exchange for territorial rights in East Africa, and it thereafter became a vital coast defence station for the Germans. All its inhabitants were removed to the mainland and strong fortifications and gun positions were built, harbours made, and airship sheds erected. It was used as a naval and aircraft base during the war, but the gun defences were never used. After the war the Germans were forced to dismantle all the fortifications and military installations on the island under the supervision of the Allied Disarmament Commission.

Heligoland Bight, Battle of naval engagement between British and German forces, 28 Aug 1914. The battle was fought in the Heligoland Bight, the stretch of water between Heligoland island and the German mainland used by the German fleet for exercises. A British force of 2 light cruisers, 33 destroyers, and 8 submarines sailed into the Bight, surprising the German vessels there. These were principally light cruisers and destroyers; as it was low tide, the heavier German warships were unable to leave their bases. The Germans attempted to cut the British fleet off from its return route, but were surprised by a second force of British light cruisers. However, these reinforcements were unable to get close to the Germans because of the British submarines between them. The Germans got over the initial shock of the raid and used their superiority in number of cruisers to begin driving the British out of the Bight. The arrival of the battle-cruiser squadron of the Grand Fleet, under Admiral ♦Beatty, reversed the situation once again and their heavy firepower sank three German cruisers. The rest of the German fleet then turned about and returned to their bases, while the British fleet sailed out of the Bight, having sunk three light cruisers and a destroyer. The success of this attack was a severe blow to German naval morale.

helmet protective covering for the head, worn by military personnel to guard against relatively low impacts. Steel helmets, primarily to protect against shell splinters and ♦shrapnel balls, although rather less effective against rifle bullets, were first issued by the French mid-1915. The idea was then taken up by the British and Germans who issued helmets early in 1916. The distinctive shapes of the French 'Adrian', the British 'bowler' and the German 'coal-scuttle' can all be traced back to national designs of the Middle Ages. Other combatants adopted one of these three patterns, although the Russians did not adopt a helmet for their troops on the Eastern Front. Only those few Russians who served on the Western Front or in Macedonia, in proximity with other Allied troops, were issued with Adrian helmets supplied by the French.

High Wood British name for a hilltop French wood, the Bois des Foureaux, in the *département* of the Somme. It became a focal point in the battle of the ◊Somme; British cavalry entered it 14 July 1916, one of their few sorties in that battle, and it was the target of a number of attacks by both sides from then on. It was finally taken by the British 47th Division 15 Sept 1916, by which time there was not a tree left standing.

Hill 60 slight rise in the ground (scarcely higher than its surroundings) SE of Ypres, near Zillebeeke, Belgium. It had great tactical importance since from it the British line in the Ypres Salient could be strafed, and the Germans could fully observe British movements. On 17 April 1915 six mines, each containing one ton of explosive, were detonated beneath the hill, and it was immediately attacked by a British force who established themselves in and around the mine craters. This force then held out against powerful German attacks and artillery bombardment until it was finally overwhelmed by a chlorine gas attack 5 May. The Germans regained the crest of the hill but were unable to dislodge British troops who had dug in on the western slope. It remained in German hands until taken as part of the ◊Messines operation June 1917, was recaptured by the Germans, and finally taken back by the British Sept 1918.

Hindenburg Paul Ludwig Hans von Beneckendorf und von 1847–1934. German field marshal and right-wing politician, president of Germany 1925–34. During World War I he was supreme commander and, with ◊Ludendorff, practically directed Germany's policy until the end of the war. Born in Posen (now Poznan, Poland) of a Prussian *Junker* (aristocratic landowner) family, he was commissioned 1866, served in the Austro-Prussian and Franco-German wars, and retired 1911. Given the command in East Prussia Aug 1914, he received the credit for the defeat of the Russians at ◊Tannenberg and was promoted to supreme commander and field marshal. Following the war he entered politics and was president of Germany from 1925 until his death. He acquiesced in the rise of Hitler and was compelled to invite him to assume the chancellorship Jan 1933.

Hindenburg Line German western line of World War I fortifications built 1916–17. It was built in order to give the German Army a shorter and easier-held line in the west, allowing them to hold off the Anglo-French attack while dealing a knock-out blow to Russia. Consisting of well-built trenches with concrete shelters and pillboxes, all protected by thick wire obstacles, the line ran from Arras to Laon. The main positions were on reverse slopes, with the advance positions on forward slopes and all were protected by artillery. The battle of the ◊Somme led the Germans to fall back to the Hindenburg Line late in 1916. Part of the line was taken by the British in the third battle of ◊Arras, but it generally resisted attack until the British offensive of summer 1918.

Hipper Vice-Admiral Franz von 1863–1932. German sailor. Holding the rank of rear-admiral in 1914, he commanded the cruiser squadron which bombarded the ◊Hartlepools. He later commanded cruisers in the battles of the ◊Dogger Bank and ◊Jutland, after which he was awarded the *Pour le Merite* by the Kaiser. He was promoted to commander in chief of the High Seas Fleet 1918.

Hog Island island in the Delaware River, Pennsylvania, USA. Almost uninhabited, and mostly swamp, it was converted 1917 into a shipbuilding yard to construct 50 7,500-ton freighters for carrying supplies from the USA to Europe. Orders were given for its construction 13 Sept 1917, work began 1 Oct, and the first ship was launched 5 Aug 1918. The yard was designed as a site at which prefabricated components from over 100 yards and factories around the USA could be assembled into complete ships and launched. Fifty slipways and seven 1000-foot fitting-out piers were built, together with 131 km/82 mi of railway track, 27 warehouses, and accommodation for 33,000 men employed in the yard.

Hogue, HMS British armoured cruiser of the Cressy class, built 1898–1901. The Hogue and its sister ships, ◊HMS Cressy and ◊HMS Aboukir were all sunk 22 Sept 1914 by the German submarine U-9 some 30 km/20 mi off the Hook of Holland, with the loss of 25 officers and 535 seamen. It is the only known occasion of three warships being sunk in succession by a single submarine.

Hohernzollern redoubt name given by the British to an intricate trench system in the German first line at the battle of ◊Loos, Sept 1915.

Strongly fortified, with a front of about 450 m/500 yds, it extruded from the German front line. It was taken by the British during the opening stages of the battle but regained by the Germans two days later.

Holbrook Captain Norman Douglas 1874–1942. British sailor. He was serving in the submarine branch at the outbreak of war. On 11 Dec 1914, commanding submarine B11, he dived beneath a minefield in the ◊Dardanelles and torpedoed the Turkish battleship Messudiyeh. He then made his escape, although pursued by torpedo boats and subjected to several attacks. He was awarded the first naval Victoria Cross of the war for this action.

Holt tractor US agricultural tractor using a 'caterpillar' track instead of wheels. The track system had been invented by the Hornsby company of Grantham, England, 1908, and in 1909 they submitted a tracked tractor to the British Army. It won a prize for its performance, but the Army did not purchase any. Finding no commercial demand for the idea in Britain, Hornsby sold the patents to the Holt Tractor Company of Stockton, California, who had considerable success with the design in the mid-west farming states of the USA. By 1915 several had been purchased by the British and French armies and were used for hauling guns and other heavy loads. It was the sight of a Holt tractor which inspired Col ◊Swinton to develop what eventually became the tank.

Horne General Henry Sinclair, Baron of Stirkoke 1861–1929. British soldier. Commissioned into the Royal Artillery 1880, he served in the South African War and became lieutenant-colonel 1905. He was inspector of artillery 1912–14, and on the outbreak of war went to France commanding an artillery brigade. He was given command of 2nd Division 1915, later went to the Middle East to report on the defences of Egypt and the Suez Canal, then returned to France and commanded 15th Corps in the battle of the ◊Somme. After this he took command of the 1st British Army until the war ended.

Knighted 1916, he was the only artillery officer to command a field army, and he also acted as an artillery adviser to General ◊Haig. He was responsible for many of the technical and tactical improvements in artillery, including the perfection of the creeping ◊barrage. In 1919 he became Eastern District commander in Britain, was awarded a grant of £30,000 and created Baron.

Hotchkiss gun French machine gun. Invented by a Baron Odkolek of Austria who sold the design and patents to the French Hotchkiss company for a lump sum 1893. Hotchkiss developed it into a workable gun which was adopted by the French army 1897. It was later adopted by the Japanese, during the Russo-Japanese War, and by the British 1915. Several models existed but the most common was a light air-cooled, gas-operated weapon fed with ammunition in metal strips, which was used as a support weapon by infantry. Heavier, tripod-mounted, versions were used for sustained defensive fire and in an anti-aircraft role.

Howitzer artillery piece mounted so as to be able to fire at elevations greater than 45 degrees. This allows the trajectory to pass over intervening obstacles and drop on to positions which would be impossible to hit with a flat-trajectory gun. In general, a howitzer fires a heavier shell, at lower velocity, than a gun of the same calibre.

Hunter-Weston General Sir Aylmer Gould 1864–1940. British soldier. He joined the Royal Engineers 1884, and served on the Northwest Frontier of India, where he was wounded, and later in Egypt and the South African War. He became assistant director of military training 1911. In 1914 he was commanding a brigade, which he took to France and commanded 29th division at ◊Gallipoli 1915, later taking command of 8th Corps. In this post he was over-optimistic and his tactics led to heavy casualties. He was invalided home July 1915, suffering from sunstroke and over-strain. After a rest he returned to France and commanded a corps during the ◊Somme battles. Knighted 1915, he left the army 1919 to enter politics as Unionist Member of Parliament for N Ayrshire.

Hutier General Oskar von 1857–1934. German soldier. Von Hutier joined the German army 1875 and by 1912 was a lieutenant-general commanding the 1st Guard Division in Berlin. Thereafter, he held various minor commands but first came to prominence in the summer of 1917, when commanding the 8th German Army, by capturing ◊Riga 3 Sept. In this battle he developed the tactic of using small armed parties of well-trained infantry to infiltrate the enemy positions, outflank and turn them, and thus force gaps for larger parties to follow up; this was assisted by well-planned artillery support devised by his artillery commander Col ◊Bruchmuller. Known at the time as 'Ludendorff tactics', since the idea was believed to have come from General ◊Ludendorff, it was not until some time later that von Hutier's part was appreciated. The tactic was refined and used later with considerable effect in the ◊German Spring Offensive 1918.

identity disc metal disc or discs worn around the neck by all soldiers. The idea, evolved during the war and eventually common to all combatants, was principally to identify the dead. Two discs were worn by British troops, one to be removed and returned to headquarters as a notification of death, the other to remain on the body to provide identification for the burial records.

Imbros (Turkish *Imroz*) island in the Aegean Sea; area 280 sq km/108 sq mi. Occupied by Greece in World War I, it was used by the British as a forward base after the evacuation of ◊Gallipoli and was bombed several times by Turkish aircraft. It became Turkish under the Treaty of ◊Lausanne 1923.

Immelmann Max 1883–1916. German aviator. Born in South Africa, he renounced his British nationality while studying medicine in Germany. Immelmann joined the German air service on the outbreak of war and rapidly became known as one of the foremost fighter pilots. He developed the 'Immelmann Turn', a manoeuvre in which, pursued, he would climb suddenly in a half-loop, roll, and then dive back at his pursuer. Decorated by the Kaiser Jan 1915, he was shot down and killed near Lens by the British pilot Lt George McCubbin 18 June 1916.

incendiary shell artillery projectile developed in Britain for use against ◊Zeppelins, the intention being to ignite the hydrogen in the airship's gasbags. The construction generally resembled that of the ◊shrapnel shell, a hollow projectile with a charge of gunpowder at the rear and a number of thermite canisters in the body, carrying a time fuse in the nose. When the fuse functioned, it ignited the gunpowder which in turn ignited the thermite and ejected the burning canisters ahead of the shell. At least three Zeppelins were brought down by this type of shell, but when bombers replaced airships the use of incendiary shells was abandoned.

Indian Army an independent force, although under British officers, with a strength of 155,000 men 1914. During the course of the war about 1 million more were enlisted and at the Armistice the army stood at 573,000. Indian troops fought on the Western Front, the Dardanelles, the Middle East, and in East Africa, coming under British control and operating either as purely Indian units or as part of larger British formations. The army was predominantly infantry, with 38 cavalry regiments and 12 mountain artillery batteries. All field and divisional artillery was British, part of the British Army in India but attached to the Indian Army.

Recruitment of soldiers was no problem; recruitment of officers far more difficult. The British officer had a special relationship vis-à-vis the Indian soldier, part officer, part father-figure. He spoke the men's language and understood their traditions and beliefs. Obtaining officers at short notice who were capable of building this relationship was almost impossible, and led to a gradual decrease in the efficiency of Indian troops on the Western Front. The number of Indian officers increased considerably during the war years, a tendency which continued in the post-war period. Approximately 700 Indian officers and 45,000 men were killed and 1,500 officers and 64,000 men were wounded during the war, plus about 5,500 of all ranks missing.

Infantry Hill Hill in the Pas-de-Calais *département* of France, 1.6 km/1 mi E of Monchy, and 103 m/340 ft high. It became a focal point of the battle of ◊Arras, April–May 1917. Two British infantry regiments held up a German attack 14 April 1917, after which the hill changed hands several times, finally being taken by the British Aug 1918.

Invincible, HMS British battle-cruiser. Completed 1908 and armed with eight 12-inch and sixteen 4-inch guns, she displaced 17,250 tons and had a speed of 25 knots. Took part in the battles of ◊Heligoland Bight and the ◊Falkland Islands, and was sunk at the battle of ◊Jutland 31 May 1916 with all hands lost.

Iron Division name commonly given to elite troops of continental armies. The French Iron Division distinguished itself in the battle of the

◊Somme. The Belgian Iron Division was heavily involved in the Allied offensive in the summer of 1918. The German Iron Division was composed of ◊Storm Troops, and was largely filled with Russians from the Baltic provinces during the military uprisings in 1919–20.

Isonzo, Battles of the series of battles between Italian and Austrian forces, 1915–17. The Isonzo river rises in the Julian Alps and runs south, more or less following the present-day border of Italy and Yugoslavia, to the Gulf of Trieste. On the declaration of war by Italy, 23 May 1915, the Austrians took up a defensive position on the east bank, facing Italy.

The *first battle* was an Italian attack across the river June 1915 which made some gains and reached a position overlooking the ◊Carso Plateau. Bad weather then prevented any further movement.

The *second battle* began July 1915 with an Italian thrust against the fortifications of ◊Gorizia, followed by an attack in the Carso region. They failed at Gorizia but took a great deal of ground and prisoners in the Carso before the battle died away Sept 1915.

The *third battle* began 18 Oct 1915 with a heavy Italian artillery bombardment along the whole line, followed by another attack against Goriza and further operations in the Carso until winter weather prevented further movement.

The front then lay quiet until Aug 1916 when the *fourth battle* was launched with another attack against Gorizia and its surrounding defences, which fell to the Italians 9 Aug. This was followed by an advance in the Carso region which gained ground in the direction of Trieste. This attack died down by the end of Aug but sporadic fighting continued until Oct 1916.

During the winter both sides made preparations for a spring offensive, and the *tenth battle* opened May 1917 with an Italian thrust against the Austrian line N of Goriza. This made some gains but was then stopped by a powerful Austrian counter-attack after which the lines stabilized and the centre of action moved elsewhere.

Italian Army a largely conscript force with a small cadre of regular officers and NCOs; at any one time the bulk of the army was from the current 'class' of conscripts who, after their service, returned home and were placed on the active reserve. In 1914 its strength stood at 289,000

The Italian Front 1915–18

1915
June 23 –Dec 2   First to Fourth Battles of the Isonzo

1916
March 11–29   Fifth Battle of the Isonzo
May 15 – June 17   Austrian Trentino offensive
June 9–28   Italian Trentino counter-offensive
Aug 6 – Nov 14   Sixth to Ninth Battles of the Isonzo

1917
May 12 – Sept 15   Tenth and Eleventh Battles of the Isonzo
Oct 24 – Nov 12   Battle of Caporetto (Twelfth Isonzo)

1918
June 15–23   Austrian Piave offensive
July 2   Beginning of Italian Piave counter-offensive
Oct 24 – Nov 4   Battle of Vittorio Veneto

all ranks; formed into 25 infantry and 4 cavalry divisions supported by 36 field artillery regiments and 30 batteries of heavy artillery plus 40 siege and fortress batteries, and the usual engineer and supply elements. By the time of the Armistice its strength was just over 5 million, with casualties of some 465,000 dead and 960,000 wounded.

Popular legend tends to denigrate the Italian solider as a poor fighter, but history belies this. Prior to the disaster at ◊Caporetto Oct 1917, which lowered morale, the Italian troops had shown great ability and bravery against the Austrians in very difficult terrain.

Ivangorod, attacks on part of the German offensive against the Russians in Poland, Sept–Oct 1914. Ivangorod (now Deblin, Poland), was a Russian fortress on the east bank of the Vistula river, besieged by the 4th German army under ◊Denkl. The first attack was defeated by a Russian counter-attack which severely mauled the Austro-German forces and forced them to retreat to Radom. They remained there until July 1915 when, commanded by ◊Woyrsch, they attacked, seized a bridge across the Vistula and invested the fortress. The advance continued around the fortress, linking up with Hungarian and Austrian troops from the south and threatening to cut the only Russian line of retreat. The Russians removed everything they could and abandoned Ivangorod 4 Aug, blowing bridges behind them as they retired.

J

Jack Johnson nickname given by British troops to describe the burst of a German 15-cm shell. The nickname is a reference to Jack (John Arthur) Johnson (1878–1946), a black US boxer who became the heavyweight champion of the world 1908, as the shellburst generated a cloud of black smoke.

Jaeger German designation for light infantry troops. They were more lightly armed than ordinary infantry and had a faster marching pace. Largely recruited from mountain and forest districts, they also carried out pioneer work and reconnaissance duties. The German army had 18 Jaeger regiments at the outbreak of war.

Japan Japan had treaties of mutual alliance with Britain, France, and Russia in force in 1914 and joined them in declaring war on Germany. The alliances only bound Japan to military assistance should the eastern colonies of Britain or France be attacked, and Germany had promised not to attack these if Japan remained neutral. However, the war provided a perfect opportunity to carve out some useful possessions and profit, so Japan occupied the German colonies of the Marshall, Caroline, and Mariana islands Oct 1914. This precipitate action caused some alarm in Australia and the USA, but there was little the British could do about it, since they needed Japanese help in dealing with German commerce raiders in the Pacific. Japan then besieged the German fortress in Tsingtao, China, with a force of 23,000 which soon forced the surrender of the 4,000-strong German garrison.

In 1915 the Japanese presented their '21 Demands' to the Chinese government, demanding control over various economic and political affairs, demands the Chinese were in no position to refuse. The Japanese Navy patrolled the Pacific and Indian Oceans during the war, cooperating with the British navy, and three groups of destroyers were deployed in the Mediterranean as convoy escorts.

Jellicoe Admiral John Rushworth, 1st Earl 1859–1935. British admiral. He joined the navy 1872, serving in Egypt and China, and was controller of the navy 1908–10. At the outbreak of war he was promoted to the acting rank of admiral and commanded the Grand Fleet 1914–16; the only action he fought was the inconclusive battle of ◊Jutland, May 1916. He was First Sea Lord 1916–17, when he failed to push the introduction of the convoy system to combat U-boat attacks. He was promoted to admiral of the fleet 1919 and created 1st Earl 1925.

Jericho town in Palestine (now Israel), about 25 km/15 mi NE of Jerusalem. Although only a village in 1914–18 it occupied a valuable strategic position, covering the eastern approach to Jerusalem and the Jordan valley. After the British under General ◊Allenby captured ◊Jerusalem Dec 1917, they advanced to take Jericho in order to secure their flank and establish a base for operations on the east bank of the Jordan. Two divisions, supported by ◊Anzac cavalry, advanced toward Jericho, clearing a number of Turkish rearguard positions en route. The two infantry divisions then attacked Jericho directly, while the cavalry swept around the south to outflank the Turkish defences and threaten their line of supply. The Turks abandoned Jericho and fell back, and the Anzac force entered the village 21 Feb 1918.

Jerusalem chief city of Palestine (now Israel), area 37.5 sq km/14.5 sq mi. Held by the Turks and attacked by the British, the fighting was complicated by a mutual desire to avoid damaging, or fighting in the vicinity of, the Holy Places. Turkish forces took up positions outside the town and were first attacked 21 Nov 1917, without success. General ◊Allenby paused to bring in reinforcements, then attacked 8 Dec from the west with some success, though part of his force was slowed down by heavy rain. Having gained some ground, the attack halted overnight to allow the delayed troops to align their positions, and in the morning Allenby found his troops were confronted only by weak rearguard positions; the Turks had abandoned the city. On 26–27 Dec the Turks made four attempts to counter-attack and regain Jerusalem, but all were beaten off.

Jewish Regiment regiment of the British Army formed 1917; officially the 38th to 42nd battalions of the Royal Fusiliers, they were popularly known as the 'Judaeans'. The regiment was able to provide the necessary dietary and religious conditions required by members of the Jewish faith and its strength was bolstered by local enlistment of Palestinian Jews and also Russian Jewish emigrants to the USA who travelled to Palestine to enlist. It was sent to Palestine 1918 and gained a reputation as a reliable fighting unit but was disbanded 1919.

Joffre Marshal Joseph Jacques Césaire 1852–1931. French soldier, Marshal of France 1916. He joined the army 1870 and was chief of general staff by 1911. The German invasion of Belgium 1914 took him by surprise, but his stand at the Battle of the ◊Marne resulted in his appointment as supreme commander of all the French armies 1915. His failure to make adequate preparations at Verdun 1916 and the military disasters on the ◊Somme led to his replacement by Nivelle Dec 1916. He became president of the Allies' War Council 1917.

Jutland, Battle of naval battle between British and German forces 31 May 1916, off the W coast of Jutland. Early on 31 May the German fleet under Admiral ◊Scheer entered the North Sea from the Baltic, intending to entice British battle-cruisers in the area of the Norwegian coast and there destroy them. Leading the fleet were five battle-cruisers under Admiral ◊Hipper; the main fleet consisted of 16 ◊Dreadnought and 6 pre-Dreadnought type battleships accompanied by 11 light cruisers and 72 destroyers. Alerted by German radio traffic, the British Grand Fleet under Admiral ◊Jellicoe sailed from Scapa Flow with 28 Dreadnoughts and 3 battle-cruisers. A further force of 6 battle-cruisers and 4 fast battleships under Admiral ◊Beatty sailed from the Rosyth naval base.

Hipper's and Beatty's scouting destroyers saw each other in the afternoon of 31 May and the German force promptly turned away to entice the British to the German fleet. Beatty took the bait and a long range gunnery duel then took place in which two British battle-cruisers were sunk and Beatty's flagship damaged. Beatty himself then turned away to draw the Germans north and bring them against Jellicoe's heavier strength. The fleets met, and a general melee ensued during

Battle of Jutland *comparison of forces by naval strength*

British fleet

1st Battle Squadron	8 battleships; 2 damaged.
2nd Battle Squadron	8 battleships.
4th Battle Squadron	8 battleships.
5th Battle Squadron	4 battleships; 3 damaged.
1st Battle-cruiser Squadron	4 battle-cruisers; 3 damaged, 1 sunk.
2nd Battle-cruiser Squadron	2 battle-cruisers; 1 damaged, 1 sunk.
3rd Battle-cruiser Squadron	3 battle-cruisers; 1 damaged, 1 sunk
1st and 2nd Cruiser Squadrons	8 cruisers.
1st, 2nd, 3rd, and 4th Light Cruiser Squadrons	26 light cruisers
destroyers	78; 8 sunk.
seaplane carrier	1.

German fleet

1st Battle Squadron	8 battleships; 3 damaged.
2nd Battle Squadron	8 battleships; 2 damaged, 1 sunk.
3rd Battle Squadron	8 battleships; 4 damaged.
battle-cruisers	5; 4 damaged, 1 sunk.
light cruisers	11; 4 sunk.
destroyers	72; 5 sunk.

comparison of forces by class of vessel

class	British vessels (sunk)	German vessels (sunk)
Dreadnought battleships	28 (0)	16 (0)
Pre-Dreadnought battleships	0	6 (1)
battle-cruisers	9 (3)	6 (1)
armoured cruisers	8 (3)	0
light cruisers	26 (0)	11 (4)
destroyers	78 (8)	72 (5)

casualties

	British		German	
	killed	wounded	killed	wounded
officers	343	51	172	41
sailors	6,104	513	2,414	49

which another British battle-cruiser was sunk. Seeing that he was out-gunned, Scheer turned away under cover of smokescreens and destroyer attacks. Jellicoe continued southwards in the hope of getting his fleet between Scheer and the German bases. Scheer turned back into range, then left four battlecruisers to cover his retreat. Jellicoe, fearful of torpedos in the failing light of evening, decided not to follow and the battle thus came to a somewhat inconclusive end. Both sides claimed victory, Germany for having sunk more ships than they lost, and Britain because the German High Seas Fleet never ventured outside harbour for the rest of the war.

There seems to be something wrong with our bloody ships today, Chatfield. Admiral Beatty to his aide, during the *Battle of Jutland*.

K

K-class submarines British submarine class, the largest submarines of the war period. Displacing almost 3000 tons, the K-class vessels were 105 m/350 ft long. They used steam propulsion on the surface at a speed of 24 knots and electric propulsion when submerged at a speed of 10 knots. Armed with one 3-inch, one 4 inch, and three anti-aircraft guns, and eight torpedo tubes, they were crewed by 6 officers and 50 men. Used only for patrol duties in the North Sea, two were sunk after being rammed during exercise manoeuvres and one while performing its acceptance trials.

Kaiser Wilhelm Geschutz German long-range gun, commonly called the 'Paris Gun' from its use to bombard Paris March–Aug 1918 from a position on railway mountings in the Forest of Coucy, 125 km/78 mi from the city. A total of 183 shells landed inside the city boundaries and 120 outside during the bombardment, killing 256 people and wounding 620. After the initial surprise, the Parisians took little notice of the shelling, and little damage was done to property. The worst single incident was on Good Friday, 29 March 1918, when a shell hit the roof of the church of St Sepulchre which collapsed, killing 88 and wounding 68 of the congregation.

Seven 21-cm guns were made, using bored-out 38-cm naval guns fitted with special 40 m-/130 ft-long inserted barrels, although for most of the war there were only two mountings so that there were effectively only two guns each with two spare barrels. As the guns wore out, due to the high pressures and temperature of the powder charge, the barrels were removed and re-bored to 24-cm calibre to be used with a fresh outfit of ammunition. The shells weighed 120 kg/264 lbs and were fired by a 180 kg/400 lb powder charge, giving them a range of up to 131 km/82 mi. The guns were withdrawn in the face of the Allied advances

Aug 1918; one spare mounting fell into American hands near Chateau-Thierry but no gun was ever found by the Allies, during or after the war.

Kaledin Alexander Maximovitch 1861–1918. Russian soldier. Kaledin joined the Trans-Baikal Cossack horse artillery 1879 and by the outbreak of war 1914 was a general commanding a cavalry division. In 1915 he took command of an army corps in Galicia, under ◊Brusilov and in the following year succeeded Brusilov in command of the 8th Russian army. He led this army during the ◊Brusilov Offensive and played a significant part in the success of the operation. After the March revolution 1917 he supported the attempts to reorganize the army and was appointed Hetman of the Cossacks Sept 1917. But the November revolution put the Bolsheviks in power and Kaledin threw in his lot with the White forces. Unable to stem the tide of Bolshevism, he committed suicide 1918.

Katshanik town in Serbia, on the railway from Skopje to the Kosovo Plain, which also gives its name to the nearby Katshanik Pass between the Kara Dagh and Shar Dagh mountain ranges. The town was the site of a battle between the Serbs and the Bulgarians 10–15 Nov 1915. After capturing Skopje, the Bulgarians pressed onward to gain the Kosovo PLain, where they could outflank the main Serbian army retreating along the valley of the Ibar river. A scratch force evacuated from Skopje managed to hold the Bulgarians in the pass for five days before they were overcome, but the delay allowed the main Serbian army to retreat in safety.

Kiel Canal (formerly *Kaiser Wilhelm Canal*) waterway 98.7 km/61 mi long that connects the Baltic with the North Sea. Built by Germany 1887–95, the canal allowed the German navy to move from Baltic bases to the open sea without travelling through international waters, though it was also of value to commercial traffic, removing the hazardous trip around the Jutland peninsula. Originally 9 m/30 ft deep and 65 m/213 ft wide, the increasing size of German warships led to it being deepened to 11 m/36 ft and widened to 100 m/328 ft 1909–14. It was declared an international waterway by the Versailles Treaty 1919.

Kiggell General Sir Edward Lancelot 1862–1954. British soldier. He joined the Royal Warwickshire Regiment 1882, served in the South

African War 1899–1902 as a staff officer, and made director of staff duties at the War Office 1909. In 1913 he became commandant of the Staff College and on the outbreak of war became director of military training. In 1915 he went to France as Chief of the General Staff and remained in that post until late 1917 when, due to the intrigues of ◊Lloyd George, most of Haig's staff was replaced. During that time, he had been knighted 1916 and promoted to lieutenant-general 1917. Kiggel then became lieutenant governor of Guernsey until his retirement 1920.

Kitchener Horatio Herbert, Earl Kitchener of Khartoum 1850–1916. British soldier and administrator. He defeated the Sudanese dervishes at Omdurman 1898 and reoccupied Khartoum. In South Africa, he was Chief of Staff 1900–02 during the Boer War, and commanded the forces in India 1902–09. He was appointed Secretary of State for War on the outbreak of World War I, and was one of the first to appreciate that the war would not be 'over by Christmas'. He planned for a three-year war and began raising new armies in anticipation. Not an easy man to work for, he would not delegate responsibility and did not work well in a team. He bears some responsibility for the ◊Gallipoli campaign, having initially refused any troops for the venture, and when it failed his influence declined. His place as military adviser to the government was taken by Sir William ◊Robertson, and Kitchener was appointed to lead a mission to Russia. He was aboard the cruiser Hampshire en route to Russia June 1916, when it struck a mine and he was drowned.

Kitchener's armies Name applied to the volunteer armies raised after the outbreak of war at the urging of Lord ◊Kitchener; also known as 'New Armies'. Kitchener issued a call for 100,000 men 7 Aug 1914 and further calls followed. There were great difficulties, since the rate of enlistments swamped the normal recruiting and training process, but within a year over 2 million men had volunteered and three new armies were in existence. By early 1916, however, volunteers had dwindled to a trickle and it became necessary to introduce ◊conscription.

kite balloon captive ◊balloon developed for military observation purposes; a spherical balloon sways and spins in gusty weather but an elongated balloon with tail fins will lie toward the wind and remain relatively steady. Devised originally by the German Army, as the

Drachen balloon, the idea was taken up by other armies. The basic form was then adapted to use as a barrage balloon.

Kluck Alexander von 1846–1934. German soldier. Joined the Prussian Army 1865 and served in the Austro-Prussian and Franco-Prussian wars. In 1913 he was inspector-general of the 8th Military DIstrict, with headquarters in Berlin, and in 1914 was given command of the German 1st Army which invaded Belgium. After taking Brussels and outflanking Antwerp, he advanced on Mons, drove out the British army, took Tournai and captured Maubeuge. Advancing toward Paris in early Sept 1914 he exposed his flank which was promptly attacked by the combined British and French armies in the battle of the ◊Marne. This led to a general retreat of the German line to the river ◊Aisne where von Kluck made a successful stand. He failed to take Soissons 1915 and was wounded in the leg by shrapnel. He saw no more field service and, by this time feeling his age, he retired 1916.

Kolchak Alexander Vasilievich 1874–1920. Russian sailor. Kolchak joined the Russian Navy 1891 and saw service in the Russo-Japanese war. In 1914 he was rear-admiral of the Black Sea fleet and was appointed vice-admiral 1916. In June 1917 his sailors mutinied in Sevastopol and arrested him, together with most of his officers, only releasing him when he resigned his post. In the winter of 1917 he organized a force of White Russians in E Siberia and established an anti-Bolshevik government in Omsk 1918. In 1918–19, at the head of a sizeable army, he marched west to the Urals and inflicted defeats on several Bolshevik forces, but late in 1919 he was captured by Bolsheviks at Irkutsk and shot 7 Feb 1920.

Konigsberg German armoured cruiser which, after commerce raiding in the Indian Ocean during 1914, was driven into the Rufiji river delta in German East Africa and blockaded there by British warships. Hiding in the labyrinth of the delta she was eventually discovered by aerial reconnaissance and destroyed by long range gunfire 11 July 1915.

Kosovo, retreat from retreat of the Serbian Army before the advancing Austrians Nov 1915. The Austrian army's sweep in N and central Serbia, combined with the Bulgarian Army's advance in E Serbia, trapped the Serbian army in the Kosovo plain, leaving only the option of retreating southwest to Scutari (now Shkoder, Albania). The suffering on the retreat was terrible, many thousands dying from starvation and cold due to the harsh winter conditions and mountainous route.

Kovess von Kovesshaza Field Marshal Franz 1859–1937. Austrian soldier. Came to prominence 1915 by his capture of ◊Ivangorod on the Eastern Front. He was then sent to Serbia to command one of the armies under ◊Mackensen; this was an Austro-German force and was chiefly responsible for the defeat of the Serbians. As a result he was given command of a force sent to conquer Montenegro early 1916. After this success, he took command of an army in the Trentino and was promoted to field marshal Aug 1917. In July 1918 he was appointed to succeed General von Hoetzendorff ◊Conrad as second-in-command under the German General von Below.

Kovno (now Kaunas) fortress town and district of Lithuania on the Niemen river. It was besieged by German troops under ◊Hindenburg as an off-shoot of his advance against ◊Warsaw. German forces arrived outside the fortifications 8 Aug 1915, and after a short bombardment attempted unsuccessfully to storm the town. This was repeated twice, after which heavy artillery was brought up and the town and fortifications were shelled for a week. An infantry attack then captured one of the smaller forts, making a gap in the defences, more reserves were thrust in and the town fell 17 Aug 1915.

Kreimhild Line German name for a fortified line of trenches and pillboxes covering St Juvin and St Georges in France. It formed a fall-back position some miles behind the ◊Hindenburg Line and was finally completed 1918.

Krithia village in ◊Gallipoli, about 6.5 km/4 mi N of Cape Helles, and the scene of several small battles for possession of the village and the adjacent hill of Achhi Baba. Neither were ever taken by the Allies, although there were periodical minor gains and losses, but the struggle for these two objectives is memorable as the casualties suffered were out of all proportion to their tactical value.

Kronstadt (now Brasov, Romania) Austro-Hungarian border fortress town in a highly valuable strategic position covering several routes into Transylvania. Initial advances by Russia and Romania led to its abandonment by the Austrians. As ◊Falkenhayn's offensive caused the Romanian armies to retreat in Transylvania Oct 1916, Kronstadt was held by a Romanian force and was attacked by German columns converging upon the fortress. Driven out of the town, the Romanians made a desperate stand on the nearby heights, but were eventually driven off and the town was regained by Austria.

Krupp German steelmaking armaments firm, founded 1811 by *Friedrich Krupp* (1787–1826) and developed by *Alfred Krupp* (1812–1887) who pioneered the Bessemer steelmaking process. In 1850 he began experimenting with making solid steel breech-loading cannon, perfected models of which proved their worth in the Franco-Prussian War 1870–71. As his designs improved he supplied the German army and navy with guns of all calibres, and also built up an enormous export trade in artillery. During the war the major part of German artillery was provided by Krupp and he developed, among others, the ◊Paris Gun, the 42 cm howitzers which reduced the forts at ◊Liège, and numerous railway-mounted guns up to 38 cm calibre.

The company supported Hitler's regime in preparation for World War II, after which the head of the firm, *Alfred Krupp* (1907–1967), was imprisoned.

Kut-Al-Imara city in Iraq, on the river Tigris; a grain market and carpet-manufacturing centre. In World War I it was part of the Turkish empire and was attacked by a British column under General ◊Townshend Sept 1915. After successfully mounting a diversionary attack in the south, Townshend was able to assault the town from the north, and broke in and routed the Turkish garrison. He then advanced to ◊Ctesiphon but was repulsed and fell back into Kut and fortified it. The Turks attacked Kut without success, but then completely encircled the town and laid siege to it 25 Dec 1915. British relief columns attempted to reach Kut but were beaten back, and Townshend surrendered his force of about 3,000 British and 6,000 Indian troops 29 April 1916. Their treatment by the Turks was barbaric and two-thirds of the British and half the Indian troops died during a forced march to captivity of some 1,200 miles. The town was eventually recaptured by a fresh British force under General ◊Maude 23 Feb 1917, remaining in British hands for the rest of the war.

L

La Basée, Battle of battle between British and German forces, Oct 1914. The British 2nd and 3rd Corps were between Aire and Béthune, about to swing west and secure Lille. Large German reinforcements had arrived in the area and while the 6th German Army advanced and captured Lille 12 Oct 1914, the 4th German Army arrived and struck at the exposed British flank near ◊Ypres. The British advanced toward Lille in the hope of recapturing it but were held, while the flank attack placed them in danger. Attempts were made in vain to straighten the British line, and a concentrated attack drove the British back until La Bassée and Neuve Chapelle were taken by the Germans. Another heavy German attack swept round Armentières, but was beaten back. By this time, (early Nov) the battle for ◊Ypres had begun. Ypres took priority with both sides, so the battle around La Bassée and Armentières died out and the line stabilized.

Landrecies French town in the *département* of Nord, on the river Sambre. It is an old fortress town and was the scene of a brief battle between British and German troops 25 Aug 1914. The 4th British Guards Brigade, retiring from ◊Mons, reached the village and were bivouacking there, when the advance guard of the 4th German Corps suddenly entered the place. Bitter house-to-house fighting ensued; British reinforcements were called up and after six hours the Germans were driven out. It was later occupied by the Germans during the general British retreat to the ◊Marne, and remained in German hands for the rest of the war.

Landsturm German third-line reserve troops composed of men who had completed their conscript or regular service, any reserve service, and any ◊*Landwehr* service. They were then transferred to the *Landsturm*, in which they remained until the age of 45. Normally the

Landsturm was only to be used for local defence and similar duties, but the shortage of men in the latter part of the war led to their use in all military capacities.

Landwehr German second-line reserve troops. All German conscripts, on completion of their mandatory service, were transferred to the 'first ban' of the Landwehr for five years, during which time they attended regular training camps. At the end of this period they passed into the 'second ban', remaining there until they were 39, when they moved into the ◊*Landsturm*.

In time of war the troops of the first ban were used as reserves for fighting formations and those of the second ban for line of communication duties, but due to the shortages of troops 1917–18 this distinction was lost. In the Austrian army the *Landwehr* was a standing reserve pool into which regular troops and recruits were drafted when there was no immediate need for them at the front.

Langer Emil German 38-cm naval gun mounted on the ground, installed on the Belgian coast 1915 and used to bombard Dunkirk, about 40 km/25 mi away. In spite of aerial reconnaissance and bombing attacks on likely places, Langer Emil was never discovered and remained a thorn in the Allied side until the war ended.

Langle de Cary General Ferdinand Louis Armand Marie de, 1849–1931. French soldier. Joined the army (Chasseurs d'Afrique) 1869, later attended staff school, and fought in the Franco-Prussian War when he was wounded. General of an Algerian cavalry brigade 1900, he then became a member of the Conseil Superior de Guerre. In 1914 he commanded the 4th Army and fought on the ◊Meuse and ◊Marne. In 1915 he commanded in the Champagne offensive and then was placed in command of the groups of armies forming the 'Army of the Centre', which he led at ◊Verdun 1916. In March 1916 he reached the official age limit and was retired.

Lanrezac General Charles Louis Marie 1852–1925. French soldier. Joined the French infantry 1870, and saw action in the Franco-Prussian War and Tunisia. Became governor of Reims 1909 and general of division 1911. In 1914, he commanded the 5th Army which was driven back from the ◊Sambre, precipitating the retreat from ◊Mons. He showed no tendencies toward the offensive and was incapable of liaising with the British, and so was relieved of his command Oct 1914 and appointed inspector of military schools. In 1917 he became inspector-general of the army and in April was placed on the reserve.

Laon French town, capital of the *département* of the Aisne and a major fortress. It was captured by the Germans 30 Aug 1914 and remained in their hands until late 1918. In Aug 1918 the 3rd, 5th, 6th, and 10th French armies, under ◊Mangin and with attached American and Italian units, advanced against the German forces holding the Laon district on a line from Soissons to Compiegne. Noyon was taken by 30 Aug and on 5 Sept the Forest of Coucy was cleared, putting an end to the threat of the ◊Paris Gun. The Laffaux plateau took most of Sept to clear, and finally, after intense artillery bombardments, the French entered Laon 13 Oct 1918. By the end of the operation, the French had advanced 56 km/35 mi over extremely well- defended country and taken some 30,000 prisoners.

Lawrence Thomas Edward ('Lawrence of Arabia') 1888–1935. English soldier and scholar. After studying Oriental languages at Oxford, Lawrence went to the Middle East and spent several years travelling in native dress in Arabia, Syria, and Mesopotamia, mastering Arabic dialects and making archaeological studies. On the outbreak of war he was recalled to England and employed producing maps of the Arab regions. When the sherif of Mecca revolted against the Turks 1916 Lawrence was given the rank of colonel and went with the British Mission to King Hussein. There he reorganized the Arab army, which he practically commanded, and conducted guerrilla operations on the flank of the British Army 1916–18. He was a guerrilla leader of genius, combining raids on Turkish communications with the organization of a joint Arab revolt, described in *The Seven Pillars of Wisdom* 1926, as well as providing intelligence about Turkish movements. At the end of the war he was awarded the DSO for his services, and became adviser to the Foreign Office on Arab affairs.

Le Cateau French town in the *département* of Nord, occupied by the Germans throughout the war. Two battles were fought in the vicinity between British and German forces.

The *first battle* took place 26–27 Aug 1914. The British 2nd Corps had reached Le Cateau during the retreat from ◊Mons. Almost worn out by three days of constant marching and fighting, the corps spread out between Le Cateau and Caudry and began digging in. General ◊Smith-Dorrien, commanding, decided to make a stand; General ◊French, the commander in chief, was afraid of exposing his flank and was in favour of continuing the retreat, telling Smith-Dorrien that he could expect no support if he stayed. Four German corps fell upon the British line, greatly outnumbering it; the British guns were brought up into the open, among the infantry, so that their visible support would aid infantry morale. The Germans had some 660 guns to the British 246, and gradually obliterated the British batteries. Eventually the Germans forces found an exposed flank and began working around, so that orders were given to retire. Thanks to the screening action of French cavalry and the rearguard of remaining British guns, most of the troops were able to withdraw. The Germans were sufficiently shaken to delay their pursuit until the next day, thus giving Smith-Dorrien's men a slight respite.

The *second battle* of Le Cateau took place 6–12 Oct 1918 across the same ground, this time as part of the general Allied advance after breaking the ◊Hindenburg line. Liberally supported by tanks and bombing aircraft, the British forces simply rolled the Germans up in front of them and it was less a battle than a pursuit action.

Leake Lieutenant-Colonel Arthur Martin 1874–1953. British surgeon and soldier. Qualified as a surgeon, he joined the Hertfordshire Yeomanry during the South African war and was awarded the Victoria Cross 1902 for his work in attending wounded men while under fire and himself wounded. He returned to a medical practice in England but later took a commission in the Royal Army Medical Corps and was posted to India. He retired and enlisted in the Serbian Army in 1912, serving as a medical officer in the Balkan Wars, then returned to India and re-joined the RAMC Sept 1914. Sent to France, he was awarded a second Victoria Cross (in fact, a clasp to his first VC) for exceptional bravery and devotion to duty in the battles around Zonnebeke Nov 1914, thus becoming one of the very few men ever to win the VC twice.

Lebel rifle French service rifle. Of 8-mm calibre, using a bolt breech action, and with a tubular magazine beneath the barrel, it was the first service rifle ever to use a small calibre bullet and smokeless powder. Introduced 1886, it was partly replaced by a Lebel-Berthier design, which used a box magazine, in the early 1900s but large number of the 1886 pattern remained in service throughout the war.

Lee-Enfield rifle British service rifle. Of .303 inch (7.7mm) calibre it used a bolt-action breech and a 10-round box magazine. Introduced 1893 it went through several minor modifications but remained the British standard rifle until the 1950s.

Leipzig redoubt German fortified position in France, between Ovillers and ◊Thiepval. Captured by the British 7 July 1916 during the battle of the ◊Somme, it was re-taken by the Germans March 1918 and not recovered until the general advance in the autumn of 1918.

Leman General Gerart Matheu Joseph Georges 1851–1920. Belgian soldier. Joined the army engineers 1872 and in 1875 was attached to the ministry of war. After being an instructor in fortification, he became director of studies in the military academy 1899 and commandant 1905. In 1914 he was a lieutenant-general commanding the fortress of Liège, and directed its defence when the Germans attacked. His head-quarters were in Fort Loncin which came under fire from the German 'Big Bertha' howitzers. One shell detonated the fort magazine, and General Leman was wounded and buried in the subsequent wreckage. He was rescued and taken prisoner by the Germans 15 Aug 1914. After a period in a prison camp his health deteriorated and he was permitted to go into internment in Switzerland 1917 and to return to Belgium Jan 1918, where he died 17 Oct 1920.

Lemberg (later Lvov, Poland, now in the Ukraine) town in Galicia, scene of fighting between Austrian and Russian forces, 1914–15. A fortress town and military HQ, the Austrian army fell back to Lemberg when defeated by the Russians at ◊Sokal Aug 1914. Three Austrian armies were advancing eastward to do battle; the 2nd was based on Lemberg, the 1st was about 15 km/9 mi S of Lemberg, and the 3rd was in SW Poland. The Russians mustered two huge armies and when the 2nd Austrian advanced, the Russians, under ◊Brusilov and ◊Russky, almost encircled it and completely defeated it, while effectively keeping the other two Austrian armies at bay. This defeat led what was left of the 2nd Army to retire and abandon Lemberg to the Russians. In June 1915 German troops under ◊Mackensen advanced on Lemberg from the south but were repulsed. Keeping the defences diverted, this attack allowed other German forces to swing north and east and thus threaten the rear of the defended zone. After a fierce battle lasting several days the Russians finally evacuated the town and fortress 22 June 1915, and it remained in German hands thereafter.

Lenin Vladimir Ilyich (adopted name of Vladimir Ilyich Ulyanov) 1870–1924. Russian revolutionary, first leader of the USSR, and communist theoretician. Russian revolutionary. Name assumed by Vladimir Ilytch Ulianov, a nobleman's son. He took to political activity as a student and was exiled to Siberia 1895. Upon his release 1900 he left Russia and travelled around Europe, fomenting revolutionary theories. During the 1905 revolution he edited the first Russian socialist newspaper. From Switzerland he attacked socialist support for World War I as aiding an 'imperialist' struggle. In April 1917 he was given passage by the Germans to return to Russia and take up his revolutionary activities, in order to remove Russia from the war and allowing Germany to concentrate her war effort on to the Western Front.

On arriving in Russia Lenin established himself at the head of the Bolsheviks, against the provisional government of Kerensky; a complicated power struggle ensued, but eventually Lenin triumphed 8 Nov 1917; a Bolshevik government was formed, and peace negotiations with Germany were begun leading to the signing of a treaty 3 March 1918 (see ◊Russian Revolution). The Germans had achieved their aim and Lenin and the Bolsheviks could now concentrate their efforts on the civil war with the 'White Russian' (counter-revolutionary) forces of ◊Denikin, ◊Wrangel, and others bent upon restoring the monarchy, a task which occupied them until the early 1920s. From the overthrow of the provisional government until his death, Lenin effectively controlled the Soviet Union, although an assassination attempt in 1918 injured his health. He founded the Third (Communist) International 1919.

Lens French town in the *département* of Pas-de-Calais, a railway junction and engineering town in a mining area. The area was the scene of almost constant battle during the war, and the town itself was taken by the Germans Oct 1914. The damage to the town and surrounding area was so great that mining operations could not re-start until 1921. The *Battle of Lens* was fought May–Aug 1917 between British and German forces, the British attempting to drive the Germans from the area and also make them fear for the safety of Lille and draw troops away from the Ypres front. Canadian troops made a determined attack on the town, gaining the suburbs, but the battle degenerated into house-to-house fighting and little real progress was made. The Germans launched several counter-attacks but the Canadians held on to their gains. A final assault was planned, but by this time the enormous British losses in the battle of ◊Ypres meant that the reserves for another attack on Lens were not available, and the Canadians were withdrawn, leaving the Germans in possession. It was finally taken 3 Oct 1918 after German defeats elsewhere led them to abandon the town.

Lettow-Vorbeck Paul Emil von 1870–1946. German soldier. Joined the German artillery 1890 and served in the Boxer Rebellion and in German Southwest Africa. In 1914 he was military commander in German Southeast Africa (now Tanzania) where he displayed tactical brilliance. With a force numbering about 3,000 German and 11,000 native troops and with virtually no support from Germany, he kept the 130,000 strong Allied force under ◊Smuts constantly at bay until he finally retired over the border into Portuguese East Africa 1917. From there he continued to wage a guerilla campaign against the Allies for the remainder of the war. He was never seriously defeated in the field, and did not surrender until two weeks after the Armistice. Promoted to general 1917, although his operations never affected the major course of the war he nevertheless kept a considerable Allied force tied down in Africa and effectively out of the rest of the war. He returned to Germany and retired 1920.

Lewis gun British light machine gun, it was gas-operated, air-cooled, and fed from a rotating drum of 47 or 97 rounds. The Lewis gun was initially designed by Samuel MacLean and was then developed and perfected by Col I N Lewis, US Army. Unable to interest the US Army in the weapon, Lewis took the gun to Belgium and set up a manufacturing company there 1913. In 1914 most of the staff fled to Britain where they were able to continue manufacture in the Birmingham Small Arms Company factory. The gun was subsequently used by the British, Belgian, and Italian armies in great numbers, both as a ground weapon and as an aircraft gun. Though generally replaced by more modern designs in the 1930s, the Lewis was still in use during World War II.

Libau German merchant ship used to run guns and ammunition to the Irish Republican Army (IRA) for the projected Easter rising 1916 under Roger Casement (1864–1916). The ship, commanded by a German naval officer, sailed to Tralee Bay 21 April 1916 where Casement was supposed to board the Libau from a U-boat, but he failed to appear. British patrol boats then appeared and escorted the Libau to Cork, but the captain was able to scuttle the ship and surrendered himself to the British. Placed in a prisoner-of-war camp, he later escaped but was recaptured.

Liberty engine US-manufactured aero engine based on a Rolls-Royce design. A V-12, water-cooled engine, it developed 405 bhp (brake horsepower) at 1,650 rpm (revolutions per minute). The weight in running order was 1,083 lbs and it was adopted for use in a number of aircraft and also in tanks. The prime feature of the engine was that it had been designed specifically for mass-production, in order to have a reliable engine which could be turned out as quickly as the rest of an aircraft.

Liberty tank American name for the British Mark VIII tank, adopted by the Anglo-American Tank Committee for production in both the UK and USA. Ambitious plans were made for sub-contracting parts to factories in both countries and building 1,550 tanks in an assembly plant in France, ready for the projected 1919 offensive but the war ended before this could be done. About 100 were built after the war, mostly in the USA, from parts made before the Armistice.

Liebknecht Karl 1871–1919. German socialist. Liebknecht practised as a barrister in Berlin, did his military service in the Prussian Guard, but turned to socialism while defending a group of agitators in Konigsberg 1904. Imprisoned for sedition 1907, he was eventually elected to the Reichstag 1912. In 1914 he refused to vote for war credits, but when called to the colours he served in a labour battalion on the

Eastern Front. After a speech against government finance for the war he was expelled from the Reichstag April 1916 and shortly afterwards sentenced to four and a half years imprisonment for sedition. Amnestied Oct 1918 he agitated for revolution, forming the German Communist Party 1918. In Jan 1919, he helped foment the Spartacist rising and was shot 'whilst attempting to escape' 15 Jan 1919.

Liège city of Belgium and principal town of the Liège province. A notable centre of gunmaking, it was heavily protected by a ring of forts and had a garrison of about 30,000 men under General ◊Leman. On 5 Aug 1914 the defences were attacked by a force of about 100,000 German troops. When a simple infantry assault failed, artillery bombardment began and a small German force managed to penetrate the ring and occupy part of the city. On 12 Aug the 42 cm 'Big Bertha' howitzers were brought up and began reducing the forts one by one. The last forts fell 16 Aug 1914, General Leman was wounded and captured, and on the following day the city was formally occupied, remaining in German hands throughout the war.

Ligget General Hunter 1857–1935. US soldier. Joined the army 1879 and saw service in Cuba and the Philippines, later becoming president of the Army War College. In 1918 he succeeded General ◊Pershing as commander of the US Army in France and conducted the successful campaign in the ◊Argonne.

Lille French town, capital of the *département* of Nord and an important industrial centre. In 1914 it was protected by 20 elderly forts, but the French government, as a result of political pressure, declared it open and evacuated all troops. Some German forces entered the town 2 Sept 1914 but left 5 Sept and for some weeks it remained in French hands. Fighting began nearby between elements of the 5th French Army and the German army 5 Oct, as a result of which the Germans bombarded the town, destroying several hundred houses and killing 80 civilians. The garrison surrendered 12 Oct 1914 and from then on it remained in German hands, becoming a prime objective of Allied strategy. The Allies refrained from bombarding it, since its factories were vital to the economy of N France and were not in use by the Germans, but when forced to retreat Oct 1918 the German army destroyed a great deal of machinery and railway installations.

Liman von Sanders Otto 1855–1929. German soldier. Joined the German cavalry 1874; in 1913 he reached the rank of general, commanded the 22nd Division, and was ennobled. In 1914 he was sent to Turkey and, appointed field-marshal of the Turkish army, commanded the Turkish forces at ◊Gallipoli 1915. He then took command of all Turkish forces in the Middle East and was in command in Palestine and Syria during 1918. Captured by the British under General ◊Allenby he was interned in Malta and returned to Germany Aug 1919.

Liquorice Factory, The British nickname for an industrial factory in ◊Kut-Al-Imara which had been converted into a fortified post and was used by both British and Turks as a machine gun position at different times. Finally used by the Turks as a small flanking fort to protect their retreat from the town 1917.

listening post sentry post, usually slightly forward of the general trench line, where the occupant can listen for signs of enemy activity such as digging, wiring, bringing in gas cylinders, etc. In cases where the trenches were relatively close, such sounds could be clearly heard at night and yielded useful information on the enemy's actions and intentions.

Little Willie prototype British tank built 1915. It consisted of little more than a rectangular box on two 'Creeping Grip' caterpillar tracks, with a two-wheeled steering unit connected to the rear, but it proved the viability of a tracked vehicle. It could not meet the War Office specification for a tank, since it could not cross a trench wider than 1.2 m/4 ft, but it gave valuable technical information and was an indispensable step in the design of the first fighting tank.

Lloyd George David 1863–1945. Welsh Liberal politician, prime minister of Britain 1916–22. A solicitor by trade he became an MP 1890 and was a pioneer of social reform. During the Boer War, he was a prominent supporter of the Boers. He held ministerial posts during World War I until 1916 when there was an open breach between him and Prime Minister Asquith, and he became prime minister of a coalition government. Securing a unified Allied command, he enabled the Allies to withstand the last German offensive and achieve victory. After World War I he had a major role in the ◊Versailles peace treaty.

In the 1918 elections, he achieved a huge majority over Labour and Asquith's followers. He had become largely distrusted within his own party by 1922, and never regained power.

The finest eloquence is that which gets things done; the worst is that which delays them.
David Lloyd George speech at Paris Peace Conference Jan 1919

Lody Carl. German spy. A lieutenant in the German Naval reserve, he travelled frequently to British ports prior to 1914 in the guise of a travel guide, making particular note of naval establishments. After the outbreak of war he was selected by ◊Boy-Ed to be his agent in England. Lody was given a stolen US passport, went to England, reported on air raid protection in London, then went to the naval base at Rosyth, to Liverpool, and finally to Ireland. He was arrested at Killarney and found to be in possession of incriminating documents and later discovered to have been responsible for the sinking of a British cruiser by reporting its sailing to the German Navy. Tried and found guilty of espionage, he was shot in the Tower of London 6 Nov 1914, the first German spy to be executed during the war.

Lódz´ (pronounced 'Wutch') industrial town in central Poland, 120 km/75 mi SW of Warsaw, a centre for textile manufacture. In 1914 it was held by the Russians in the face of strong attacks by German forces under ◊Mackensen, during ◊Hindenburg's second attack on Warsaw. Fierce Russian resistance kept the Germans out of the town, but the German forces passed on both sides for some distance, so that Lódz´ became a prominent salient, difficult to defend and in danger of being pinched off if the German columns moved together. It was therefore evacuated without loss 5 Dec 1914. The Germans continued to bombard it for most of the following day before they realised the Russians had left. It remained in German hands thereafter.

Lohner aircraft Austrian flying boat, extensively used in the Adriatic, made by Jakob Lohner & Sons of Vienna. Since it had also been built under license in Italy prior to Italy's entry into the war, it was also used by the Italians in the same theatre, leading to no little confusion. The principal characteristic of the Lohner was its swept-back biplane wings, giving the aircraft an arrow-head shape in plan.

Long Max nickname for the German 38-cm railway gun. Used principally for long range interdiction fire at ◊Verdun, it was also used as the starting point for the development of the ◊Paris Gun.

Longwy French town in the *département* of Meurthe-et-Moselle, about 40 miles NW of Metz, on the Belgian frontier. Called 'The Iron gate of France' by Louis XIV, it controls the approach from Luxembourg via the Chiers valley, a traditional invasion route. Defended by a fort, in Aug 1914 it was garrisoned by two infantry battalions and a small artillery force. On 3 Aug the German army appeared in the area but did not attack until 21 Aug when an intense artillery bombardment destroyed most of the town. On 26 Aug there was only one operating French gun left and the fortress commander surrendered. The town remained in German hands for the rest of the war.

Loos, Battle of offensive carried out by British and French forces against the Germans Sept 1915 with the intention of recovering the mining district around the towns of Loos and ◊Lens and, if possible, capturing ◊Lille. At the same time as the French offensive in Champagne, it was hoped to divert German forces from there to aid the French.

The German positions were well-fortified, with large numbers of steel and concrete pillboxes and shelters. The British forces included numbers of battalions of the ◊Kitchener armies, being used for the first time, and was also the first occasion on which the British used gas. Unfortunately the wind shifted and the gas was blown back into the British lines, but the cylinders were rapidly shut off and little damage was done. The attack managed to drive a salient some way into the German lines, but the reserves were badly organized and before they could be brought up a German counter-attack drove the British back to their start line. A second attack, south of the ◊Hohernzollern redoubt, managed to gain some 3,200 km/3,500 yds and this was retained. About 250,000 British and a similar number of French troops were engaged in the battle; British losses were about 60,000, among them three generals. French casualties are not known since they were included with other actions at the same time, but they were probably heavier than the British.

Lorraine, Campaigns in the French district of Lorraine bordered the German district Lothringen, which had been Lorraine prior to the end of the Franco-Prussian war 1871. In July 1914 German border troops began erecting field defences and wire; on the outbreak of war French troops were forbidden to go within 10 km/6 mi of the border so as not to provide the Germans with an excuse to invade. The Germans invaded anyway, taking up the French self-imposed exclusion zone and thus gaining the mining district of Briey and the Vosges mountain passes. Three French armies were mobilised in Lorraine, holding a front from ◊Verdun to the ◊Vosges. Initial advances by the French were quickly defeated, but a German advance against Nancy was held and driven back, and a German attempt to advance so as to outflank the armies forming for the battle of the ◊Marne was similarly repulsed. After this most of the sector remained a quiet front until the last weeks of the war when large forces were concentrated against ◊Metz; there was also continuous fighting in the west of the sector around ◊Verdun and some battles in the Vosges 1915–16.

Lossberg General Friedrich Karl von 1868–1934. German soldier. Lossberg became a colonel 1915 but was virtually unknown until selected as Chief of Staff of the German 3rd Army during the fighting around ◊Champagne Sept 1915. He handled his duties well and was given a similar post during the battle of the ◊Somme. At ◊Arras in 1917 he was Chief of Staff of the German army which took most of the British attack. He was then moved to Flanders as Chief of Staff there and promoted to major-general, and late in Oct 1918 replaced ◊Ludendorff as the chief of the general staff. Although little known, contemporaries have said that he had probably the finest brain in the army and was regarded as the master of German defences in the west.

Louvain central Belgian university town on the river Dyle, 32 km/20 mi from Brussels. It was occupied by German troops 19 Aug 1914. On 25 Aug, while some desultory fighting was going on north of the town, shots were heard in the town itself. Their source has never been found, but the German troops took alarm and began firing indiscriminately and then burning houses. Next day the town was systematically cleared of its civil population, most of the people being shipped to Germany as labourers, while others were shot. The town was then systematically looted and burned, the library of the university being one of the most valuable targets.

Ludendorff General Erich von 1865–1937. German soldier. He joined the infantry 1882, and in 1898 joined the General Staff, lecturing at the Berlin Kriegsakademie and working in the planning section of the Staff. In 1914 he was a major-general and became Chief of Staff to von ◊Bulow's 2nd Army in the attack on Belgium. He was sent to the Russian Front to act as Chief of Staff to ◊Hindenburg 22 Aug and was largely responsible for the victory at ◊Tannenberg and the successes of 1915. He then accompanied Hindenburg to the Western Front where they executed the attack on ◊Verdun 1916. When that failed, he and Hindenburg became the commanders in chief of all German forces and were broadly responsible for the conduct of the war from then on.

Ludendorff reorganized the German Army and planned the strategy which advanced the Eastern Front while he held the French and British in check in the west; with von ◊Hutier he devised new methods of attack, and finally planned the ◊German Spring Offensive of 1918. The collapse of the ◊Hindenburg Line under British attack Sept 1918 and the collapse of Bulgaria shortly afterwards caused him to lose confidence and he called for peace negotiations, but when talks were opened he changed his mind, refused to cooperate, and was dismissed by the Kaiser 26 Oct 1918. In postwar years he was active in right-wing politics. He took part in the Nazi rising in Munich 1923 and sat in the Reichstag (parliament) as a right-wing Nationalist.

Lusitania ocean liner sunk by a German submarine 7 May 1915 with the loss of 1,200 lives, including some Americans; its sinking helped to bring the USA into the war.

Lutsk (now Luck, Poland) Russian town, one of three Russian fortresses known as the 'Volhyn Triangle'. Captured by the Austrians 31 Aug 1914 after a battle with retreating Russians, the Russians mounted a counter-offensive on the ◊Styr river line Sept 1914, and were able to retake Lutsk 24 Sept. However, lack of supplies and ammunition led them to evacuate it again 28 Sept and it remained in Austrian hands until the ◊Brusilov offensive April 1916. As part of the general Russian gains in this campaign, Lutsk was recaptured 7 June 1916, holding it until they retired from the war 1917.

Luxembourg although guaranteed neutrality by all the European powers 1867, Luxembourg was invaded by the German Army 1 Aug 1914 on the pretext that French invasion was imminent. The population was placed under German law, men conscripted into the German Army, and civilians seized as hostages, though none were executed. It remained in German hands until the Armistice.

Lyddite British explosive, used for filling artillery shells. Actually molten and cast picric acid, the name was adopted in order to conceal the nature of the substance and taken from the initial trials which were conducted at Lydd, in S England.

1. An Austrian 30.5cm heavy howitzer in action on the Italian Front. This type was given the ironic nick-name *Schlanke* ('Slim') *Emma*.

2. A British Sopwith Camel single-seater fighter. The Camel helped Allied pilots recover air superiority after the decimation of the Royal Flying Corps during 'Bloody April' 1917.

3. British troops in early PH ('phenol helmet') gas marks on the Western Front. Restrictive and ineffective, these were ultimately replaced by box-respirator masks.

4. Paul Ludwig von Hindenburg, Field-Marshal and chief of the German general staff from August 1916. Hindenburg and Erich Ludendorff were virtually military rulers of Germany 1917–18.

5. A corner of Anzac Beach on the Gallipoli peninsula, Turkey, 1915. The Allied position was almost intolerably cramped and exposed to constant Turkish bombardment.

6. Sir Douglas Haig, Field-Marshal and commander in chief of British forces on the Western Front from 19 December 1915. He was an unimaginative commander whose reputation suffered further from the animosity felt towards him by Lloyd George, the British Prime Minister.

7. A British Mark I 'male' tank near Thiepval (Somme), 25 September 1916. The Somme offensive saw the first, unsuccessful, use of tanks in warfare.

8. Erich Ludendorff, Quartermaster General and *de facto* commander in chief of the German Army from 1916, though his rank was technically inferior to that of Hindenburg.

9. Ferdinand Foch. An early proponent of French offensive spirit, Foch had proven himself one of the most flexible and realistic commanders of the war by the time of his appointment on 14 April 1918 as Allied commander in chief.

10. A German UB48-class medium U-boat at the commencement of a patrol. The prominent Utof 10.5cm deck gun indicates a date of 1918.

11. Lenin addressing a crowd of revolutionary troops in 1917. Trotsky is visible beside the rostrum.

M

McCudden James Byford 1895–1918. British fighter pilot. McCudden enlisted at the outbreak of war as a mechanic in the Royal Flying Corps. Promoted to sergeant, he trained as a pilot and rapidly became adept as an air fighter, winning the Military Medal Sept 1916. He was then commissioned and won the Military Cross Feb 1917, earning the bar to it Aug 1917. In Nov 1917 he received the DSO, and shortly afterward the bar to the DSO as well, followed March 1918 by the Victoria Cross. McCudden was on his way to France to take over command of a squadron when he was killed in a flying accident 8 July 1918. Up to 31 March 1918, he had shot down 54 enemy aircraft.

MacDonogh General Sir George Mark Watson 1865–1942. British soldier. MacDonogh joined the Royal Engineers 1884, rose to colonel, and then became a staff officer 1912. Promoted to major-general, he became director of military intelligence at the war office late 1915 where he remained until the war ended, after which he became adjutant-general. He was knighted 1917 and promoted to lieutenant-general 1919.

machine gun automatic weapon, capable of continuous fire, used in support of infantry operations, as an air defence weapon, and as armament on tanks and aircraft. Combined with barbed-wire obstacles, the machine gun became one of the most powerful defensive weapons of the war and, indirectly, was the reason for the development of the tank.

In 1914 most machine guns were heavy, water-cooled weapons, fed with belts of ammunition and used in a defensive role or as barrage weapons to support an attack. The ◊Maxim gun was the first weapon of this class, followed by the ◊Vickers, Schwarzlose, ◊Browning, and other makes. During the course of the war the need for an efficient machine gun capable of being carried by one man became apparent and the *light machine gun* came into use. Allied light machine guns included the ◊Lewis and ◊Hotchkiss, while the German Army converted their Maxim into a more portable form.

Machine Gun Corps British regiment, raised 1915. The unit was a consolidation of infantry machine gun companies into a separate, specialist unit, reflecting the growing importance of the machine gun.

The principal role of the unit was to provide massed machine guns which could lay down suppressive fire on areas during an attack so as to prohibit the enemy forming up or advancing across them. It was divided into infantry, cavalry, heavy and motor branches, the latter becoming the Tank Corps. The unit was disbanded 1919, and machine guns were returned to infantry companies, since the peculiar tactical problems which had led to its formation were felt to be unlikely to reappear.

Machine Gun Guards British military unit, formed 1918 as the 6th (or Machine Gun) Regiment of Foot Guards. It consisted of five battalions, and was virtually the Brigade of Guards' own version of the ◊Machine Gun Corps, for employment with other Guards regiments. Like the Corps, it was disbanded after the war.

Mackensen General August von 1849–1945. German soldier. Von Mackensen joined the German army 1869 and by 1908 was general of cavalry and commander of the 17th Army Corps. In 1914 he became one of Hindenburg's generals and came to prominence in the second battle for ◊Warsaw. He became the supreme commander of the Austro-German forces operating in ◊Galicia 1915, then advanced into SE Poland and was involved in the operations which drove the Russians from Warsaw. He was subsequently promoted to field-marshal and overran Serbia late 1915.

Following Romania's entry into the war he commanded the force which invaded the Dobruja Aug 1916, and, with ◊Falkenhayn, invaded Romania itself. His offensive against the Russo-Romanian armies 1917 was less successful but after the collapse of Russia and the treaty of ◊Brest-Litovsk, he was able to consolidate his positions in Romania and became the de facto ruler of the country until the Armistice. After the Armistice he was interned in Hungary but was permitted to return to Germany 1919.

Magdeburg German cruiser. It had a displacement of 4,410 tonnes/4,480 tons, a speed of 25 knots, and was armed with 12 105-mm guns and four torpedo tubes. While attempting to evade a Russian naval force 27 Aug 1914, it ran aground in the Gulf of Finland. Discovered and fired on by Russian ships, the captain attempted to scuttle the vessel and then abandoned ship. Russian sailors went aboard and were able to save the naval code-books, which were then taken to Britain. The salvage of these code-books was instrumental in allowing the Allies to read German Naval codes for much of the war.

Maistre General Paul Andre Marie 1858–1922. French soldier. Maistre joined the infantry as a lieutenant 1879 and by 1912 was a brigadier-general on the general staff. He commanded the 21st Army Corps Sept 1914 and was promoted to full general Oct 1914. He took command of the 6th Army May 1917 and of the 10th Army Dec 1917. In June 1918 he was given command of the group forming the Armies of the North and became president of the Committee of Higher Defence. Following the end of the war, he became inspector-general of the French Army June 1919. Although never a famous name, he was among the most competent and reliable of French commanders.

Mametz French village and wood occupying a commanding position in the *département* of the Somme, 8 km/5 mi from ◊Albert. The village was captured by the British 1 July 1916, followed by the wood 10–12 July, as part of the British offensive during the battle of the ◊Somme. Both were lost to the ◊German Spring Offensive March 1918 and recovered in the Allied offensive in the autumn.

The wounded were being carried back in streams, all covered from head to foot with the mud in which they had been fighting, shining like seals.
　　　　　R. Fielding on the fighting for *Mametz* Wood, in *War Letters*.

Mangin General Charles Marie Emmanuel 1866–1925. French soldier, a 'fire-eating general' who was always full of the offensive spirit, he sometimes bit off more than he could chew. Mangin joined the army 1886 and saw service in Senegal, the Sudan, and French Indo-China.

In 1914 he was commanding an infantry brigade in Morocco, but returned to France and commanded a division in the first battle of the ◊Marne. He then commanded a division at ◊Verdun, recapturing the forts of ◊Douaumont and ◊Vaux-Fossoy. He was subsequently promoted to general, taking command of the 6th Army Dec 1916. His part in the ◊Nivelle offensive in the Champagne sector 1917 was disastrous and was one of the factors which led to the serious ◊mutiny in the French army later in the year. However, he redeemed himself sufficiently to take command of the 10th Army June 1918 and played a leading role in the counter-offensive which drove the German army from the ◊Aisne and ◊Marne. Following the war, he commanded the French Army of Occupation in Germany 1919.

Whatever you do, you lose a lot of men.
General *Mangin* on comparing divisional casualty figures at Verdun

---

Mannlicher rifle Austrian rifle, standard arm (in various versions) of the Austro-Hungarian, Romanian, Bulgarian, Greek, and Balkan armies. The Austro-Hungarian weapon was an 8-mm calibre weapon and used an unusual 'straight-pull' bolt mechanism and a five-round clip-fed magazine. Carbine versions were also produced for artillery, engineers, and cavalry.

Mannock Edward (Mickey) (d. 1918). British fighter pilot. Originally serving in the Royal Engineers, he transferred to the Royal Flying Corps and rapidly became one of Britain's foremost fighter pilots. He was awarded the Military Cross 1917, later earning a bar to it, and the DSO and two bars 1918. He was shot down and killed 26 July 1918, with his score standing at 50 German aircraft. He was posthumously awarded the Victoria Cross July 1919.

Maraçesti, Battle of battle between Austro-German and Russo-Romanian forces, Aug 1917, the greatest battle fought by the Romanian army during the war. After defeating the Russians in Galicia 1916, von ◊Mackensen attacked the Russo-Romanian defences on the river Sereth with 12 divisions, heading toward Maraçesti, an important railway junction. He was stopped close to the town by a strong Russo-

Romanian force and the battle continued for some days, Eventually, the Russian element of the defences, under the influence of Bolshevik agitators, broke and ran. By this time, though, Romanian reinforcements were arriving and in spite of heavy fighting defeated Mackensen's force and prevented him taking Moldavia.

March General Peyton Conway 1864–1955. US soldier. Joined the US Artillery 1888, served in the Philippine Insurrection and on the general staff, and became adjutant-general of Missouri 1911. In 1917 he went to France as commander of the US Artillery and was appointed acting Chief of Staff March 1918, being promoted to general and Chief of Staff in May. He resigned from the army 1921.

The Marne Campaign 1914

Aug 16	German capture of Liège
Aug 20	German capture of Brussels
Aug 22–23	Battle of the Sambre
Aug 23–24	Battle of Mons
Aug 26–27	Battle of Le Cateau
Aug 29	French counter-attack at Guise
Sept 5–9	Battle of the Marne

Marne, Battles of two unsuccessful German offensives. In the *First Battle* 5–9 Sept 1914, three German armies were swinging round from Belgium to sweep through France and encircle Paris. After some initial uncertainty, Marshal ◊Joffre began to see what the German strategy was and ordered the 1st and 2nd French Armies to hold the Germans around Verdun and Nancy. Meanwhile he formed two new armies, the 6th and 9th, in preparation for a counter-attack and drew back his left flank to entice the Germans further south. The French 6th Army under ◊Gallieni moved against the exposed flank of General von ◊Kluck's 1st German Army which halted its southward drive and turned aside to deal with Gallieni. This opened a 48 km/30 mi gap between the German 1st Army and the 2nd Army under von ◊Bulow. Joffre now threw his counter-attack force against von Bulow who retired, forcing von Kluck to retire in order to avoid being totally surrounded, and the German advance was halted and turned back. Although tactically inconclusive, the first battle of the Marne was a strategic victory for the Allies.

The *Second Battle* 15 July–4 Aug 1918 formed the final thrust of the ◊German Spring Offensive. Ludendorff threw 35 divisions across the Marne, planning to encircle Reims. The French were prepared for the attack, with four armies under good generals, together with a strong US force, and although the Germans initially gained ground they were eventually halted and turned back. The Allied counter-attack, beginning 18 July, is sometimes referred to as the *Third Battle* of the Marne and it forced the Germans back to a line running from Reims to Soissons.

Marshall General Sir William Raine 1865– 1939. British soldier. Joined the army 1886 and served on the NW Frontier of India in the Tirah campaign 1897–98, and in the South African war 1899–1902, where he was wounded. In 1914 he was commanding an infantry battalion in India, but 1915 was given command of the 87th Brigade which he led at ◊Gallipoli. He later commanded a division, and was made a corps commander in Mesopotamia Sept 1916. On the sudden death of General ◊Maude Nov 1917, he assumed overall command in the area and successfully completed the campaign. Knighted 1917, he was appointed to command of the Northern Armies in India 1920.

Martinsyde British aircraft made by Martinsyde Ltd of Woking. The company began making monoplanes 1908 and after the outbreak of war produced several extremely good biplane scout–fighter aircraft for the Royal Flying Corps. Their final model, the F.4 'Buzzard' was a single-seat biplane powered by a 300 hp Hispano engine which had a top speed of 235 kph/145 mph, faster than any other single-seat aircraft of the period. The Buzzard was armed with two Vickers machine guns firing through the propeller arc.

Orders were given for the manufacture of about 1,700 machines, but only about 50 had been made before the war ended. The contracts were cancelled, but the company were able to build a further 200 which were bought by the air forces of Portugal, Finland, Japan, and Spain.

Marwitz General Georg von der 1856–1934. German soldier. Joined the German cavalry 1875 and by 1903 was chief of staff of an army corps. Became general of cavalry 1908 and by 1912 was a divisional commander. On the outbreak of war he was active on the Eastern Front, first in the Carpathians and later led the attack on ◊Przemysl 1915. He commanded the German 2nd Army in France and defeated the British at ◊Cambrai Nov 1917. He later led the same army in the ◊German Spring Offensive 1918, and ended the war commanding the 5th Army in the ◊Verdun sector.

Mata Hari (stage name of Gertrud Margarete Zelle) 1876–1917. Dutch courtesan, dancer, and probable spy. She had affairs with highly placed military and government officials on both sides during the war and told Allied secrets to the Germans. She may have been a double agent, in the pay of both France and Germany. She was eventually tried by the French on espionage charges and shot in Paris 1917.

Maubeuge French town and fortress in the *département* of Nord, on the river Sambre close to the Belgian border. The town was an important strategic point as it was at the junction of five railway lines, and so it was protected by 15 detached forts and gun batteries, mounting 435 guns. Garrisoned by about 35,000 French troops, it was selected as the advance base for the British Expeditionary Force in 1914, but was besieged by the Germans from 25 Aug and after 13 days was surrendered to a force of about half the garrison's strength. After the war, a court-martial tried the commander but acquitted him on the grounds that he had, at least, managed to keep some German forces out of the battle of the ◊Marne.

Maude General Sir Frederick Stanley 1864–1917. British soldier. Maude joined the Coldstream Guards 1884, served in the Sudan, joined the staff 1897, and then served in the South African War, winning the DSO. In 1909–12 he served as assistant director of the Territorial Forces. He went to France Aug 1914 as a staff officer with 5th Division and commanded a brigade Oct 1914, but was wounded and returned to England. He then took the 13th Division to ◊Gallipoli, Egypt, and Mesopotamia. He was given command of the forces in Mesopotamia Aug 1916 and subsequently drove the Turks from ◊Kut-al-Imara and captured ◊Baghdad. He successfully carried out follow-up operations but then contracted cholera and died Nov 1917, being replaced by

General ◊Marshall. Well-liked and skilful, Maude was an effective general and his sudden death was a great loss to the army.

Mauser rifle service rifle of the German Army, adopted 1898. A 7.92mm calibre, bolt-action rifle, it had a five-shot magazine. The original design, the Gewehr '98, was a full-length rifle; it was supplemented by a short-barrelled version known as the Karabiner '98 which gradually replaced the longer weapon and became the standard rifle for all arms of the services.

Maxim gun machine gun invented by Sir Hiram Maxim and first developed 1884. It became the standard machine gun of Britain, Germany, Austria, Russia, and several other countries. Recoil-operated and water-cooled, it was a heavy, belt-fed, tripod-mounted weapon, and could deliver sustained fire for hours on end at a rate of about 600 rounds per minute. The British replaced it with the Vickers, a modification of Maxim's design, 1912, and the Germans developed the Parabellum, a similar modification at much the same time, but the Maxim remained the principal German and Russian machine gun throughout the war.

Megiddo fortress town in N Israel, site of several important Biblical battles. The British field marshal Allenby broke the Turkish front here Sept 1918 and Turkey capitulated almost immediately after. It is identified with the Armageddon mentioned in the Biblical book of Revelations.

Menin Belgian town in the province of West Flanders, on the river Lys ⅃⅃⅃ the French frontier. In 1914 a British force made up of one infantry and one cavalry division, sent to assist the Belgian army, entered Menin but found their path blocked by five German corps which promptly attacked them. Seeing that his position was hopeless, the British commander withdrew what was left of his force to Ypres and the Germans occupied the town. Menin remained in German hands until 1 Oct 1918.

Mesopotamia the area bounded by the Tigris and Euphrates rivers; broadly, the area which is now the country of Iraq. In 1914 it was Turkish territory and operations against the Turks in the area began with the landing of a British force from India at Bahrain Nov 1914.

The Campaign in Mesopotamia

1914
Nov 21   British occupation of Basra

1915
July 24   Allied victory at Battle of Nasiriya
Nov 22–26   Inconclusive Battle of Ctesiphon
Dec 7   Turkish investment of Kut

1916
Apr 29   Surrender of Allied forces in Kut

1917
Feb 24   Turkish evacuation of Kut
March 11   Allied capture of Baghdad
Sept 27   Allied victory at Battle of Ramadi

1918
Nov 3   Allied occupation of Mosul

This force had driven the Turks from Basra, Shaiba, and Amara by June 1915, thus establishing a cordon of security around the Basra oilfields, the object of the expedition. Political considerations then prevailed and the force went on toward ◊Baghdad, taking ◊Kut-al-Imara but being repulsed at ◊Ctesiphon. Reinforcements were sent, but by the time they appeared the British forces in Kut-al-Imara were besieged and eventually surrendered. In early 1916 the fresh force advanced but poor organization, lack of supplies, and above all lack of strength, meant that they achieved very little. Eventually, two army corps under General ◊Maude were established in the theatre Dec 1916, and began a slow advance to Baghdad. The Turks resisted stubbornly but the British gradually extended their control of the country, driving the Turks northward and reaching Mosul and Kirkuk by Oct 1918, when the Turks were granted an Armistice.

Messines Belgian village and ridge in West Flanders, 9.5 km/6 mi S of Ypres. The village was occupied by the Germans Nov 1914, enabling them to hold a dominant position overlooking the British lines. An attempt by the 2nd British Army, under General ◊Plumer, to take the ridge led to the ***Battle of Messines*** 7–15 June 1917, against the 4th German Army, under General von Arnim. A significant factor in the battle was the unprecedented scale of ◊mining operations by the British; some 20 mines were excavated and charged with 600 tons of explosive, although one was discovered by the Germans before the battle and neutralized. The battle began with an exceptionally heavy artillery bombardment, lasting from 28 May to 7 June, which did considerable damage to the German defences. The mines were detonated at 3.10 a.m. on 7 June, immediately followed by a joint infantry and tank assault preceded by a creeping barrage. By 10 a.m. the entire German front line was in British hands, and the second line had been secured by 8 p.m. A German counter-attack was thrown back and the position was secured. Another innovation in this battle was the use of supply tanks to carry forward ammunition for the infantry and both ammunition and fuel for the 76 tanks which were deployed in the battle itself. Messines remained in British hands until the ◊German Spring Offensive 1918, but was re-taken, again by General ◊Plumer's forces, Sept 1918.

Meuse, Battles of the battles between French and German forces, Aug 1914. After the German invasion of Belgium and N France, the 4th French Army was ordered to hold the left bank of the river Meuse and maintain contact with the 5th French Army, then in headlong retreat from Charleroi. However, there was a 48 km/30 mi gap between the two armies, into which the German 2nd and 3rd Armies advanced. Troops of the 4th German Army bridged the river Meuse at Remilly, Torcy, and Donchery, establishing a large bridgehead south of Sedan. This was extended by taking other bridges and the Germans advanced along the whole Meuse front. The 4th German Army was checked by the French at Noyers and demanded assistance from the 3rd Army. However, the 3rd was paralysed by von ◊Moltke's demand to send some of its best troops to the Eastern Front, and had also been told to mount an attack on a fresh objective to the southwest. As a result, the German 4th Army was driven back over the Meuse by the French 4th Army, who gained a considerable victory. At this point Marshal ◊Joffre ordered a general retreat; General Langle de Cary, the French commander in the field, promptly obeyed, pulling back rapidly and abandoning large areas which could have been used to delay the subsequent German advance.

Meuse-Argonne campaign US-French offensive against the Germans Sept–Nov 1918. The 1st US Army attacked from the west side of the river Meuse 26 Sept 1918 with complete success, capturing Varennes and Montfaucon, while the 4th French Army attacked in Champagne. The attack was renewed 4 Oct, eventually breaching the ◊Kreimhilde Line and capturing Grandpré. By 1 Nov the US troops had advanced some 6 km/4 mi, taking Buzancy 2 Nov, and the Germans were in rapid retreat. By 7 Nov the Americans held the left bank of the Meuse opposite Sedan, and the bridge at Stenay was taken 10 Nov.

Although the Allied forces did not advance quickly, they achieved vital strategic results; the Montmedy-Sedan and Metz-Mézières railway lines were rendered useless to the Germans, depriving them of a valuable lifeline, and the German left wing was secured while the British advance in Flanders rolled back the right. However, the US forces paid a heavy price for their gains: some 26,227 dead and 96,788 wounded.

Mills bomb ◊hand grenade invented by William Mills of Birmingham 1915. It consisted of a cast-iron body filled with explosive and a central tube into which a detonator, fuse, and percussion cap were inserted. Above the cap was a striker pin, held against the pressure of a spring by means of an external lever, which was locked in place by a split pin. The user gripped the grenade so as to hold the lever depressed and withdrew the pin. As the grenade was thrown, the lever flew off and allowed the spring to drive the striker against the cap, igniting the fuse. After four seconds the grenade detonated, delivering blast and fragments over a wide area.

The Mills bomb entered service as the No. 5 grenade, but was then modified so that it could have a steel rod screwed into its base and be fired as a ◊rifle grenade; in this form it was called No. 23 grenade. Finally, it was altered again, having a 6.3 cm/2.5 in disc screwed to the base to allow it to be fired from a muzzle cup fitted to a rifle – the No. 36 grenade. It remained in British service in this form until the 1960s.

Milne Sir George Francis, 1st Baron 1866–1948. British soldier. Milne joined the Royal Artillery 1885 and served in both the Sudan campaign and the South African war, winning the DSO. In 1914 he was the artillery commander of the 4th Division, then took command of an infantry brigade and, in Feb 1915, a division. After a period as chief staff officer to the 2nd Army he was sent to ◊Salonika and took command of the British troops there May 1916. Under General Franchet d'Esperey, the French supreme commander, Milne was responsible for the defensive operations against the Bulgarian army 1917 and for the offensive which led to the collapse of Bulgaria 1918. He then took command of the army of the Black Sea, and retired Sept 1920 to become lieutenant of the Tower of London. Knighted 1918, he was promoted to general 1920.

mine explosives planted as traps in both land and naval warfare. As a *naval* weapon it is a spherical casing containing explosives and fitted with contact fuses, attached to a 'sinker' so that it will float at a fixed depth below the surface of the sea, which is detonated by a ship brushing against it.

In *land* warfare the term originally meant a tunnel driven beneath an enemy position and packed with explosives which were then detonated to coincide with an attack, a tactic used in many places on the Western Front (see ◊mining). However, toward the end of the war the term was used to describe explosive devices laid in the ground to impede the progress of tanks, and it is this meaning which has survived.

minefields areas where ◊mines have been planted to trap an unwary enemy or prevent them from crossing or gaining access to the area, both at sea or on land. Minefields would often be laid outside enemy ports to sink ships attempting to enter or leave. They were also laid in large numbers by the Allies in the North Sea, Irish Sea, and similar areas in order to prevent German warships entering or to channel submarines into areas where they could be more easily detected and attacked by surface vessels.

minenwerfer (lit. 'mine-thrower') German trench warfare weapon, the fore-runner of the trench mortar. The original *minenwerfers* were complex short-range breech-loading howitzers, but these were gradually supplemented by simpler muzzle-loading ◊mortars which took the same name.

minesweeping removing sea ◊mines so as to allow ships to move in the area in safety. The operation was usually carried out by dragging some form of cable device through the water so as to catch the cables attaching the mines to their 'sinkers', pulling the mines to the surface, or to cut or snap the cables, allowing the mines to float up. Once on the surface, the mines could be detonated safely by gunfire.

mining military term meaning to drive a tunnel beneath an enemy position. The end of the tunnel is filled with explosives which are then detonated so as to destroy the position and its occupants. The technique was frequently employed by both sides on the Western Front, but its drawback was that the enormous crater created could often be defended by unharmed troops quicker than the attackers could reach it.

Gentlemen, we may not make history tomorrow, but we shall certainly change the geography.
                    General Plumer to his staff before the battle of Messines,
                              which saw unprecedented use of *mining*.

Mishich Field Marshal Zivoyin 1855–1921. Serbian soldier. He joined the Serbian infantry as a lieutenant 1876, fought in the Serbo-Turkish wars and the war against Bulgaria 1885–86, and was chief of the general staff during the Balkan Wars 1912–13. In 1914 he commanded the Serbian 2nd Army and played a major role in resisting the Austrian invasions. Appointed field-marshal 1914, he retained command of the 2nd Army during the great retreat of 1915. He was given command of the re-constituted 2nd Army 1916 and outflanked ◊Monastir, aiding its capture by the Allies. He commanded the Serbian forces which played a part in the subjugation of Bulgaria Sept 1918. He died from illness 20 January 1921.

'moaning minnie' nickname given by British soldiers to shells fired from a German ◊*minenwerfer*, from the peculiar noise made by their flight and a corruption of the word *minenwerfer*.

Moltke Helmuth Johannes Ludwig von 1848–1916. German soldier. Nephew of the great von Moltke of Franco-Prussian War fame, he entered the German infantry 1869 and served in the Franco-Prussian war. He served as aide-de-camp to the Kaiser for some time, and became general of infantry and chief of the general staff 1906. On the outbreak of war it fell to him to execute the famous ◊Schlieffen Plan, but despite warnings he made modifications to the plan which diluted its effect. Once operations had begun he failed to keep in contact with the various formations, delayed decisions, shifted troops from one flank to another, withdrew others to reinforce the Eastern Front, and in general showed himself to be incapable of discharging the duties of his office. He was removed and replaced by ◊Falkenhayn Oct 1914, and, his reputation ruined, died June 1916.

Monash Sir John 1865–1931. Australian civil engineer, army officer, and administrator. He was a colonel at the outbreak of World War I and commanded the 4th Infantry Brigade through the Gallipoli campaign 1914–15. He established his reputation while in command of the 3rd Australian Division in France 1916 and in 1918 was promoted to lieutenant-general and succeeded ◊Birdwood in command of the Australian Corps. He gained recognition as one of the most capable of the British corps commanders in battles such as Amiens, Mont St Quentin, and the breaking of the Hindenburg Line. After the war he was chairman of the State Electricity Commission of Victoria, as well as holding several other public positions and acting as a spokesperson for the Jewish community and active Zionist. He retired from the army 1930.

Monastir Serbian town (now Bitola) 217 km/135 mi NW of ◊Salonika, a rail junction and military depot. It was occupied Nov 1915 by the Bulgarians who held two ridges alongside the town and others in front to defend it. A mixed French and Russian force advanced toward Monastir Sept 1916 after capturing Florina, assisted by a Serbian army under General ◊Mishich which moved around the eastern flank and captured the Bulgarian positions. A series of Allied frontal attacks, all aided by Serbian flanking moves, gradually drove back the Bulgarian defences until, their supply line threatened by yet another Serbian encircling movement, they abandoned the town 19 November 1916.

Mondragon rifle automatic 7.92 mm calibre rifle with a 10-shot magazine, designed by General Mondragon of the Mexican Army 1908.

Prior to 1914 it was manufactured by the Schweizerische Industrie Gesellschaft in Neuhausen-am-Rheinfalls, Switzerland, and shipped to Mexico. However the outbreak of war prevented further shipment and the remainder were bought by Germany. It was initially issued as a sniper weapon but was found too delicate for the trenches and was then taken up by aviators before machine guns became standard aircraft armament.

Monitor class of armoured warship of slow speed, shallow draught, and a limited number of very large guns, used for operations in shallow waters. They had a low freeboard (i.e., the deck was designed to be close to the water) and so provided a very small target and had greater stability when firing guns. On the outbreak of war three such ships were under construction in Britain for the Brazilian Navy; they were commandeered by the Admiralty and named Severn, Humbers, and Mersey. Armed with two 12-inch guns, they were successfully used to bombard German defences on the Belgian coast and more were built, some carrying 18-inch guns. The Mersey was also sent to East Africa 1915 to bombard the German cruiser ◊Konigsberg in the Rufiji delta.

Mons, Battle of battle between British and and German forces, Aug 1914. On 22 Aug the British Expeditionary Force was positioned on a line running from Mons to Conde, two towns in Belgium. The British, in conjunction with French troops on the left and right, were to attack the German forces under von ◊Kluck and possibly envelop them.

However, the French force due to operate on the British left did not arrive, leaving the flank open. A German thrust, estimated at some 160,000 men, broke in between the British right flank and the French 5th Army under ◊Lanrezac, which broke and began to fall back, leaving the British with both flanks open to encirclement. Assuming that the French would soon return, the British dug in and resisted German attacks but by the afternoon of 24 Aug it was obvious that the French would not return and the British would be overwhelmed. They therefore fell back to a prepared defensive position but the German momentum forced them out. They then gradually retreated southward in a series of leap-frogging rearguard actions until the Germans overstretched their supply lines and slackened their pursuit. The British formed a fresh line and the retreat was over.

Morane-Saulnier aircraft French aircraft made by company of the same name. The company began 1910 and settled on a 'parasol' monoplane design, so called because the wing was mounted above the fuselage on struts. Among the earliest of purpose-built military aircraft, the Type L was a two-seat reconnaissance and bombing machine used by British, French, and Russian forces. Roland ◊Garros used one to develop his propeller bullet deflectors, allowing him to fire a machine gun forward and Lt Warneford used one to bring down the first Zeppelin in air combat. The Type N was a single-seat fighter, known as the 'Bullet' from its shape, and deviated from the original Morane design in being a low-wing monoplane.

Morhange French town in Lorraine, SE of Metz; site of a battle between French and German forces Aug 1914. On 14 Aug the French armies in Lorraine opened an offensive, aiming to advance down the valley of the river Sarre to attack Metz. The Germans were expecting such a move and had prepared a deep defensive zone on their side of the border. The French walked into the trap and were torn to pieces by machine gun and heavy artillery fire. The Germans then counterattacked in strength and drove the French some 16 km/10 mi behind their original starting line, capturing Luneville, crossing the Meurthe river, and threatening Nancy. The French reached a suitable defensive line and managed to dig and the front then stabilized.

mortar strictly, any short ◊artillery piece which is fired only at elevation angles greater than 45°. In common usage, the term is used for muzzle-loaded, smoothbore weapons firing a fin-stabilized bomb, largely used as an infantry support weapon. Mortars began to be developed when the trench lines came into use 1914, so that missiles could be pitched into the enemy trenches.

The German ◊*minenwerfer* was an early and complex design, but the archetypal weapon was developed by Sir Wilfred Stokes for the British Army. This was a simple tube with a fixed firing pin at the bottom end, into which a bomb carrying a blank shotgun cartridge and some smokeless powder was dropped. The cartridge hit the pin, ignited the powder, and blew the bomb from the barrel. Adopted 1915, Stokes' mortar was seized on and copied by several inventors and became a universal weapon.

Mort Homme French hill in the *département* of the Meuse. In March 1916, as part of the battle of ◊Verdun, the Germans attempted to take the hill by frontal assault. They sustained enormous casualties but the attack failed, and they then tried a flank attack with similar results. Another attack in April also failed, but eventually a further attack in May caused the French to abandon the hill. They were able to recapture it Aug 1916.

'Mother' name given to the prototype British fighting tank built by Foster of Lincoln 1916. Originally called 'Big Willie' (cf ◊Little Willie), the name was changed once it was apparent that this was the definitive design. It was first run 29 Jan 1916 at Hatfield Park and then demonstrated 2 Feb in front of Lloyd George, Haig, Robertson, Kitchener, and other luminaries.

Murmansk expedition British, French, and US expedition to N Russia 1918. The object was to occupy part of the Kola peninsula and protect the Murmansk–Petrograd railway line from Finland which was then an ally of Germany and was bargaining with the Bolshevik government for an enlargement of Finnish territory to include the Kola peninsula. The regional Soviet authorities cooperated with the Allies in protecting the railway line and the Allies, for their part, undertook not to interfere in the area politically and to provide food for the population. Shortly afterward the Supreme Soviet changed its mind and ordered the local Soviet not to cooperate, but the locals ignored the order. The Allied force moved south Oct 1918 and cleared the area of various renegade Finn and Bolshevik groups, eventually reaching Lake Onega summer 1919. By this time the original purpose of the expedition had been achieved, and, the war being over, evacuation was ordered. By the end of 1919 the entire force had been withdrawn.

Murray General Sir Archibald 1860–1945. British soldier. Entered the Royal Inniskilling Fusiliers 1879, served in South Africa, and was Director of Military Training 1907. In Aug 1914 he went to France as Chief of Staff but returned to Britain Oct 1915 to become Chief of the Imperial General Staff. Shortly afterward he was appointed to command the Mediterranean Expeditionary Force, went to Egypt, and led the advance into Palestine. His organization of the defences of Egypt was superb, as was his advance, but he made serious errors in his failure to capture Gaza, largely due to failures by his subordinates. He returned to Britain 1917 to take over the prestigious Aldershot command which he retained until 1919.

Mustapha Kemal Pasha ('Ataturk') 1881–1938. Turkish soldier and statesman. Commissioned as a lieutenant from military academy 1904 he was immediately exiled due to his revolutionary leanings, but he recanted and devoted himself to a military career. Commanding a division in Gallipoli 1915 he displayed considerable tactical ability and eventually commanded the entire Turkish defences there with outstanding success. He was less successful on other fronts but he emerged from the war with a considerable reputation as a military commander.

After the war he moved into politics, gained a notable victory over Greek expansionist policies and eventually became president of the First Turkish Republic 1924, when he took the name 'Ataturk' – 'Father of the Turks'.

mustard gas (dichlorethyl sulphide) war gas. Developed by the Germans, they first used it 12 July 1917; the Allies only adopted it about a year later, being delayed by the need to build plant for its production. A vesicant and systemic poison, its early use was highly successful as its full effect only became apparent some hours after an attack. It attacks the lungs when inhaled, while the vapour attacks the eyes, causing blindness, and in liquid form causes suppurating blisters on the skin. During the first three weeks of mustard gas attacks by the Germans, 14,276 troops suffering cases of gas poisoning were admitted to British military hospitals and about 500 men died.

mutiny organized act of disobedience or defiance by two or more members of the armed services. In naval and military law, mutiny has always been regarded as one of the most serious of crimes, punishable in wartime by death.

Minor mutinies occurred in almost every army during the war, generally triggered by some ostensibly small grievance such as non-delivery of mail, bad food, or at ◊Etaples 1917 replacement camp staff neglecting to send men to their 'own' regiments. The most serious mutinies occurred in the French Army 1917, when whole battalions refused to conduct offensive operations. This was largely due to poor rations, lack of home leave, and an apparent lack of respect for human life on the part of some senior French commanders. The affair was successfully contained and kept quiet, neither the Germans nor the rest of the Allies having much inkling of the extent of the problem. However, after the war rumours were rife and stories of whole battalions being marched to the front line and shelled by their own artillery as punishment were common.

N

Namur Belgian town, capital of the Namur province, 56 km/35 mi SE of Brussels. Standing on the confluence of the Meuse and Sambre rivers, it is also an important rail junction and garrison town and in 1914 was defended by a ring of nine outlying forts. On 19 Aug 1914 the German Army brought up heavy artillery and began bombarding these forts. The Belgian garrison, supported by 3,000 French troops, attempted to attack the German gun positions but were driven back. On 23 Aug the French troops retreated to escape being surrounded and on the following day the Belgian field army also retired for the same reason. What remained of the garrison was overcome by a German attack and the last three forts were silenced 25 Aug. Namur remained in German hands for the remainder of the war.

Nancy French city, capital of the *département* of Meurthe-et-Moselle, some 355 km/220 mi E of Paris. After the battle of ◊Morhange Sept 1914 the French line stabilized just in front of Nancy, having lost a large sector to the Germans. A German attack was launched at the southern end of this front, and this was met by a strong counter-attack by fresh troops under ◊Castelnau from the north, taking the Germans by surprise. By this time the Germans were tiring and Castelnau urged his force to one more effort. The French began to gain ground and eventually began entrenching on a line from Nancy, through Luneville to Baccarat. The Germans then launched another assault, coinciding with von ◊Kluck's final attempt to gain Paris. This met with some success, but again Castelnau sensed that the Germans were just as desperate as he and managed to get his troops to counter-attack and regain several lost positions. Eventually the Germans began to pull back, the French re-occupied Luneville, and the front line stabilized roughly on the original German border.

Narev, Battle of the battle between German and Russian forces in Poland, July–Aug 1915. Early in July, ◊Gallwitz decided on an attack across the Narev river and drove the Russian forward troops back to a line on the south side of the river, although the Russians managed to hold a number of bridgeheads on the north side. On the night of 23 July Gallwitz stormed the river, secured a crossing, and managed to get astride the main road and rail lines leading to Warsaw, about 32 km/20 mi away. The Russians succeeded in holding him there, and in spite of receiving reinforcements Gallwitz made no further progress, turning instead to force a crossing of the river Bug.

Naroch, Lake, Battle of battle between Russian and German forces March–April 1915. Lake Naroch is in Byelorussia (now Belarus), about 110 km/70 mi E of Vilnius, and in 1914 was in a Russian province. In Feb 1915 the French were hard-pressed at Verdun and asked Russia to launch a diversionary attack. Russia had been contemplating action in the Lake Naroch area anyway and mounted an attack on German positions at the Lake 18 March 1915. Even though the Germans had spent the winter building strong defences, the attack met with some initial success, capturing parts of the German front line close to the Lake, but the inevitable counter-attack followed. The battle moved back and forth for some weeks until the Germans felt they had determined the Russian plans. They then brought in reserves and, in particular, called up more artillery under the command of Col ◊Bruchmuller, which began heavily bombarding the Russians. This barrage, combined with the greater weight of the German attacks, the appalling conditions of the spring thaw, and general weakening of the Russian troops, led to the Germans completely regaining the territory they had lost and the Russians fell back to their original line, having lost about 110,000 men.

Nernst Professor Walter 1864–1941. German physicist. The first scientist to propose the use of a chemical agent as a weapon, in 1914 Nernst suggested putting an irritant powder, dianisidine chlorsulphonate, among the bullets in shrapnel shells to obtain an additional lachrymatory effect. The idea was accepted, Nernst supervised the filling of the shells, and they were first fired during an attack at ◊Neuve Chapelle 27 Oct 1914. The idea proved a failure; the Allies noticed nothing unusual in the bombardment and General Falkenhayn's son is said to have won a case of champagne for remaining in a cloud of the substance for five minutes without showing any signs of discomfort. Nernst returned to his laboratory and played no further part in the German chemical warfare programme, although his ideas were further developed and adapted by others so that chemical warfare became a significant weapon in the latter stages of the war. He received the Nobel Prize for chemistry 1920.

Nery French village in the *département* of Oise, near Compiègne. On the morning of 1 Sept 1914 part of the British 1st Cavalry Brigade, retreating from ◊Mons, were bivouacked in the village, among them 'L' Battery of the Royal Horse Artillery. At about 5 a.m. the battery, with horse teams hooked to the guns, was waiting to move off in the mist when they were surprised by a German force on nearby hills which poured heavy fire into the area. The guns were immediately unhooked and brought into action under fire in the open. For two hours they kept up a rapid fire against the German positions, losing guns and men throughout the action, until only one gun remained served by two wounded men. At 7.15 a.m. reinforcements arrived and were able to drive the German force from its commanding position. L Battery lost 45 officers and men killed and wounded out of a strength of 170, and won three Victoria Crosses. The battery now carries 'Nery' as its honour title and annually celebrates the battle.

Neuve Chapelle French village in the *département* of Nord, SW of ◊Armentières. Taken by the Germans Oct 1914 it became the objective in a battle between British and Germans March 1915. In order to prevent the movement of German troops to the east and also to assist the French at ◊Arras, the battle was begun 12 March with a 40 minute artillery bombardment by 480 guns, followed by a barrage behind the German trench line to prevent the arrival of reinforcements. The infantry assault was a success, carrying four lines of German trenches and taking the village. However, due to failure of communications the reserve troops which should have followed up the attack failed to arrive in time, enabling the Germans to reform their line. The British artillery no longer had sufficient ammunition to produce a superiority of fire, and the battle died away as the British dug in to their new line.

New Armies alternative name of the ◊Kitchener Armies.

Newton Pippin British ◊hand grenade developed early 1915. It consisted of a serrated iron body filled with explosive and a fuse made from a cut-down rifle cartridge, a piece of mining fuse, and a detonator. A spring cap carrying a pin fitted on the end, and when struck against a hard surface this fired the cartridge and lit the fuse; the grenade was then thrown immediately. It takes its name from its inventor, a Lt Newton, and a facetious reference to a popular type of apple, the 'Pippin'. Newton also developed a ◊rifle grenade on similar lines. Both were superseded by the ◊Mills grenade.

Nieuport French aircraft, built by Edouard de Nieuport but designed by Gustave Delage. The Model 10 single-seat biplane fighter was developed 1915 from a 1914 design of racing aircraft and was widely used by the British, French, Belgian, and Russian air forces. The Model 17 of 1916, another single-seat biplane, was one of the best fighting aircraft of the war and effectively countered the German ◊Fokker machines. With a 130 hp engine it could attain a speed of 177 kph/110 mph, had a range of about 300 km/185 mi, and was armed with one synchronised machine gun firing through the propeller and another machine gun on the top wing firing over the propeller. Some were also armed with rockets for attacking observation balloons. Widely used by all the Allies, it was the chosen machine of many of the prominent 'aces'.

   The final design, the Model 28 of 1918, was initially given an unreliable engine but after modifications became another success, being widely used by the US air force until superseded by the ◊SPAD fighter. In its final form it used a 170 hp engine to reach a speed of 196 kph/122 mph and was armed with two fixed synchronised machine guns.

Nivelle Robert Georges 1856–1924. French soldier. Joined the French artillery 1878 and saw active service in Algeria, Tunisia, and China. In 1911 he was promoted to colonel and became Chief of Staff of the Algerian division. In 1914, commanding an artillery regiment, he took part in the invasion of Alsace and the battle of the ◊Aisne, and was promoted to brigadier-general. He was promoted to full general 1915 and took command of the 3rd Army Corps. In April 1916 he was given command of the 2nd Army and played an important part at ◊Verdun; as a result of this success he replaced ◊Joffre as commander in chief of the armies of the North and Northeast 12 Dec 1916. He then planned a massive offensive in the Craonne-Reims area for April 1917, but his public boasting about it reached German ears and the offensive itself was a disaster, with enormous French casualties which precipitated the later French ◊mutinies. Nivelle was removed, replaced by ◊Pétain, and sent back to command the troops in North Africa.

No Man's Land old term for any piece of waste or unowned ground, used at least as early as the 14th century. During the war it was used to identify the space between the opposing trenches of the combatants.

It is pock-marked like the body of foulest disease, and its odour is the breath of cancer.No Man's Land under snow is like the face of the moon, chaotic, crater-ridden, uninhabitable, awful, the abode of madness.

Wilfred Owen on *No Man's Land*, letter 19 Jan 1917.

Nungesser Lieutenant Charles 1883–1927. French fighter pilot. A trained engineer, he was working in South America as an aircraft designer and builder when the war broke out. He returned to France and fought as a cavalryman and later in the trenches; after being wounded several times he was invalided out of the army as unfit for further service. He enlisted in the air corps and became a specialist in aerial bombing, later becoming a prominent fighter pilot with 45 German aircraft downed. He was killed while attempting to fly the Atlantic 1927.

O

Observatory Ridge Belgian ridge in the province of Flanders close to Hooge. It passed into German hands Sept 1914, was the focus of several minor struggles, and was finally captured by Canadian troops July 1917 during the battle of ◊Ypres.

'Old Contemptibles' name adopted by soldiers of the British regular army who survived the retreat from ◊Mons and other early battles of the war. The name came from the Kaiser Wilhelm's angry outburst at his forces in Belgium being held up by 'Sir John French's contemptible little army'. The troops seized on this with delight and named their post-war veterans' association 'The Old Contemptibles'.

Ostend Belgian town in the province of West Flanders, seaport and fishing harbour. It was occupied by the Germans 14 Oct 1914 and remained in their hands for the rest of the war. The Germans developed the port as a submarine and light destroyer base for the German Navy and in 1918 the British made two attempts to block the harbour entrance so as to bottle up the German vessels.

The first attempt was made 23 April but failed when the wind changed and the two blockships destined to be sunk in the harbour mouth drifted away and were blown up outside. In the second attempt, 10 May, HMS ◊Vindictive was run against the eastern pier with the intention of swinging the hull across the entrance and then sinking the vessel. But as Vindictive hit the pier, its bridge was struck by a German shell, killing the captain and wrecking the controls so that it proved impossible to swing the ship across. She was blown up and only partially blocked the harbour. The Germans were later able to drag the wreckage aside, leaving them a 9 m/30 ft entrance.

Otranto Barrage Barrier across the mouth of the Adriatic Sea from Otranto, Italy, to Corfu on the Albanian coast. The barrage was made up of nets supported by floats, and patrolled by 120 fishing vessels, each armed with a light gun, and 30 armed motor launches. It was intended to prevent Austrian and German submarines from leaving their base at Cattaro (now Kotor, Yugoslavia) and entering the Mediterranean, but was of doubtful effectiveness. The Austrians made several small attacks on the line, but mounted their most serious attack May 1917 when three cruisers and two destroyers first attacked an Italian supply convoy and severely damaged it and then systematically sailed along the barrage and shelled the patrol vessels, sinking 14 patrol craft and damaging many more. They then set off to return to Cattaro, but a combined British/French/Italian flotilla left Brindisi to try and cut them off. In the ensuing battle, inept Allied tactics led to indecisive results, and the Allied force eventually withdrew when they saw heavy Austrian reinforcements approaching from Cattaro. As a result of this fiasco the Otranto Barrage was abandoned by the Italian naval commander in chief as being incapable of being defended, after which the German and Austrian submarines had the run of the Mediterranean and Allied shipping losses increased.

Ovillers French village in the *département* of the Somme, 4.8 km/3 mi NE of Albert. A German strongpoint during the battle of the Somme, the British reached it on the first day of the battle but took a further 15 days to capture it. It was again lost to the Germans March 1918 and finally re-taken by the British in the autumn.

Owen Wilfred 1893–1918. English soldier and poet. Owen was in France at the outbreak of war but returned to England to enlist 1915. He was killed in action a week before the Armistice. His verse, owing much to the encouragement of Siegfried ◊Sassoon, expresses his hatred of war, for example *Anthem for Doomed Youth*, published 1921.

P

Pakenham Admiral Sir William Christopher 1861–1933. British sailor. Joined the Royal Navy 1874 and served with the Japanese fleet during the Russo-Japanese war 1904. In 1914 he was promoted to rear-admiral and commanded the 3rd cruiser squadron, later commanding the 2nd battle-cruiser squadron at ◊Jutland. He succeeded ◊Beatty as commander of the battle-cruiser force Dec 1916. Knighted 1916 and promoted to vice-admiral 1918, he became president of the Royal Naval College 1919–20 and then commander in chief North Atlantic and West Indies.

Palestine, Operations in In 1914 Palestine was part of the Turkish Empire and operations in this area began Feb 1915 with a Turkish attack on the Suez Canal, followed by another in March, both of which were repulsed. In response, the British mounted an expeditionary force to invade the Sinai Peninsula and safeguard the canal. This force entered the Sinai late 1915 but there was a lull until April 1916 when a sudden Turkish attack delayed, but did not halt, the advance. By Dec 1916 the British had taken El Arish and by Jan 1917 they had completely cleared the Sinai.

They then continued into Palestine towards ◊Gaza, laying a railway as they went. After two attacks on Gaza had failed, changes were made in the British command, General ◊Allenby replacing General ◊Murray. Several months were then spent in preparations before Allenby renewed the offensive, allowing the Turks to fortify a line from Gaza to Beersheb. Allenby attacked again Oct 1917, bombarding Gaza to draw the Turks into the area and then launching a sudden attack against Beershebas, which he took 31 Oct 1917. He then rolled up the Turkish line and took Gaza itself 7 Nov. The British force now advanced up the coast to take Jaffa and then turned to attack ◊Jerusalem which they entered 11 Dec. After beating off a Turkish counter-attack, the line was advanced and ◊Jericho fell 21 Feb 1918.

The ◊German Spring Offensive 1918 created an urgent need for reinforcements on the Western Front, so there was a considerable delay in operations in Palestine as experienced units were replaced with fresh troops from India, who needed time to settle in and complete their training. Allenby resumed the offensive 18 Sept 1918, driving the Turks northward and destroying two of their armies and shattering a third. By 29 Sept 1918 the British were advancing on ◊Damascus and the conquest of Palestine was complete.

Papen Franz von 1879–1969. German diplomat. In 1914 he was military attache in Washington, with the rank of captain, and he subsequently assisted ◊Boy-Ed in organizing a ring of spies and saboteurs in the USA. He was exposed for his part in a plot to destroy the Welland Canal, and, at the request of the US government, was recalled to Germany 1915. After this promising start he became Chancellor of Germany 1932, envoy to Austria 1934, and ambassador to Turkey 1939–44.

paravane British anti-mine device, used for ◊minesweeping. Resembling a torpedo with wings, the paravane was towed from the bows of a ship and was so designed that at a preset depth it would pull the towing wire taut. When this wire struck a mine cable, the cable was deflected down the wire to the paravane where it met a powerful cutter blade. This cut the mine free to float to the surface some distance from the ship, where it could be destroyed by gunfire. One paravane on each side of a ship's bow virtually guaranteed safety against moored mines.

Paris Gun common name for the German long range gun officially called the ◊Kaiser Wilhelm Geschutz.

Passchendaele village in W Flanders, Belgium, near Ypres. The nearby Passchendaele Ridge, some 60 m/200 ft high, was captured and then fortified by the Germans Oct 1914. It was a vital strategic gain as it gave them command of the Allied lines. It was captured by the British against strong resistance Oct–Nov 1917 as part of the third battle of ◊Ypres. It was then re-taken by the Germans March 1918 and recovered again by the Belgians Oct 1918. The name is frequently, and

wrongly, applied to the whole of the battle of Ypres; Passchendaele
was but a part of that battle

Patton Major George S 1885–1945. US soldier. Though better known
for his exploits during World War II, Major Patton served as a cavalry
soldier during World War I. He virtually founded the US tank corps, to
which he was appointed by General ◊Pershing 19 Nov 1917, at which
time he was its only member. He attended the British tank school,
learned to drive and command a tank, attended the French tank school,
and then set up an American school at Langres which trained two battalions. These were then equipped with French ◊Renault tanks which
Patton led into action in the Saint Mihiel sector 12 Sept 1918 with
mixed success. He then led another tank attack in the ◊Argonne 26
Sept, in which he was wounded, only leaving hospital on Armistice
Day, but winning the DSC, the DSM, and the rank of colonel.

periscope optical instrument designed for observation from a concealed position such as from a submerged submarine. In its basic form
it consists of a tube with parallel mirrors at each end, inclined at 45° to
its axis. Although most often thought of as a submarine observation
device, periscopes were widely used in the trenches to allow observation without exposing the observer, and special versions were also
developed to be attached to rifles, allowing the rifle to be fired over the
parapet while the firer sighted it by means of the periscope from under
cover.

Pershing General John Joseph 1860–1948. US soldier. Pershing
joined the 6th Cavalry 1886 and served action in the Indian campaigns
and the Spanish-American war, led the expedition against the Moros in
the Philippines 1902, observed the Russo-Japanese war from the
Japanese side 1905, and 1916 led the punitive expedition against
Pancho Villa in Mexico. On the entry of the USA into the war he was
appointed commander in chief of the US expeditionary force with the
rank of major-general. From the start he stuck to the principle of using
the US forces as a coherent formation, and refused to attach regiments
or brigades to British or French divisions; he modified this slightly to
allow the attachment of some US units to the French in an emergency,
but otherwise held out until he had assembled a sufficient American

force to undertake operations. The first such operation was the ◊St Mihiel offensive Sept 1918, followed by the ◊Meuse-Argonne operation. At the end of the war he was promoted to the obsolete but revived rank of 'General of the Army' and succeeded General ◊March as Chief of Staff 1921.

Ils ne passeront pas! (They shall not pass!)
Henri-Phillipe Pétain on the German Army at Verdun 1916.

Pétain Henri-Phillipe 1856–1951. French soldier and politician. Entered the infantry 1878, and reached the rank of colonel 1912, commanding an infantry regiment. In 1914 he commanded a brigade, then a Corps at ◊Arras and was engaged in operations in ◊Artois 1915. He was an Army commander by Sept 1915 and took part in the ◊Champagne offensive and Feb 1916 took command at ◊Verdun, where his calm fortitude and organizing ability were essential to the success of the operation. It was Verdun that made him into a national figure. In May 1916 he took command of the Armies of the Centre and after the disastrous period of ◊Nivelle he took command of the armies of the North and Northeast as well, eventually becoming commander in chief of all French forces March 1918.

He was instrumental in restoring morale after the Nivelle offensive and the subsequent mutinies; skilled at man-management he attended to the soldiers' complaints about rations and leave, and also made it clear that he would no longer support vainglorious attacks. Although subordinate to Marshal ◊Foch, he did not always agree with him, but nevertheless brought the French Army back to a fine pitch, held it firm in the face of the ◊German Spring Offensive, and led it well in the subsequent Allied advance. He was promoted to Marshal of France Nov 1918. His reputation after the war was unfortunately destroyed after he collaborated with the Germans during World War II.

Pfalz German aircraft built by the Pfalz Fluegzeugwerke of Bavaria. The firm initially built aircraft designed by others, under license, but in 1917 developed its own design, the D3, a single-seat biplane fighter which became popular with German aviators. Driven by a 160 hp

Mercedes engine it could reach 164 kph/102 mph and carried two for-ward-firing machine guns. In 1918 it was succeeded by the D12, a strengthened model with some technical improvements, which many considered a better aircraft than the popular ◊Fokker D7, but relatively few were built before the war ended.

phenyldichlorarsine war gas introduced by the Germans Sept 1917. One of the most toxic gases, it acted against the lungs to cause pul-monary oedema; it also acted as a sneezing gas and in contact with the skin raised blisters. It was the first lung injurant used in the war and was later adopted by the French under the name 'Sternite'. It was generally used in conjunction with other gases, to penetrate the protection afforded by ◊gasmasks.

phosgene war gas; common name for carbonyl chloride. First used by the Germans in a cloud attack Dec 1915, it was rapidly adopted by the other combatants and became the principal battle gas of the Allies. More than 80% of the gas casualties of the war were caused by phos-gene. It is not immediately irritating when inhaled but causes an acute inflammation of the lungs; victims frequently felt quite well after a short rest but then died suddenly a few days later.

Piave river in N Italy, rising in the Carnic Alps and flowing 200 km/125 mi to the Adriatic about 32 km/20 mi N of Venice. After the battle of ◊Caporetto Oct 1917 the Italian army retreated to a defensive line on the Piave. The *first battle* of the Piave took place when the Austrians attacked the Italian line Nov 1917; the Italians managed to hold their line and repel the attackers.

The front then remained quiet until the *second battle* June 1918. The Austrians crossed the river under cover of smoke and gas and managed to establish a bridgehead, but were thrown back by an Italian counter-attack July 2. Close to the sea they managed to pierce the Italian line and advanced about a mile but were again driven back to their starting line. The Piave then flooded suddenly, which put an end to the Austrian assault.

In the *third battle* 23 Oct 1918 (also called the battle of Vittorio Veneto) the Italians, together with British troops, massed on the river and attacked the Austrians. Three Italian armies crossed the river and within two days the Austrians were in general retreat, pursued by the Italians, until the Austrians called for an Armistice 4 Nov 1918.

Pilsudski General Josef Klemens 1867–1935. Polish soldier and statesman. Although of Lithuanian stock he espoused the cause of Polish independence and was exiled to Siberia by the Russians 1887–92 but returned to lead the National Socialist party. When the war broke out he emerged as a general of a Polish force which invaded Russia 6 Aug 1914. After the Russians had been evicted from E Poland he became a member of the Polish Council of State Nov 1916, but soon resigned, whereupon he was arrested by the German authorities and imprisoned. He was released Nov 1918 and re-entered politics, governing for a time as a dictator, but then was elected president Feb 1919, and given the rank of Marshal. In 1920 he led the Poles against the Bolsheviks, driving them out of Poland after the battle of the Vistula. He retired 1923 but, despairing of the political scene, in 1926 led a coup d'état and took power as dictator until his death.

Pinsk town in W Russia about 160 km/100 mi E of Brest-Litovsk. In 1915 the Russian forces retreating from ◊Brest-Litovsk fell back on Pinsk, pursued by von ◊Mackensen's armies. The town was taken by the Germans 16 Sept 1915; von Mackensen pushed further east but was soon stopped by the Russians who had settled on a defended line. The Germans handed Pinsk over to the Poles but it was recovered by the Bolsheviks 1920.

Plug Street British soldiers' name for the Belgian village and wood of Ploegsteerte, 5 km/3 mi N of Armentières and 13 km/8 mi S of Ypres. Both the village and the wood featured prominently in the various battles of ◊Ypres. After changing hands several times during 1914 they remained in British possession until taken by the Germans in the March 1918 offensive, after which they were re-taken by the British Sept 1918.

Plumer Hubert Charles Onslow, 1st Baron 1857–1932. British soldier. Joined the York and Lancaster Regiment 1876, and served Africa throughout the 1890s, culminating in the South African War 1899–1902, at the end of which he was promoted to major-general. Knighted 1906 he held various commands in Britain, became quartermaster-general and served on the Army Council. Plumer spent much of the war on the Western Front around the Ypres area, scene of much heavy fighting. He was highly popular with his troops (who referred to him as 'Daddy ') as he planned carefully, organized meticulously, and generally executed his plans at far less cost in lives than any of his contemporaries could have managed.

He took command of the 5th Army Corps Jan 1915 and in May 1915 the 2nd Army. He was responsible for the planning and execution of the attack on ◊Messines 1917, generally considered to be one of the best organized British operations of the war. He commanded the British forces in Italy Nov 1917–March 1918, then returned to the 2nd Army in France. After the Armistice he marched his army to the Rhine as part of the forces of occupation. He was made a field-marshal and created a baron 1919, and was appointed governor of Malta.

Pomeroy bullet explosive machine gun bullet developed for use against ◊Zeppelins. Designed by John Pomeroy, a Canadian engineer, it was adopted by the British air service. The bullet was filled with nitro-glycerin which would ignite the hydrogen gas escaping from the hole in the gas-bag made by the passage of the bullet.

Pom-Pom gun 1-inch calibre Maxim machine gun mounted on a wheeled carriage and used as a light support gun. It was first used by the Boers during the South African War 1899–1902, where it acquired the name from the sound it made when firing. By 1914 it no longer had any tactical use as a field weapon and most were put to use as light anti-aircraft guns.

Poperinghe Belgian town in the province of West Flanders, 9.5 km/6 mi W of ◊Ypres. During the war it was the principal centre of the British forces on the Flanders front and was surrounded with camps, hospitals, supply depots, canteens, and other military establishments. It fell into German hands Aug 1914 but was retaken by the British 15 Oct 1914 and retained thereafter, though it was frequently bombarded and came close to being overrun in the German Spring Offensive March 1918.

Portugal Portugal declared its support for the Allies 7 Aug 1914, and authorized military participation 23 Nov, but the unstable government of the day, together with severe financial problems in the wake of the 1910 revolution, meant that it was impossible to actually provide troops except to reinforce the Portuguese African colonies. In Feb 1916 Britain urged Portugal to seize some 36 German ships then lying off Lisbon, as a result of which Germany declared war on Portugal 16 March. British and French military missions went to Portugal and began training the Portuguese army, and in early 1917 two divisions were sent to France where they were attached to the British army. This force was later increased and eventually 65,000 officers and men were sent to France of whom 1,800 were killed and about 12,000 wounded or listed as missing. A further 25,000 Portuguese troops, accompanied by about 100,000 native troops, took part in the Allied campaign for ◊German East Africa.

Pozières village in N France 6.5 km/4 mi E of Albert, on rising ground which gave the Germans valuable command of the ◊Somme battlefield. It was captured by Australian troops during the Battle of the ◊Somme July 1916. By the time the Australians withdrew Sept 1916, they had suffered 23,000 casualties.

Prieux rocket incendiary rocket devised by a Frenchman of the same name and used by fighter aircraft to attack observation balloons and airships. Stabilized by a long stick, in the same way as common firework rockets, they were fired electrically and were highly effective, though limited in range.

Przasnysz Polish town about 72 km/45 mi N of Warsaw, an important road junction. The Germans captured it from the Russians and quickly lost it again Dec 1914. In Feb 1915 Hindenburg brought up two army corps to recapture it, attacking from three directions. The Russians held the town with a comparatively small force and so evacuated it 25 Feb 1915, but the troops were by then surrounded and had no escape route. They were only saved by the arrival of troops collected from the various Russian border fortresses who deployed west and north of the town and began surrounding the encircling German forces. Battered on both sides by Russians, the Germans fought for two days before disengaging and retiring to their original positions near Mlava, having lost at least 10,000 prisoners to the Russians. This put an end to

Hindenburg's offensive against the ◊Narev river line, and the town remained in Russian hands until later in 1915 when a fresh German advance captured it.

Przemysl Polish border town and Austro-Hungarian fortress in Galicia, on the river San, 125 miles E of Kraków. In the initial Russian campaign the Russians encircled the fortress Sept 1914 and settled down to a formal seige. But at about the same time the Austrian resistance in ◊Galicia suddenly stiffened and the German invasion of Poland got under way, both of which factors threatened the Russian advance and began to drive it back. By Oct 1914 this movement had opened a route into Przemysl for the Austrian Army to reinforce and attempt to relieve it. After bitter fighting this attempt failed, the Austrians were pushed back, and the siege lines were closed around the fortress once more. The garrison attempted to break out Nov–Dec but they were always defeated by the besieging force. The shortage of food now began to make itself felt as the Russian pressure tightened and eventually the garrison blew up the major forts and magazines and surrendered the fortress 22 March 1915 along with 9 generals, 2,600 officers, 117,000 men and 700 guns.

By May 1915 the tide had turned against the Russians and von Mackensen was besieging them; they had not had time to repair the various forts and were unable to withstand the serious attack which took place in the first days of June. By 3 June the fortress was in German hands and remained so for the rest of the war.

Putnik Field Marshal Radomir 1847–1917. Serbian soldier. He fought in the Serbo-Bulgar war 1885 and was professor in the military academy 1886–92. He was promoted to general 1903 and for a time acted as minister of war. During the Balkan Wars 1912–13, he was commander in chief of the Serbian Army and was appointed field marshal. At the outbreak of war he was convalescing at an Austrian spa but was permitted to return to Serbia where he became Chief of Staff to Prince Alexander, the nominal commander in chief. In practice, Putnik was in command and in the first months his tactics outfought the Austrians at almost every turn. However, eventually the greater numerical strength of the Austro-German combination told and he was forced to retreat across the mountains of Montenegro and Albania to the Adriatic Oct–Nov 1915. Thousands of soldiers died of exposure and starvation, and Putnik himself made the final miles on a stretcher. He survived, but his health was irretrievably broken and he died at Nice 1917.

Q

QAIMNS see ◊Queen Alexandra's Imperial Military Nursing Service.

Q-Boat British ships used to trap submarines, also called 'mystery ships'. They were small freighters with guns concealed in a collapsible deck structure. On being hailed by a U-Boat, a 'panic party' would hastily abandon the ship by lifeboat, leaving a fighting party concealed on board. The U-Boat would then be lured into sailing closer to the seemingly abandoned ship to ensure sinking it with the minimum amount of gunfire, and as soon as it was within range the deck structures would fall, revealing the guns already manned and they would open fire immediately. Several U-Boats were sunk by this ploy, but once it became known it was less successful and had to be abandoned.

Quast General Ferdinand von 1850–1934. German soldier. Entered the German infantry 1870, became a lieutenant-general 1910, and in 1913 became general of infantry commanding the 9th Army Corps. A competent and unassuming soldier, he held a series of commands without prominence and probably reached his zenith in commanding the 6th Army against the British on the river Lys April 1918, an action which is generally obscured as part of the ◊German Spring Offensive.

Quéant French village in the *département* of Pas-de-Calais, about 14 km/9 mi from Bapaume. It was the southern end of the German 'Wotan' Line, running north to Drocourt and forming part of the ◊Hindenburg Line. Strongly fortified, it was stormed and captured by the Canadian Army 2 Sept 1918. This 'Wotan' Line is often referred to in documents of the period as the 'Quéant Switch line'.

Queen Alexandra's Imperial Military Nursing Service (QAIMNS). British military nursing organization, founded 1902 from the Army Nursing Service. They provided staff nurses, sisters, and matrons for military hospitals throughout the world.

R

race to the sea, the expression used to describe the entrenchment of the two sides Sept–Nov 1914 as they tried to outflank each other in Flanders, finally reaching the sea. The trench line then expanded in the other direction until it formed a continuous front from the North Sea to the Swiss border.

Radom Polish manufacturing town 112 km/70 mi S of Warsaw. After their defeat at Ivangorod the Austrian army fell back to Radom 24 Oct 1914, closely pursued by the Russians, and a fierce battle developed close to the town. The area was thickly forested so that German and Austrian troops became separated from their parent units and split up into smaller units which the Russians, more experienced in forest fighting, were able to tackle and defeat one at a time. The Russians finally took the town 28 Oct and the Austrians continued their retreat.

RAF abbreviation for ◊Royal Air Force.

Rainbow Division nickname for the 1st US Infantry Division, so-called because it had been deliberately assembled from troops from all the 48 states of the union, so that each state would be represented in the first US division to reach France.

rationing restricted allowance of provisions or other supplies in time of war or shortage. Food rationing was introduced in Germany early in the war but not until 1917 in Britain. Basic foods such as sugar, butter, lard, tea, and cheese were rationed to a specified amount per person per week. Meat was rationed by value rather than quantity so as to allow the consumer some degree of choice. After the Armistice food supplies became easier, but rationing did not officially end until 1919.

Rava Russka, Battles of battles between Austrian and Russian forces Sept 1914; sometimes referred to as the battle of the Grodek

Line. The Austrians had retreated to a line from Tomasov (now Tomaszow Lubelski, Poland) via Grodek (now Gorodok, Ukraine) to Rava Russka (now Rawa Russkaja, Ukraine). The Austrian line continued further north but with several gaps, and the Russians were able to infiltrate thorough these to make flank attacks. This destabilized the Austrians as parts of their line fell back, while others remained isolated and attempted to make their own way out of the encircling Russians. A series of battles up and down the line ensued, resulting in a general retreat by the Austrians with estimated losses of 250,000 casualties and some 100,000 troops along with 400 guns and quantities of stores captured by the Russians. Rava Russka itself fell 8 Sept 1914.

Rawlinson Henry Seymour, 1st Baron of Trent 1864–1925. British soldier. Joined the Rifle Brigade 1884 and then transferred to the Coldstream Guards 1892 after service in India and Burma. He served in Africa in the late 1890s, including service in the South African War 1899–1902. He became a divisional commander 1910 and in 1914 was made director of recruiting but within a month went to France at the head of 7th Division which he led through Belgium to ◊Ypres and ◊Neuve Chapelle. In 1915 he was given command of the 4th (New) Army and was responsible for the main attack on the ◊Somme 1916. In early 1918 he he became British representative at the Council of ◊Versailles but was hastily recalled in March, to take command of the 4th Army again. With this army, he played a decisive part in stemming the ◊German Spring Offensive and in the Allied offensive which ended the war. He was knighted 1915, and made full general, awarded ∠50,000 for his war service, and created baron 1918. In 1920 he was appointed commander in chief of the army in India.

redoubt small enclosed trench work employed in conjunction with a system of infantry trenches. It formed a strong point of resistance even after the rest of the trenches had been destroyed or captured.

Renault tank French two-man tank armed with a ◊Hotchkiss machine gun. It fitted the French tactical concept of rapid advance, and it was hoped that several hundred would eventually be available to operate in swarms. This never came about, partly because they were easily stopped by obstacles and rough country due to their small size, and they acted as light support vehicles for foot infantry.

Rennenkampf General Paul Karlovitch 1854–1918. Russian soldier. Joined the cavalry 1873, became colonel 1893, and general 1905, having served in China and the Russo-Japanese war. In 1914 he was commanding the Vilna military district; he took command of the army of the Niemen and invaded E Prussia. After some initial success he was forced to retreat following the defeat of ◊Samsonov at ◊Tannenberg Aug 1914. He attacked again with reinforcements, drove the Germans back from the river Niemen line, and once more invaded E Prussia. He was then transferred to the Warsaw Front where he defeated the first German attack. However, he had a violent disagreement with General ◊Russky when the Germans made their second attempt Nov 1914; he could not cooperate properly with Russky and so was retired. He lived in retirement for the rest of the war until he was murdered by the Bolsheviks 1918.

Repington Charles à Court 1858–1925. British soldier and journalist. Entered the Rifle Brigade 1878 and served in Afghanistan, Burma, and the Sudan before being on the staff during the South African war 1899–1902. In 1902 he had an affair with a fellow officer's wife and was forced to resign. He became a journalist with the *Times*, transferring to the *Morning Post* 1918. His military service gave him many valuable contacts who were still in the army during the war, and it was thanks to them that he exposed the ◊shell scandal 1915.

RFC abbreviation for ◊Royal Flying Corps.

Richthofen Manfred, Freiherr 1888–1918. German aviator. Originally a cavalryman (Lancer) he transferred to the air corps and eventually became the most famous 'ace' of the German service. A phenomenal shot, he relied more upon that than upon any tactical skill, and by Feb 1917 had over 20 Allied aircraft to his credit. Promoted to captain he commanded the 11th Pursuit Squadron, known as ***Richthofen's Flying Circus***, and throughout 1917 increased his reputation. He scored his 80th victory April 1918, when he received the Order of the Red Eagle with Crowns and Swords. He was shot down behind British lines on the Somme 21 April 1918 and buried with full military honours.

Rickenbacker Edward V 1890–1973. US aviator. A well-known racing motorist, he went to France 1917 as General Pershing's driver, then transferred to the Army Aviation Corps as an engineering instructor. He qualified as a pilot and joined the 94th Squadron 4 March 1918. He soon became a skilled fighter pilot, commending the squadron, and by the end of the war had 26 enemy machines to his credit. In postwar years he became a successful businessman and was awarded the Congressional Medal of Honor 1930 for his wartime activities.

rifle grenade small missile, containing an explosive or other charge, similar to ◊hand grenades, but fired from a rifle rather than thrown. Rifle grenades were developed in order to achieve a greater range than was possible with the hand grenade, for use where the trench lines were too far apart for grenades to be thrown. The first models were cast-iron cylinders of explosive, fitted with a simple impact fuse, and attached to a steel rod. The rod was inserted into the barrel of a rifle and the chamber loaded with a blank cartridge (i.e., one without a bullet). On firing, the explosion of the cartridge blew the rod from the barrel and sent the grenade to a range of about 100–150 yds. This system, however, damaged the rifles and was gradually replaced by a cup which attached to the rifle muzzle and into which a grenade could be placed. A blank cartridge was then fired to blow the grenade out.

Riga Baltic seaport and capital of Latvia. It was attacked by the Germans Aug 1915 but successfully defended by Latvian troops of the Russian army. A fresh German offensive Oct 1915 failed to reach the city after severe fighting and the area then fell quiet. In late 1917 a new German offensive began, in which ◊Ludendorff and ◊Bruchmuller devised a new infiltration tactic. Artillery would fire on specific targets, rather than make a general bombardment, and parties of storm troops would then pass through the defences and take them from the rear or attack headquarters and supply points, thus breaking holes in the defensive line through which the mass of German infantry could pour. This succeeded and the Germans took the city 3 Sept 1917, retaining it for the remainder of the war. Latvia proclaimed independence in Riga Nov 1918 but Soviet troops captured the city Jan 1919. They were expelled with the aid of German troops who promptly took the city themselves until the Latvians and Estonians attacked the Germans June 1919. Under orders of the Allied mission to the Baltic the Germans evacuated the city later that year.

River Clyde British steamship, converted into a troop carrier and used to land troops at 'V' Beach, ◊Gallipoli. Gangways and ramps were built along the sides and bows so that the ramps could be lowered once the ship had beached to allow troops to deploy quickly under fire.

RNAS abbreviation for ◊Royal Naval Air Service.

Robertson Sir William (1860–1933. British soldier; the only man ever to rise from private to field marshal in the British army. Robertson enlisted as a trooper in the cavalry 1877 and had risen to troop sergeant-major by 1885. He was commissioned 1888 and went to India to join the 3rd Dragoon Guards, remaining there until 1896, by which time he was a staff captain. He moved to the intelligence branch and served on the staff in South Africa, and became Director of Military Training 1913. He went to France 1914 as quartermaster-general and was Chief of Staff throughout 1915. He was appointed Chief of the Imperial General Staff Dec 1915, a position he held until 1918 when he resigned after a difference of opinion with Lloyd George over the direction of the war. He then commanded Eastern Command in England before going to Germany to command the British Army of the Rhine until 1920. Knighted 1913, he was promoted to full general 1916 and field marshal 1920. He was awarded £10,000 and a baronetcy for his war services 1919.

Robinson Lieutenant William Leefe, VC 1895–1919. British fighter pilot. Commissioned 1914 he joined the Royal Flying Corps (RFC) the following year. On 3 Sept 1916 during a German air raid he unsuccessfully attacked a Zeppelin, then attacked the Schutte-Lanz airship SL11 and shot it down over Cuffley, Herts. This was the first German airship to be shot down over England and Robinson was awarded the Victoria Cross. He was then posted to France but was shot down near Douai May 1917 and became a prisoner of war until returning to England 14 Dec 1918. He contracted influenza and died at Stanmore 17 Jan 1919.

Romania, German conquest of Romania remained neutral until 27 Aug 1916, when she declared war on Austro-Hungary, immediately setting in motion an invasion of Transylvania which met with considerable success. Bulgaria in turn declared war on Romania, which diverted some forces to deal with this threat. Meanwhile Germany assembled 250,000 troops in Hungary under ◊Falkenhayn and this force set about driving the Romanians back to their frontier 20 Sept–7 Oct. Next the Bulgarians attacked from the south with German aid and under the command of von ◊Mackensen. By the end of Nov 1916, Mackensen and Falkenhayn had joined forces and began sweeping the Romanians, who had now been joined by Russian force, northwards. Bucharest was occupied 6 Dec. On 5 Jan 1917 the Germans reached the line of the Sereth river which was firmly held by a very strong Russian force, and at that point the Germans stopped. They renewed the offensive Aug 1917 but the joint Russian/Romanian defences on the Sereth defeated Mackensen at the battle of ◊Maraçesti. However, the November Revolution caused the Russian army to collapse, leaving the Romanians to face the Germans alone. They requested an armistice 6 Dec 1917 and signed a peace treaty 7 May 1918.

Room 40 room in the British Admiralty building for the ◊cryptanalysis staff who deciphered German naval signals under the command of Admiral ◊Hall. It was they who deciphered the ◊Zimmermann telegram.

Ross rifle Canadian military rifle of extreme accuracy and power, using a unique 'straight-pull' bolt mechanism. In .303 inch calibre it became the service rifle of the Canadian Army, but when exposed to the mud and foul conditions of the Flanders trenches it was found to be dangerously defective. It was withdrawn late 1915 and replaced for active service by the ◊Lee-Enfield rifle, although it was retained for service in Canada for some years.

Rosyth British naval base on the Firth of Forth. Established 1909, it became important as a docking and repair base for the Grand Fleet during the war and as the headquarters of the cruiser squadrons.

Royal Air Force (RAF) British air arm, established 1 April 1918 by merging the ◊Royal Flying Corps and the ◊Royal Naval Air Service, giving a total of 188 squadrons by the time of the Armistice. It continued the fighter and tactical bomber roles of the original services and also instituted an 'Independent Air Force' of strategic bombers which carried out over 500 raids over German territory.

Royal Flying Corps (RFC) air arm of the British army, created 1912 from the Air Battalion, Royal Engineers, which had originally been formed to operate observation balloons. Until July 1914 it also provided air support for the Royal Navy. It was organized in squadrons, each of three flights of four aircraft; at first these were mixed, but as the war progressed squadrons became dedicated to fighter, bomber, reconnaissance, training, or other roles. The RFC was merged into the ◊Royal Air Force 1 April 1918.

Royal Naval Air Service (RNAS) air arm of the British navy, formed July 1914 from naval officers and elements of the ◊Royal Flying Corps. The RNAS performed patrol duties over the North Sea, pioneered the use of aircraft carriers, and was also responsible for the air defence of Britain until 1916. It pioneered strategic bombing, attacking German airship bases as early as 1914. In order to protect its forward bases in Flanders, the RNAS also operated an armoured car squadron and provided a great deal of input to the early tank development programme.

Ruffey General Pierre Xavier Emmanuel 1851–1932. French soldier. He joined the French artillery 1873, served in Madagascar and as a professor at the Ecole de Guerre, becoming a colonel 1901. He was made general of division 1905 and then a corps commander. In 1913 he became a member of the Superior Council of War and 1914 took command of the French 3rd Army, holding the line from Montmedy through Sedan to Rocroi. Toward the end of Aug 1914 he was driven back by the Germans after severe fighting and was obliged to retreat to the Argonne. Shortly afterwards he was replaced by General ◊Sarrail and held no field command thereafter.

Rufiji river in German East Africa (now Tanzania), flowing into the Indian Ocean via a large delta with many branches. It was here the German cruiser ◊Konigsberg concealed itself 1915. Blockaded by British warships, she was finally destroyed by gunfire from the ◊monitor Severn.

Rumpler German aircraft built by the Rumpler works, Berlin. The company began by building ◊Taube monoplanes under licence, then developed a number of two-seater reconnaissance biplanes, trainers, seaplanes, and three-seater bombers. Among the more remarkable designs was the C7 high-altitude photo-reconnaissance machine which pioneered the use of oxygen and heated suits for the two-man crew.

Rupprecht Crown Price of Bavaria 1869–1955. European princes were often given high commands, but Prince Rupprecht was unusual in also having sound military ability. He joined the German army 1886 and worked his way up, becoming general 1904 and inspector-general of the Bavarian Corps 1913. He commanded the 6th Army, largely composed of Bavarian units, in Lorraine 1914 then fought on the Lys and in the first battle of ◊Ypres Oct–Nov 1914. He later held the German line from Ypres to Arras and fought many battles against the British. In 1917 he commanded the German front from the North Sea to the river Oise and led his army group in the ◊German Spring Offensive. He went into exile upon Bavaria declaring itself a republic 1918. He was a descendant of Charles I of England and, according to some authorities, the rightful heir to the throne of England.

Russian Revolution actually two revolutions of Feb and Oct 1917 (by the Julian calendar) that began with the overthrow of the Romanov dynasty and ended with the establishment of a communist soviet (council) state, the Union of Soviet Socialist Republics (USSR).

By 1917 the Russian economic situation was grim, and food riots in Petrograd in Feb (March by the Western calendar) set off a wave of unrest against the Tsar's autocratic government. The Army leaders forced the abdication of Tsar Nicholas and in the *February Revolution* a Provisional Government under the principal influence of Kerensky, nominally Minister of Justice, took over. This body had no experience of government and soon became enmeshed in political strife with the Peasants and Workers' Soviet of Petrograd and similar extreme left organizations, in particular the Bolsheviks, who had gained control of the soviets and advocated land reform (under the slogan 'All power to the Soviets') and an end to Russian involvement in the war.

◊Lenin's return from Switzerland sharpened the dispute between the government and the Bolsheviks, culminating in the *October Revolution*, a Bolshevik coup on the night of 25–26 Oct (6–7 Nov Western calendar). The People's Soviets were established as the ruling authority and elected Lenin the new leader of Russia. The new government immediately began peace talks with the Germans which led to an armistice 17 Dec 1917 and a peace conference commenced at Brest-Litovsk 22 Dec. For all practical purposes the Russians ceased to play

any part in the war from now on. Trotsky, the principal Bolshevik nego-
tiator, made excessive and arrogant demands of the Germans who
eventually repudiated the armistice and resumed their attacks on
Russia. This brought Trotsky to his senses; he rapidly re-convened the
conference, accepted the German terms and the peace treaty was signed
3 March 1918. A bitter civil war ensued for some three years as the
'Red' Soviet government struggled agains the 'White' counter-revolutionary forces led by ◊Denikin, ◊Wrangel, ◊Kolchak, and others, aided
by military support from the Allies until late 1919. Seeing no prospect
of the various 'White' commanders settling their differences and adopt-
ing sensible policies, the Allies removed their troops and left the
Russians to determine their own destiny. The civil war lasted until
1922, when the Red Army, organized by Trotsky, finally overcame
'White' opposition, but with huge losses, after which communist control was complete. Some 2 million refugees fled during these years.

Russky General Nicholas Vladimirovitch 1855–1919. Russian soldier. He joined the infantry 1874 and held the rank of general in the
Russo-Japanese war 1905, serving as Chief of Staff to the 2nd Russian
army. After this he served for a time as minister of war. In 1914 he
commanded the 2nd Army on the Galician front and won considerable
acclaim for his victories over the Austrians and the capture of
◊Lemberg (now Lvov). He then took command of the army of the
Niemen and forced the Germans to retreat in E Prussia. In 1916 he fell
ill and spent some time convalescent but by early 1917 was again commanding the northern group of armies. After the March Revolution he
assisted in procuring the abdication of the Tsar, but he fell foul of the
Council of Workers' and Soldiers' Deputies and was dismissed, to be
murdered Jan 1919.

S

St Chamond tank French tank manufactured by the Compagnie des Forges et Acieres de la Marine et d'Hommecourt at their St Chamond factory 1917–18. It was based on the ◊Holt tractor suspension, with a hull having a prominent front overhang and a 75 mm gun centrally mounted in the front face. It was driven by a petrol engine driving a dynamo which in turn drove electric motors connected to the track wheels. The armament was impressive but the overhang meant that it easily became stuck when attempting to cross trenches. The design was abandoned after about 400 had been built.

Saint-Etienne town in S central France in the *département* of the Loire. Centre of the gunmaking trade, it became one of the principal French arsenals, particularly for the manufacture of small arms. During the war years an automatic rifle and a medium machine gun were developed here, though neither was particularly successful.

St Mihiel salient triangular protrusion of the German front line, with its tip at St Mihiel on the river Meuse and its base stretching 48 km/30 mi from Fresnes to Pont-à-Mousson. French attempts to drive the Germans back from 1915 onward had met with heavy losses and no success until Sept 1918.

On 11 Sept seven US divisions lay on the north side and two US divisions plus the 15th French Colonial Corps lay on the south, while the 2nd French Colonial Corps fronted the tip and two US divisions lay in support. The plan was a simultaneous attack on both sides of the base to cut off the salient while the French launched a frontal holding attack. Assisted by tanks and ground attack aircraft, the US assault went forward on schedule, leading to hard fighting. On the morning of 13 Sept the 1st and 26th Divisions (coming from the south and north respectively) met at Vigneulles, neatly cutting off the bulk of the German forces. Pershing's troops took over 13,000 prisoners and 200 guns, the salient was flattened out, and the US forces went on to drive the Germans from the heights of the Meuse.

Sakharov General Vladimir Viktorovitch 1853–1924. Russian soldier. Joined the army 1869 and served in the Russo-Turkish and Russo-Japanese wars. He was made general 1897 and first came to prominence during the ◊Brusilov offensive. In 1916–17 he commanded the combined Russian/Romanian forces in the Dobruja and Moldavia, and in 1919 commanded an army under ◊Kolchak against the Bolsheviks.

Salmond General Sir John Maitland 1881–1968. British aviator. Entered the army 1901 and served in the South African war. He then learned to fly at his own expense and joined the Royal Flying Corps 1912 as an instructor. He took charge of, and thoroughly re-organized, the system of training pilots and was appointed director general of Military Aeronautics and a member of the Army Council 1917. In 1918 he succeeded ◊Trenchard as commander of the Independent Air Force in France and was responsible for much of the strategic bombing campaign that followed. Promoted to major-general 1918 he transferred to the Royal Air Force, became air vice-marshal, and was knighted 1919.

Salonika, expedition to joint Anglo-French force dispatched to help Greece against Bulgaria Oct 1915, which remained in the area, reinforced by Serbs until the end of the war. In Sept 1915, fearful of Bulgaria's intentions, Greece requested a reinforcement of 150,000 troops from the British and French governments. The Allies agreed and the first troops landed at Salonika 3 Oct 1915, including British troops from ◊Gallipoli. By the end of Oct there were about 40,000 troops in Salonika, mostly French. On Oct 11 Bulgaria invaded Serbia and the Allies advanced to make contact with the S Serbian army and halt the invasion. They failed due to the greater numbers of the Bulgarian forces and the Allies retreated back into Greece 12 Dec.

Despite having been of no assistance to the Serbians, it was decided to maintain a force in Salonika against future possible needs, and the strength was increased to three French and five British divisions. Reinforcements added to this and by summer 1916 there were 300,000

Allies and 100,000 Serbians plus elements of Russian and Italian troops present. In July this force advanced up the Struma valley, the French linking up with the Serbians near Vardar. The Bulgarians attacked the centre of the Allied line but in spite of some local successes they were eventually driven back, with the Serbians and French pressing on their right and the British turning their left flank.

◊Monastir fell to the Allies Nov 1916, after which the lines stabilized and trench warfare ensued until the spring of 1918 when General ◊Franchet d'Esperey took command of the Allied forces in the area. By this time the Greek Army had been re-organized and had 150,000 troops available, and after careful planning a fresh offensive was begun Sept 1918 which, within two weeks, obtained Bulgaria's unconditional surrender. After this the Allied force cleared all German and Austrian troops from the Balkans, and on 9 Nov a strong Serbian force crossed the Danube and was headed for Bucharest when the war ended.

Sambre French river which rises in the *département* of the Aisne, flows NE and joins the Meuse at Namur. Lanrezac was badly defeated by von Bulow here 1914, precipitating the retreat from ◊Mons. The *Battle of the Sambre* opened 1 Nov 1918 and formed the final part of the British advance across Flanders.

The British 1st, 3rd, and 4th Armies were pitched against the 2nd and 18th German Armies. The battle began by the British and Canadians taking the town of Valenciennes, then advancing through Le Quesnoy to attack the main German defensive line, known as the '*Hermann Stellung*', which ran along the Sambre. By 8 Nov this line had been broken and the town of Landrecies taken; German troops began destroying stores dumps and burning equipment, and Canadian troops entered ◊Maubeuge 9 Nov with no German resistance. On the night of 10 Nov the Canadians entered Mons, drove out the German occupants and pressed their advance until three minutes before 11 a.m. 11 Nov, when the ◊Armistice took effect.

Samsonov General Aleksandr Vassilievitch 1859–1914. Russian soldier. He joined the cavalry 1875, served in the Russo-Turkish war, became a general 1902 and commanded a Siberian Cossack brigade in the Russo-Japanese war 1905. In 1914 he was given command of the Army of the Narev and invaded E Prussia. After some initial victories, advancing as far as Allenstein (now Olzstyn, Poland), he was completely defeated at ◊Tannenberg and committed suicide 31 Aug 1914.

San Polish river; rising in the Carpathian mountains it flows NW to join the Vistula near Sandomierz, a length of about 420 km/260 mi. The *Battles of the San* were a series of engagements between the Russians and Austrians 1914–1915.

In the first battle Oct–Nov 1914 the advancing Austrians met the Russian defensive line on the river and were beaten off, allowing the Russians to begin advancing towards Cracow. The second battle took place May–June 1915 after the Russians had been defeated on the ◊Dunajetz and retired to the San line. Once again they beat off several Austrian attacks, but a German army under von ◊Mackensen then crossed the river and began advancing towards ◊Przemysl. The Russians counter-attacked but were unable to cross the San again; Mackensen made another determined attack, the Austrians did likewise, and the Russians were driven back on the fortress of Przemysl. A flanking movement by Mackensen threatened the Russians' supply lines and they abandoned the fortress and fell back to the east.

Sarajevo capital of Bosnia-Herzegovina. A Bosnian, Gavrilo Princip, assassinated Archduke ◊Franz Ferdinand here 1914, thereby precipitating World War I.

Sari Bair hill in Gallipoli midway between ◊Suvla Bay and ◊Gaba Tepe. Although strongly defended by the Turks it was taken by ◊Anzac troops 9 May 1915, but they in turn were driven out by a counter-attack the next day. Constant fighting raged around this hill until it was again taken by the Anzacs in a night attack 12 Aug. The Turks recaptured it following the Allied evacuation from ◊Gallipoli 1916.

Sarikamish, Battle of battle between Russian and Turkish forces, Dec 1914–Jan 1915. The Turkish offensive in the Caucasus was a bold scheme to advance from Erzerum via Sarikamish to Kars over a 3,000 m/10,000 ft mountain range in the depths of winter. Although by Dec 1914 they had reached Sarikamish, their progress was slow and they had been unable to bring up heavy artillery. This allowed the Russians to bring up reinforcements and guns, and they were attacked by the Turks 25 Dec, who took the town the following day. The Russians fell back, re-grouped, and then counter-attacked, regaining the town. They pursued the Turks back on their tracks and the Turkish offensive collapsed.

Sarrail General Maurice Paul Emmanuel 1856–1929. French soldier. He joined the army as a lieutenant 1876 and served in Algeria; he then transferred to the Foreign Legion and fought in Tunisia and Algeria. Became director of infantry 1907 and general commanding the 12th infantry division 1911. In 1914 he was given command of the 3rd French Army and took part in the first battle of the ◊Marne. He was appointed commander of the Army of the Orient, the French element in the ◊Salonika expedition, Aug 1915 and became commander in chief of the Allied forces in Salonika Jan 1916. He made little impression in this role and was replaced 1917, then placed on the reserve early 1918.

Does it matter? - losing your sight? ...
There's such splendid work for the blind;
And people will always be kind,
As you sit on the terrace remembering,
And turning your face to the light.
                                        Siegfried Sassoon, *Does it Matter?*

Sassoon Siegfried 1886–1967. English writer and soldier. Sassoon enlisted in the army 1915, serving in France and Palestine. His *War Poems* 1919 express the disillusionment of his generation. He wrote the autobiography *Memoirs of a Foxhunting Man* 1928.

Scapa Flow expanse of sea enclosed by the Orkney Islands, Scotland. The main base of the Grand Fleet during World War I, it was, at first, undefended against German submarine attacks and on several occasions the fleet put to sea after warnings of possible submarine attacks. Gun batteries and booms were later installed to seal off most of the potential entrances. Its role as the main fleet base was abandoned 1919 and the fleet based upon Rosyth, in the Firth of Forth, but it was brought back into use during World War II. The German fleet was interned here after its surrender 1918, and 71 warships were scuttled there by their crews 22 June 1919.

Scarpe French river. Rises near St Pol, flows E past Arras and Douai to join the Scheldt near the Belgian frontier. The ***Battle of the Scarpe*** took place Aug 1918 between British and German forces; it is sometimes called the fifth battle of ◊Arras.

The British, under General ◊Horne, were attempting to prepare the ground for a general advance by driving the Germans out of a sub-section of the ◊Hindenburg Line. They attacked along both sides of the river, taking several villages and completing the operation with the capture of Bullecourt 31 Aug. The battle then died down into a series of local skirmishes until the opening of the final battle for ◊Arras 2 Sept.

Scharnhorst German armoured cruiser, built 1907. It displaced 11,600 tons, had a top speed of 23 knots, and was armed with eight 21 cm guns, six 15 cm guns, twenty-four smaller guns, and four torpedo tubes. The Scharnhorst was Admiral von ◊Spee's flagship when he sank a British squadron at ◊Coronel Nov 1914 and was itself sunk during the battle of the ◊Falkland Islands 8 Dec 1914.

Scheer Admiral Reinhold von 1863–1928. German sailor. He joined the German Navy 1882 and served as Chief of Staff for the High Sea Fleet 1909–11. He commanded a battle squadron at Keil at the outbreak of war and was appointed commander in chief of the High Sea Fleet 1915. He commanded the German forces at ◊Jutland May 1916. He was appointed Chief of the Admiralty Staff 11 Aug 1916, and resigned 1919.

Schlanke Emma Austrian 305 mm howitzers, similar in concept to the German ◊Big Bertha. Developed by Skoda 1911–13 it was moved in three parts by road tractors and assembled at the firing point. Capable of firing a 380 kg/840 lb shell to a range of 12 km/7.5 mi, two were loaned to the German Army to supplement the Big Berthas attacking Belgian and French forts 1914, and others were used against the Italians and Russians at various times.

Schlieffen Plan military plan produced Dec 1905 by the German chief of general staff, General Count Alfred von Schlieffen (1833–1913), that formed the basis of German military planning before World War I. It involved holding off the Russians with a relatively weak defensive force while using seven-eighths of the German Army to drive through Belgium and then swing southwards to outflank the French defences, pass round Paris and thus trap the French Army between the wings of the German forces. Having thus defeated France, the army would be redeployed by rail to deal with the Russians who, due to their great size and lack of organization, would be slow to mobilize. The plan was sound, but was altered by von ◊Moltke, who reduced the strength of the army's right wing and thus made it incapable of carrying out the Plan when it was implemented 1914.

Schneider tank French tank manufactured by the Schneider-Creusot company 1917–18. Based on the ◊Holt chassis, it was an armoured box with upswept and pointed nose and with a 75 mm gun mounted on the right side. It was better at trench crossing than the ◊St Chamond design and was first used in the ◊Chemin des Dames operation April 1917, where losses were heavy due to petrol tank explosions. The armour thickness was improved and some 400 were eventually built, some of them as ◊supply tanks.

Schneiderite explosive used by the French army for filling artillery shells, composed of dinitronaphthalene and ammonium nitrate. Adopted as an economy measure as a substitute for TNT which was both more expensive and more difficult to manufacture.

If you are a gunnery man you must believe and teach that the world will be saved by gunnery and only by gunnery.
Admiral Sir Percy Scott when commanding
HMS Excellent, Naval Gunnery School.

Scott Admiral Sir Percy 1853–1924. British sailor. He joined the Royal Navy 1866 and became the principal advocate of gunnery training and improvements. He then commanded a cruiser squadron 1907–09, was knighted 1910, created a baron, and retired with admiral's rank 1913. Recalled to duty 1914 he was given command of London's air defences and placed them on a sound footing before retiring for a second time. He was also a strong believer in the future of the submarine.

SE-5a ('Scouting Experimental 5a') British fighter aircraft.It was developed by the Royal Aircraft Factory as a single-seat fighting scout biplane and was the best aircraft that factory ever produced. One of the great combat machines of the war it was agile, robust, and easy to fly, though the first models suffered from an unreliable Hispano-Suiza engine. Later models had the 200 hp Wolseley Viper engine, giving them a top speed of 190 kph/120 mph and a range of 480 km/300 mi. Armed with a synchronized Vickers machine gun firing through the propeller and a Lewis machine gun mounted on the top wing, it could also carry four 25 lb bombs. About 5,000 were built in Britain for the Royal Flying Corps and US Army, and the US company Curtis were starting on a contract for 1,000 when the war ended.

seaplane aeroplane capable of taking off from and landing on water. There are two major types, floatplanes and flying boats. The floatplane is similar to an ordinary aeroplane but has floats in place of wheels; the flying boat has a broad hull shaped like a boat and may also have floats attached to the wing tips. Both types were widely used during the war, particularly by naval flying services for patrolling and anti-submarine operations.

Sedd-el-Bahr village in the ◊Gallipoli peninsula on the N side of the entrance to the Dardanelles. It is of great strategic importance and had been fortified by the Turks since the 17th century. On the outbreak of war the old forts were refurbished and re-armed. Allied landings took place here and it was the scene of heavy fighting to establish a beach head and supply dump.

Seeckt General Hans von 1866–1936. German soldier. Entered the army 1874 and by 1914 had reached the rank of colonel. On the outbreak of war became Chief of Staff 3rd Army Corps and planned and executed the German offensive at ◊Soissons Jan 1915. He then served as Chief of Staff to ◊Mackensen and planned the Austro-German campaign in Galicia and the conquest of Serbia 1915. He became commander in chief of the new German Army 1921 and throughout the 1920s concentrated upon building up the 100,000 strong army into a highly-trained cadre which, from 1933 onward, was able to expand into the Reichswehr.

Selle, Battle of the successful Allied operation, 17–25 Oct 1918. The German 2nd and 18th armies were encamped in positions on the

line of the river Selle in front of ◊Cambrai. The British 4th Army with
two attached US divisions attacked this position from a line from Le
Cateau to Bohain; the 1st French Army mounted a similar attack on
their right. Tanks, specially waterproofed and adapted for crossing the
river, led the attack and drive the Germans back across the canal forming their second line obstacle. The attack was then extended northward
and eventually the German line was pushed back to Valenciennes and
Landrecies and the Scheldt river. The Allies captured 475 guns and
20,000 troops.

Serbian Army originally set up as a conscript army, the Serbian
forces were in the throes of re-organization after the Balkan War when
the events of 1914 overtook them. Their nominal strength was 21
infantry divisions and a cavalry division plus supporting artillery; a
total of about 350,000 men divided into four field armies. In 1915 the
Austro-German forces drove the Serbs back across the mountains in a
disastrous retreat in which as many as 200,000 soldiers and accompa-
nying civilian refugees are estimated to have died. They fell back into
Albania and Montenegro, from where Allied warships evacuated them
to Corfu. Here they were re-equipped and retrained, and then taken to
the ◊Salonika front where they operated in conjunction with British and
French troops with great success.

shell scandal largely manufactured furore in the British press 1915
over supplies of ammunition to artillery units in the field. In early 1915
the British Army was suffering a shortage of artillery ammunition, due
to the heavy demands of the war combined with the technical difficulties of expanding the manufacturing base to bring in engineering firms
with no previous experience of ammunition manufacture.

   Sir John ◊French cited this shortage as a reason for his failure at
◊Neuve Chapelle in a conversation with Col ◊Repington, the *Times*
correspondent. The *Times* proprietor, Lord Northcliffe, encouraged by
◊Lloyd George, seized the opportunity to claim that it was the fault of
bad direction by the War Office and called for the resignation of Lord
◊Kitchener, headlining the 'Shell Scandal' in both the *Times* and *Daily
Mail*. By this time the bottle-neck had been overcome and ammunition
was arriving in increasing quantities so that the press campaign's main
achievement was a boycott of the two newspapers. However, when the

coalition government was formed in May, Lloyd George achieved his aim and became minister of munitions.

shellshock term used to describe the various forms of mental disorder exhibited by soldiers after heavy bombardment or the shock of an explosion; originated in the early part of the war. At first thought to be physical and due to blast and carbon monoxide poisoning, it was later realised that the symptoms – mental confusion or frenzied terror – were neurotic in origin and similar to those found after civil accidents such as train wrecks or factory explosions. Most soldiers returned to normal after a rest away from the front line, but some never recovered and exhibited peculiarities of gait, hysterical loss of voice or sight, paralysis of limbs, and other symptoms. In postwar years stories abounded of soldiers suffering from shellshock being executed for cowardice and desertion, but there is little factual evidence of this.

Short British aircraft made by Short Brothers of Rochester and Bedford. The firm began by making balloons 1898 and only turned to aircraft 1908. The Type 184 seaplane 1914 was the first aircraft to carry a torpedo and, off ◊Gallipoli, was the first aircraft to sink an enemy ship with a torpedo. Other models were designed to carry anti-submarine bombs. The company also manufactured a number of airships for the Royal Flying Corps and Royal Naval Air Service in their Bedford factory.

shrapnel artillery projectile consisting of a hollow shell loaded with lead or steel balls and a small charge of gunpowder. While the shell was in mid-air over enemy lines the charge would be ignited by a time fuse, ejecting the balls forward like a shotgun blast and spraying bullets down onto the troops below. An efficient killer when used against troops in the open, it lost its efficacy when troops began to entrench and take cover and was gradually superseded by high explosive shells.

Siegfried Line German fortified line in France, running behind the main ◊Hindenburg Line roughly between ◊Arras and ◊Cambrai. When the Germans built their fortified lines 1916–17 the whole complex was originally called the Hindenburg Front. It was later subdivided into the main Hindenburg line and subsidiary lines such as the Brünnhild, Hunding, Siegfried, and Wotan lines, all named from Wagnerian Norse mythology.

Siemens-Schukert German fighter aircraft, built by a subsidiary of the Siemens electrical company. The first model was a copy of the French ◊Nieuport 17 biplane fighter, the D1. This was then modified with a greater wingspan and more powerful engine into the D2, and then, by changing the wingspan yet again, the D3 and D4. The D3 and D4 were initially dogged by engine trouble and although this was eventually put right the perfected models did not appear until 1918 and never in sufficient numbers to materially affect the war.

Sikorsky Igor 1899–1972. Russian aircraft designer. He designed the world's first four-engined aircraft, the Russian Knight 1913. He then improved this into the Ilya Mourometz, a massive bomber of which about 75 were built and which were extensively used by the Russian aviation service to raid E Prussia and Lithuania. Heavily armed with up to 7 machine guns, and carrying over 1,000 kg/2,200 lb of bombs, they had a top speed of about 135 kph/85 mph and a range of about 565 km/350 mi.

Following the Russian revolution, he emigrated to Paris and then to the USA 1919, where he founded a highly successful aircraft company and designed the first helicopter 1939.

Sims Admiral William Sowden 1858–1936. US sailor. He joined the US navy 1878, was naval attache to France 1898, and later became fleet intelligence officer to the Asiatic Fleet. Promoted to captain he commanded a battleship, then attended the Naval War College and in 1914 commanded the torpedo flotilla of the Atlantic Fleet. On the entry of the USA into the war he was placed in command of all US naval operations in European waters and was made a vice-admiral 1918. He won the Pulitzer Prize for his book *Victory at Sea* 1920.

Skoda Austrian engineering company, the principal manufacturer of artillery and ammunition for the Austro-Hungarian forces. The factory at Pilsen, Bohemia (now Plzen, Czech Republic) was founded 1859 and by 1913 covered 360 acres and employed 7,500 people; by 1918 it employed 40,000. Manufacturing all types of armament from machine guns to the heaviest artillery, it was notable for the design and production of the ◊Schlanke Emma 305 mm howitzers used to bombard Belgian forts 1914. In 1918 the factory was handed over to Czechoslovakia and again played an important part in World War II.

small arms firearms of calibre smaller than 0.6 inch (15 mm) which can be carried by troops on the battlefield. The group is divided into pistols, sub-machine guns, rifles, and machine guns.

Pistols were largely symbols of officer rank and saw some use in trench raiding; *sub-machine guns* were scarcely used in the war, the ◊Bergmann Musquete being the pioneer of a movement which did not begin to grow until the 1920s. The *rifle* was the universal soldier's weapon (e.g., ◊Lebel, ◊Mauser, ◊Lee-Enfield, ◊Springfield), and was invariably a bolt-action, magazine-fed weapon, though a few experimental self-loading rifles were tested at various times. The ◊*machine gun* was originally a heavy, water-cooled, belt-fed weapon (such as the ◊Maxim and ◊Vickers guns) for support in fixed positions, and proved decisive in defence, but it was later supplemented by lighter and more portable models (such as the ◊Lewis and ◊Hotchkiss models) which could accompany the infantry in an attack.

Smith-Dorrien Sir Horace Lockwood 1858–1930. British soldier; potentially one of Britain's best generals, he was denied the opportunity to realise this potential by petty spite. He joined the Sherwood Foresters (infantry) 1876 and served in the Zulu war, Egypt, the Sudan, the Northwest Frontier of India, and the South African war 1899–1902. In 1914 he was commander in chief Southern Command in England and went to France to take command of 2nd Corps in the ◊Mons retreat. He held the Germans at ◊Le Cateau Aug 1914, which incurred the displeasure of Sir John ◊French, since it was against his orders; later French refused to allow him to shorten his line at Ypres in order to avoid unnecessary casualties. After the first gas attacks at Ypres he was instructed to direct fresh attacks, which he considered wasteful of lives; he protested to French, who took the opportunity to relieve him. He then went to take charge of operations in East Africa but suffered from pneumonia and was invalided home. He became Governor of Gibraltar 1918.

'Orace, you're for 'ome!

General Robertson, upon relieving
General Smith-Dorrien of his command.

smoke screen cloud of smoke released by means of ◊smoke shells or chemical generators. It drifted in the wind and obscured the view of the enemy so as to conceal movement of troops or ships.

smoke shell artillery projectile carrying a charge of some chemical capable of producing smoke so as to form a ◊smoke screen. Such shells almost invariably used white phosphorus since this ignited spontaneously when released and thus did not require a complicated time fuse.

Smuts Jan Christian 1870–1950. South African politician and soldier. He supported the Allies in both world wars and was a member of the British imperial war cabinet 1917–18. Of Boer descent, he became a lawyer and in 1898 state attorney of the South African republic. He held military command in the South African War 1899–1902 and led a Boer column into Cape Colony, damaging the British line of communications and waging successful guerrilla war until 1902. He thereafter devoted his efforts to improving South African prosperity and held various posts in successive governments.

In 1914 he combined government with military action, leading a column into German Southwest Africa, then conducting a recruiting campaign for South African contingents to fight in Europe and elsewhere. He took over the British command in German East Africa when General ◊Smith-Dorrien's health failed and successfully completed the occupation of that country. In 1917 he was called to London to give assistance to the British government; among other tasks he was given the job of examining and reporting upon the air defences of Britain, and one result of his report was the formation of the ◊Royal Air Force 1918. He became prime minister of South Africa 1919–1924, and again 1939–48. He was made a field marshal 1941.

sniper soldier specially trained in accurate long-range shooting, scouting, and reconnaissance. The sniper's function is to shoot at 'high-value' targets such as officers and specialists, to observe the enemy's activities and report upon them, and to seek out and kill enemy snipers. Snipers are usually controlled directly by battalion or higher headquarters and are at liberty to move about the battlefield as they see fit in order to pursue their role. They were a particular scourge to both sides in the trench warfare of 1915–18.

Soignies Belgian town in the province of Hainault, a junction on the Brussels–Mons railway line 35 km/22 mi SW of Brussels. It was the site of the first clash between British and German troops, a skirmish between scouting cavalry units in the woods south of the town Aug 1914.

Soissons French town on the Aisne river, 65 miles NE of Paris and one of the oldest in France. Always fortified as a barrier against invasion from the north, it has always been among the first to suffer in war. It was taken by the Germans early in the war but recaptured 12 Sept 1914, after which they bombarded the town and caused great destruction. In Jan 1915 a French attack drove the German line back a few miles, but a German counter-attack 10 days later drove the French back to their original line, with considerable losses on both sides. The line then stabilized until the German advance of May 1918 captured the town again, and they were finally driven out by the French 2 Aug 1918.

Sokal town in Galicia (now in the Ukraine) about 30 miles NNE of ◊Lemberg (Lvov) and on the then Austrian/Russian border. In 1914 the 2nd Austrian Army of about 300,000 men mobilized on Lemberg and advanced to Sokal preparatory to invading Russia. The Russians mobilized more quickly than the Austrians thought possible and had two armies ready, one of 400,000 men under ◊Russky and one of 300,000 under ◊Brusilov, both of which attacked the Austrians at Sokal 13 Aug 1914 and defeated them. The remains of the Austrian force fell back to Lemberg.

The Army had been fought to a standstill and was utterly worn out.

General Erich Ludendorff on the Battle of the *Somme*.

Somme, Battle of the Allied offensive July–Nov 1916 at Beaumont-Hamel-Chaulnes, on the river Somme in N France, during which severe losses were suffered by both sides. It was planned jointly by Marshal ◊Joffre and General ◊Haig. The German offensive around St Quentin March–April 1918 is sometimes called the Second Battle of the Somme.

In 1916, the Allies decided to launch a coordinated offensive on the
Western, Eastern, and Italian Fronts in the summer. In the event, the
Germans pre-empted the Allied strategy with an attack on ◊Verdun Feb
1916; by the summer it had become obvious that the French were occupied fighting off this attack and any offensive on the Somme would
have to be primarily a British effort. The *First Battle* of the Somme was
launched 1 July by the British 4th Army, supported by the 3rd and the
French 8th Army Group, in an attack on the German 2nd Army which
was well-protected by deep dug-outs. The British had made obvious
preparations for the assault, including a week-long artillery bombardment of the well-entrenched German positions which had little effect
other than to warn the Germans of an impending action. Consequently,
the Germans were able to man their defences prior to the arrival of the
infantry assault, so that the Brltish suffered the heaviest casualties in
their history; 19,000 men were killed on the flrst day. In spite of this,
the attack continued and several small gains were made – the German
line was almost breached 14 July. After a lull, the battle started again
15 Sept when tanks were used for the flrst tlme; some 47 tanks were
available to the Allies of which most broke down. This attack made
some progress but when the battle finally died away mid-Nov the total
Allied gain was about 13 km/8 mi at a cost of 615,000 Allied and about
500,000 German casualties.

The *Second Battle* of the Somme 21 March 1918 was the first act of
the ◊German Spring Offensive; it was intended to capture Amiens and
split the French and British armies. The attack forced the British 5th
Army under Gough to fall back, which in turn forced the flanking
British 3rd and French 3rd Armies to retreat. The Germans advanced as
far as Montdidier and were within a few miles of Arras before they
were finally held.

Sopwith British aircraft built by the Sopwith Aviation Company,
established 1911. Producer of some of the best fighting aircraft of the
war, the first of these·was the Tabloid, a small two-seater biplane which
was used by the ◊Royal Naval Air Service to bomb Zeppelin sheds at
Dusseldorf 8 Oct 1914. The 'One-and-a-half Strutter' (1915) was the
first aircraft to be designed with a synchronized frontal gun and
appeared in both single and two-seater forms; it was the first aircraft to

fly off from a ship platform and was widely used by Britain and Russia. The Sopwith Pup (1916) was small, simple, reliable and easy to fly, and enabled the Royal Flying Corps to gain a measure of superiority over the Western Front. The Pup was the first aircraft to land on a carrier under way at sea. The Triplane (also of 1916) could out-climb any other machine in existence and was copied by ◊Fokker. The most famous Sopwith aircraft of the war was the Camel which appeared early 1917 and went on to shoot down over 1,200 enemy aircraft, though it was also renowned as being difficult to fly. The final wartime fighter was the little-known Sopwith Dolphin, a powerful and agile machine with four forward-firing machine guns.

Southwest Africa, conquest of German Southwest Africa (now Namibia) became a German protectorate 1884. In 1914 the South Africans began operations to conquer the area which went well for about two months until a Boer rebellion diverted South African attention to affairs at home. During this time the Germans sent reinforcements, but South African forces made a landing at Walvis Bay 25 Dec 1914 and marched on Swakopmund, taking it 14 Jan 1915. There was then a delay while local railway lines were repaired and connected so as to provide a supply line, especially to ensure water supplies to forces in the field. Four columns then converged on Windhoek, which was taken May 1915. The German force, about 10,000 strong, retreated north but was pursued by South African premier Louis Botha (1862–1919) and surrendered 9 July 1915.

SPAD French fighter aircraft, made by the Société Anonyme Pour l'Aviation et ses Dérivés (originally known as Deperdussin et Cie). They produced several designs but the first successful design in operation was the SPAD VII, a single-seat biplane with a Hispano engine and a single forward-firing ◊Vickers machine gun. This entered service with the French 1916 and was eventually used by almost all the Allies, about 6,000 being built. The SPAD XIII, a much improved model with two guns and a more powerful engine, appeared 1917. This was built in greater numbers (almost 8,500) than any other Allied fighter, was used by the French and US services, and was the chosen machine of many aces.

Spandau suburb of Berlin, site of the principal German arsenal. Among other things it manufactured ◊Maxim machine guns, marked with the arsenal's name, so that they were called 'Spandau' machine guns by the Allies.

Spee Admiral Maximilian, Count von 1861–1914. German sailor. One of the creators of the German Navy, in 1914 he commanded the Far Eastern Squadron and sailed from Chinese waters to destroy whatever Allied warships he could find. He met and defeated Admiral Cradock's squadron at ◊Coronel 1 Nov 1914, then sailed around Cape Horn in order to scour the South Atlantic. En route he decided to bombard the ◊Falkland Islands, not knowing that Admiral ◊Sturdee's squadron was there. In the resulting battle the Germans were defeated and von Spee was drowned when his flagship, SMS Scharnhorst, was sunk.

Springfield rifle US service rifle, adopted 1903 and retained in service until the 1940s. Of .30 inch calibre, it used a ◊Mauser bolt mechanism and five-shot magazine. The name came from the Springfield, Massachusetts, arsenal where it was designed and originally manufactured.

Staaken German heavy bombing aircraft made by the Zeppelin Werke Staaken. The largest aircraft used in the war, these four-engined biplanes had a wingspan of 42.2 m/138.5 ft and weighed about 16,000 kg/8 tons empty. Though relatively slow, with a top speed of 130 kph/80 mph they had an enormous range (800 km/500 mi) and could carry up to 2,000 kg/4,400 lb of bombs. They were principally used on the Eastern Front and against London 1917–18.

star shell artillery projectile containing a magnesium flare and parachute, intended for illuminating the battlefield during night operations. It was fused so as to burst in the air and release the ignited flare to float to the ground, illuminating the area beneath. This allowed sentries to see patrols or an approaching enemy and could also be used during an attack to allow supporting weapons to fire at specific targets. Coloured star shells were also used for signalling purposes; these contained a varying numbers of coloured pyrotechnic stars without parachutes which simply fell through the sky to give a visual signal.

Stefanik General Milan Ratislav 1884–1919. Slovakian soldier and airman. In 1914 he joined the French Army as a private soldier and rapidly rose to the rank of general. He went to the Italian front 1916 and flew several missions to drop propaganda pamphlets on Czech troops of the Austro-Hungarian army. Active in rallying Czech and Slovak troops from all areas he worked with the Czech legion in Siberia 1918 and on the formation of the Czechoslovakian republic 1918 he became commander in chief and war minister. He was killed 1919 in a flying accident while on his way to Prague.

Stokes mortar trench ◊mortar invented by Sir Wilfrid Stokes 1915. It consisted of a smooth-bore steel barrel with a closed end, resting upon a baseplate and held up at about 45° by a bipod. A screw mechanism allowed the barrel to be adjusted for angles of elevation. It fired a simple cylindrical bomb with a perforated tube at the rear end into which a shotgun cartridge filled with powder was fitted. The front of the bomb carried a simple fuse based on that of the ◊Mills grenade. The bomb was dropped down the barrel, to strike a firing pin fixed at the base; this ignited the shotgun cartridge and the explosion of the powder ejected the bomb. The first bombs weighed about 9 kg/20 lb and had a range of about 900 km/1,000 yds; later bombs were lighter and had a greater range. The Stokes design was the prototype of every mortar designed since.

Stokhod Polish river, rising near Luck and flowing N to join the Pripet. In July 1916 the Russians, having driven the Austro-German forces from the ◊Styr, advanced on the Stokhod, crossed the river and broke through the Austrian defences, taking about 4,000 prisoners.

Sturdee Admiral Sir Frederick Charles Doveton 1859–1925. British sailor. He joined the navy 1871 and served in the Egyptian war 1882. By 1910 he was rear-admiral of the first battle squadron and then of the second cruiser squadron 1912–13. He became chief of the war staff 1914 and was sent by Lord ◊Fisher to find and defeat von ◊Spee after the battle of ◊Coronel, which he did at the battle of the ◊Falkland Islands 8 Dec 1914. He commanded the fourth battle squadron at ◊Jutland 1916 and was promoted to full admiral 1917. He was commander in chief of the important naval command at the Nore on the

Thames Estuary 1918–21, and became Admiral of the Fleet 1921. Knighted 1913, he was created a baron 1916 and received a grant of £10,000 for his war services.

Styr Polish river rising in Galicia and flowing N past Luck to join the Pripet near Pinsk. The ***Battles of the Styr*** were fought between Russian and Austro-German forces 1915–16.

The first battle followed the withdrawal of the Russians from Luck 28 Sept 1915 and was a fluctuating struggle in which the Russians gained ground to the north of the sector and the Austro-Germans to the south. The lines then remained relatively stable until the second battle June 1916 when Russian forces attacked a prominent Austro-German salient at Czartoryszk, cut it off, crossed the river and advanced on the ◊Stokhod.

submarine underwater warship. The first underwater boat was constructed for James I of England by the Dutch scientist Cornelius van Drebbel 1572–1633 in 1620. A naval submarine, or submersible torpedo boat, the Gymnote, was launched by France 1888. The conventional submarine of World War I was driven by a diesel engine on the surface and by battery-powered electric motors under water. The diesel engine also drove a generator that produced electricity to charge the batteries.

submarine warfare deployment of submarines during the war as a distinct form of naval tactics. Those belligerents with submarines entered the war with few clear ideas of how they should be employed. The most common view was that they were destroyers capable of submerging to fight, and it was felt that they should operate formally as part of a fleet, patrolling, scouting, and convoying. However, experience was to show that they operated best as individuals attacking enemy merchant shipping and warships with equal facility. It was also thought that their ability to submerge made them invulnerable, but this, too, was found to be false and they were a ready prey to depth charges and gunfire providing they could be located; it was the detection and location of submarines which formed the principal technical problem in defeating them. See also ◊U-boat, ◊Q- boat.

Suez Canal, defence of the British operations against the Turks 1914–15. Britain declared war on Turkey 5 Nov 1914 and proclaimed a protectorate over Egypt 17 Dec, thus making Britain responsible for defending Egypt and the Suez Canal. There were large Turkish forces in Syria with outposts close to the Egyptian border in the Sinai. On 2 Feb 1915 the Turks launched an attack on the canal between Lake Timsah and the Great Bitter Lake, but it was resisted and a joint British, Anzac, and Indian counter-attack drove them back into the desert. The Turks attempted another attack near Suez 22 March, but this was also beaten off. The British expedition into ◊Palestine then got under way, and there was no further threat to the Canal.

Sukhomlinov Vladimir 1848–1926. Russian soldier. He first came to prominence during the Russo-Japanese war 1904–05, after which he re-organized the Russian Army and became minister for war 1909–15. He was responsible for the mobilization plans of 1914 which put the Russian Army into the field much faster than the Germans expected, but early Russian defeats were blamed upon his failure to stockpile sufficient munitions and equipment, and he was charged with accepting bribes from army contractors. He was found guilty and sentenced to life imprisonment but was released 1918 and went into exile in Finland.

supply tank armoured vehicle used to carry ammunition, rations, water, and similar vital necessities to forward troops during an attack. It was usually a battle ◊tank without guns, but the British developed a special design, the Mark IX, which was longer than a normal tank and could carry 50 fully-equipped soldiers or 10 tons of supplies. Although 200 were ordered, only 3 had been built by the Armistice and only a further 20 were built.

Suvla Bay bay in ◊Gallipoli, W of the Dardanelles. Four British divisions were landed here with the object of capturing the Anafarta Hills, in conjunction with an Anzac attack on ◊Sari Bair; had the operation been successful it would have given the Allies complete control of the central heights of the peninsula. The landing was made during the evening of 6 Aug 1915 and reinforced on the following day; initial progress was good, and some commanding heights were taken, but the overall command was not sufficiently forceful and the opportunity to advance further in the face of weak Turkish opposition was not taken. By the time that General ◊Hamilton realised the situation and gave orders to attack, the Turks had been strongly reinforced with more troops and artillery and the subsequent British attack failed. More attacks were mounted over the next few days and a fresh commander brought in to try and break the deadlock, but no impression could be made on the Turkish positions and the Allied lines settled down to defend what they had.

Till long after dusk the troops struggled with a gallantry that richly deserved success, and they got none, not a shred that was worth a grenadier's bones.

Sir George McMunn on *Suvla Bay* in
Behind the Scenes in Many Wars.

Swinton Sir Ernest Dunlop 1868–1951. British soldier and historian, designer of the ◊tank. Swinton joined the army 1888, served in South Africa, and in 1914 became 'Eyewitness', the official war correspondent. Returning to London on leave Christmas 1914 he was pondering the problem of overcoming trenches and barbed wire when he saw a ◊Holt tractor towing a gun. This inspired him to draw up a paper proposing a 'power-driven, bullet-proof, armed engine capable of destroying machine guns, breaking through entanglements and climbing earthworks'. This paper eventually reached ◊Churchill, who set up the Admiralty Landships Committee, and from it emerged the tank. Swinton later commanded tanks in action, and drew up the tactical and operational manuals which governed their employment. He was promoted to major general 1919, knighted 1923, and was Chichele professor of military history at Oxford, 1925–39.

Sydney, HMAS Light cruiser of the Australian Navy. She caught the German cruiser Emden at Cocos Island 11 Nov 1914, opened fire, and drove the German vessel ashore in the first action ever fought by an Australian warship. The Sydney later served in the cruiser squadron under Admiral ◊Beatty.

Syria, operations in British operations against the Turks Sept–Dec 1918. After completing the conquest of ◊Palestine Sept 1918, General

◊Allenby crossed the Syrian border and advanced on Damascus, which was taken 1 Oct 1918. The Turkish garrison retreated north and by 8 Oct Beirut was in British hands. Homs was occupied a week later and with the entire railway system of S Syria in his control, Allenby's supply line was secure and he rapidly pushed columns forward. By 26 Oct he was in Aleppo and had taken 75,000 prisoners, 360 guns, and vast quantities of stores.

The Turks signed an Armistice 31 Oct 1918 under which they were to evacuate the entire country by 15 Dec, though it took pressure from Allenby to make them adhere to this condition. After 1919 the country passed into French control.

T

T-Stoff German chemical agent ◊xylyl bromide, so-called for security reasons after Dr von ◊Tappen who developed it as a war gas. It was first used against the Russians at ◊Bolimov 31 Jan 1915 – the first use of gas in any major operation in the war, pre-dating the more commonly known cloud attack at ◊Ypres by some four months – and then against the British at Nieuport March 1915.

Tank Production 1916–18

	Britain	France	Germany	Italy	USA
1916	150				
1917	1,277	800			
1918	1,391	4,000	20	6	84

tank armoured fighting vehicle moving on tracks rather than wheels, developed independently in Britain and France 1915–16. The British development programme arose from a proposal by Lt Col ◊Swinton, the French from a Col Baptiste Etienne who made a similar proposal to Marshal ◊Joffre Dec 1915.

The tank's supporters saw the need to mass produce the new vehicle before swamping the Germans with a massive attack, but in desperation at the stalemate in the battle of the ◊Somme, the first 47 tanks were sent into action there 15 Sept 1916. The first French tanks went into action 16 April 1917. The Germans, though at first impressed by British tanks, later decided they were unreliable devices and did not promote any research or development until the spring of 1917. Their first design, the A7V, appeared in prototype May 1917 but the shortage of raw materials and Hindenburg's poor opinion of the tank's value made production slow and only a handful were ever made.

The British design was developed and built by Foster's of Lincoln, makers of agricultural tractors. In an endeavour to keep the project secret, the test model was described as a 'water carrier for Mesopotamia', from which it became known in the factory as 'that tank thing'. This led Swinton to refer to the new machine in a progress report by the cover name tank and the name stuck. The French simply called it *char* (lit., 'car').

Tannenberg village in E Prussia (now Grunwald, Poland) 145 km/90 mi Ne of Warsaw; site of a victory by a German force under ◊Hindenburg over Russian armies under Generals ◊Samsonov and ◊Rennenkampf 1914.

In Aug 1914 General ◊Samsonov attacked E Prussia, defeating the Germans at Frankenau. Hindenburg concentrated a force of about 100,000 around Gumbinnen against both the immediate threat posed by Samsonov and that of Rennekampf's army which he knew was approaching from the north. Hindenburg was waiting for Samsonov's attack, resisted it, turned the Russian left flank, and drove him back to Hohenstein. The Russians attempted to make a stand there but were driven into retreat. Hindenburg now extended his left flank through Allenstein, with the intention of encircling Samsonov and driving a wedge between him and Rennenkampf. He surrounded Samsonov on three sides at Tannenberg, the fourth being swamps and lakes, and tore his army to shreds; only about 60,000 troops managed to escape back to Russia. The Germans took 90,000 prisoners and several hundred guns. Hindenburg then struck north against Rennenkampf but he, having seen what had happened to Samsonov, retreated to his base on the Niemen river line.

Tappen Dr Karl von 1879–1941. German chemist; member of the Kaiser Wilhelm Institute for Physical Chemistry in Berlin. In Oct 1914 he suggested to his brother, a staff officer at Army Headquarters, that ◊xylyl bromide put into artillery shells might be used as a chemical weapon. Tappen also interested Professor ◊Haber in the idea, and Haber was thus introduced to the idea of chemical warfare, in which he became a major figure.

Tappen was given the task of supervising the design and filling of the shells, which were first used against the Russian army at ◊Bolimov 31 Jan 1915. However, due to the severe cold the substance failed to

government and his offers to serve as an intermediary with
was refused. He never received another military appoint-
etired 1920.

d Hugh Montague, 1st Viscount, 1873–1956. British avia-
lice commissioner. He joined the army 1893 and served
mperial Yeomanry in the South African War 1899–1902
handed the Northern Nigeria Regiment 1908–13. In 1912
l to fly and became an instructor at the Central Flying
coming assistant commandant 1913.

outbreak of war he became commandant of the military
he ◊Royal Flying Corps◊ and Chief of the Air Staff July
cted to command the ◊Royal Air Force on its formation, he
ith his political masters and resigned, returning to France to
nand of the Independent Air Force, nine strategic bombing
which carried out over 500 raids on German targets. In
ecame Chief of Staff, RAF. He was made a baronet and pro-
air marshal 1919. In postwar years he became a strong
n the efficacy of strategic bombing, but left the RAF 1929,
Commissioner of the Metropolitan Police 1931–35.

ever infectious disease first observed in troops on the
front Dec 1914. It persisted throughout the war, attacking all
e impartially. The principal symptoms were headaches,
he legs, skin rash, and mild inflammation of the eyes but
mplications rarely occurred.

ease initially puzzled doctors since although it was one of
st causes of sickness among troops serving in the war it had
en seen in civil communities, though it resembles a mild
yphus. Conveyed by lice, it was characterized by a sudden
ing five or six days, after which the victim recovered with
nt after-effects. A second strain emerged 1917 in which the
uration of the fever became longer, and in 1918 there was a
number of victims suffering relapses more or less regularly
ls of a few days.

oot ailment afflicting the feet caused by prolonged standing
et conditions; in severe cases it was sometimes necessary to

vaporize as it should have done and so had no effect on the Russians.
The shells were tried again in March, this time against the British at
Nieuport, but once more failed. After this Tappen appears to have taken
no further interest in chemical warfare.

Tarnopol town in Polish Galicia (now Ternopol, Ukraine) about 70
miles SE of Lvov, one of the first sites of the more general collapse of
the Russian armies following the ◊Russian revolution 1917.

The Russian offensive had been halted by July 1917 and the Austro-
German forces began a counter-attack 19 July. At first they made little
progress, until the 6th Grenadier Division of the 11th Russian Army
deserted en masse due to Bolshevik agitation, leaving a gap in the
Russian line some 40 km/25 mi wide. Panic spread through the rest of
the 11th Army and many more men disappeared. ◊Brusilov was in
Tarnopol and had just ordered a change of command, so there was no
senior officer at the front capable of repairing the damage caused by the
desertions. The Austro-Germans attacked 20 July and were able to go
straight through the gap, as the Russian troops on their route showed no
inclination to obey their commanders or make any defence. In spite of a
last-minute stand by some loyal Russian regiments, there was little they
could do to stop the advance and Tarnopol fell to the Germans 22 July.
Within two days the whole Russian front was beginning to crumble.
The Austro-German forces kept up their advance until they reached the
Russian frontier at Husiatyn (now Gus'atyn), where they halted and
awaited the outcome of the dramatic events overwhelming Russia.

Taube German military aircraft. The Taube, a monoplane with a
Mercedes-Benz engine giving it a top speed of about 70 mph, was
designed by the Austrian Dr Etrich 1908. It was manufactured under
licence in Germany by the ◊Rumpler company and was adopted by the
German Army 1912. At the outbreak of war it was the principal aircraft
of the German Army and performed useful service as a scout, notably
in the detection of Russian movements which resulted in Hindenburg's
victory at ◊Tannenberg. It was also used to bomb Paris, though this
appears to have been with nothing larger than hand grenades and did
little damage. Soon outclassed as a fighting machine, it was adopted as
the basic training aircraft and several hundred were built by most
German aircraft companies.

Territorial Force British second-line reserve army, established 1907, absorbing the Yeomanry and Volunteer regiments. It was organized into 14 divisions, 14 brigades, and other units based upon county organizations. Men between the ages of 17 and 35 could enlist for a period of 4 years, during which time they underwent training in their spare time and attended a military camp each year. These volunteers undertook to serve in Britain in case of invasion but not abroad. The force's strength in 1914 was 255,864 and wartime recruitment up to 28 June 1916, when conscription was introduced, totalled 888,989. The 'not abroad' rule was waived during the war and territorial units were embodied, trained, and sent to France to reinforce the Regular Army. Total territorial casualties during the war came to 541,245 killed, wounded, and missing.

Thompson General John Tagliaferro 1860–1940. US soldier and weapons designer. Thompson joined the artillery 1882, transferred to the Ordnance Department 1890, and spent the rest of his military career in developing small arms, particularly the ◊Springfield M1903 rifle and Colt M1911 pistol.

He retired from the army Nov 1914, joined the Remington Arms Company as chief engineer, and began work on an automatic rifle. When the Remington company received orders for rifles from Britain late 1914 he set up a factory at Eddystone, Pennsylvania, to produce the ◊Enfield rifle, and in 1916 set up another to manufacture the Mosin-Nagant rifle for the Russian army. When the USA entered the war 1917 he was recalled to duty and to convert the British Enfield rifle production plants to make the US Enfield rifle (of •30 calibre). He was promoted to brigadier general and given responsibility for supplying small arms and ammunition to the American Expeditionary Force in France, and was awarded the Distinguished Service Medal for his services. He retired from the army again Dec 1918 and returned to his rifle design. For technical reasons it was impractical but, with the aid of his assistant engineers Eickhoff and Payne, he went on to develop the Thompson sub-machine gun 1920, which became famous as the 'Tommy-gun'.

Tirpitz Admiral Alfred Friedrich von 1849–1930. German admiral. He served in the Prussian Navy from 1865 until he became Prussian

minister of state 1898 when he devoted al navy capable of challenging Britain. He t the German Navy and chief of naval staff 1 a strong navy were undermined by opposit the programme and to his virulent anti-Brit

Consequently, when war threatened h not feel the navy was yet ready. When war of an immediate British invasion was pro face navy was not ready, shortly after announced a campaign of unrestricted subn Allies, but this was not widely supporte excluded from strategic conferences. He l treatment by tendering his resignation M it accepted, after which he played no sig devoting his time to politics.

Toc H British social organization, named at centre and canteen for officers and soldiei centre was at Talbot House in Poperinghe, 'Toc H' came from the phonetic telegraphic The Toc H organization was established aft religious organization for young men and throughout Britain.

Townshend Sir Charles Vere Ferrers 186 He joined the Royal Marines 1881 and India, where he came to prominence by his before returning to Africa. He was in Ind and was promoted to major general an Mesopotamia.

He was in charge of ◊Kut-al-Imara and a when it was besieged by the Turks Dec 191 Turks April 1916 after a siege of 147 days. T brutally, being forced to march 1,200 miles of them died. Townshend, however, was trea no representations about the treatment of his he was released by the Turks to plead their obtain favourable terms for a Turkish surren

the British
the Turks
ment and

Trencha
tor and p
with the
then com
he learne
School, b

On the
wing of t
1915. Sel
clashed w
take com
squadrons
1919 he b
moted to
believer i
becoming

trench
Western
sides qui
pains in
serious c

The dis
the greate
never be
form of t
fever last
no appar
average
rise in th
at interva

trench f
in cold, w

amputate the toes. It was a persistent problem for all armies fighting in the conditions of the Western Front, but could be alleviated by greasing the feet, frequent changes of socks, and waterproof footwear.

trench warfare general term covering the various new tactics and weapons developed to adapt to the largely static battlefronts which resulted from the two sides digging into continuous trench lines. Such tactics included wire entanglements, bombing raids, armour-plated loopholes for ◊snipers, provision of supply trenches, bombing trenches, listening posts, the provision of close-range shotguns, clubs and knives for raiding parties, and ◊mining and countermining.

Trentino, Campaigns in operations between Austrian and Italian troops 1915–18. Trentino was a district of the S Tyrol in Austria during the war, now a province of Italy; broadly, the area between Lake Garda and the Brenner Pass. This area was the Italian Army's first objective after declaring war on Austria and they began their advance 24 May 1915. By the end of the year they held a line a few miles past the north end of Lake Garda.

In May 1916 the Austrians assembled a force of about 350,000 and swept down between Trento and Roverino, destroying the Italians' line and driving them back to a line in the mountains SW of Roverino. The Austrian offensive then slackened and stopped. The Italians counter-attacked June 1916 and regained much of what they had previously held. More fighting in the summer of 1918 was inconclusive; the severe nature of the mountainous country and supply difficulties often cancelled out purely military considerations, and the struggle continued until the Austrian armistice 3 Nov 1918.

Troubridge Admiral Sir Ernest Charles Thomas 1862–1926. British sailor. He joined the navy 1878, was naval attache in Vienna, Tokyo, and Madrid 1901–04, captain and Chief of Staff Mediterranean fleet 1907–08, chief of Admiralty war staff 1911–12, and commanded the Mediterranean cruiser squadron 1912–13. In 1914 he was second-in-command of the Mediterranean fleet and was severely criticised for allowing the ◊Goeben to escape. He was court-martialled and acquitted of any fault but in 1915 was made head of the British naval mission to Serbia and he remained in this backwater for the rest of the war. In 1918 he was made president of the International Danube Commission, was knighted and promoted to admiral 1919 and retired 1921.

Tsingtao German colony in China (now Qing Dao) leased for 99 years from 1898 in recompense for the murder of two German missionaries. The Germans fortified the area and constructed a port and naval base. In 1914 the Japanese declared war on Germany and demanded the surrender of Tsingtao. The Germans refused and a Japanese force of 23,000 men and 142 guns besieged the colony 2 Sept 1914. The Japanese were joined 23 Sept by a combined British and Indian force of about 1,500 men. The siege was conducted in the traditional manner by trenching and mining, until the final assault was prepared 6 Nov. The fortress surrendered the following day and was handed over to the Japanese 10 Nov, whereupon the British withdrew. By an agreement of 25 May 1915 the Japanese undertook to hand the area back to the Chinese 'under certain conditions', most of which were the 'Twenty-One Demands' which were aimed at obtaining full control of Chinese economic and political affairs. China agreed to most of the demands, but Anglo-American objections to this self-aggrandizement led to the fall of the Japanese government.

Turkish Army although technically a conscript force, most of the male population escaped duty due to gross inefficiency. After the Balkan Wars 1912–13 showed up many of the defects in organization, training, and equipment, German instructors and guidance were sought. This had some effect; by 1914 the Turks were able to field four armies, although the actual number of men has never been accurately determined due to inefficient record-keeping. Administration and supply were the Turks' weakest links; the fighting quality of the soldiers was never in dispute. The force expanded to nine armies during the war years, and it has been estimated that about 2.5 million men served during the war, though the actual fighting strength at any one time was never more than about 700,000.

Turner General Sir Richard Ernest 1871–1948. Canadian soldier. He served in the South African war 1899–1902, where he won the Victoria Cross. During World War I he commanded a brigade, then a division in France until he was appointed General Officer Commanding Canadian forces in Britain and chief military adviser to the Canadian government Dec 1916. Knighted 1917, he became Chief of the Canadian General Staff responsible for all overseas forces May 1918.

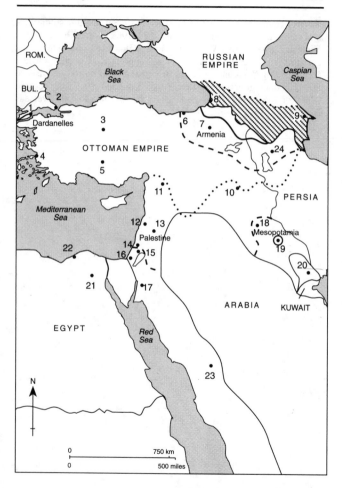

THE MIDDLE EAST 1914–18

Key

——— Maximum Allied advance 1915

– – – Allied advance by Dec. 1917

• • • • • Turkish line at surrender 30 Oct. 1918

▨▨▨ Turkish gains against Russia 1918

Cities/towns

1	Gallipoli	13	Damascus
2	Constantinople	14	Megiddo
3	Ankara	15	Jerusalem
4	Izmir	16	Gaza
5	Konya	17	Aqaba
6	Trabzon	18	Baghdad
7	Erzerum	19	Kut-al-Imara
8	Batum	20	Basra
9	Baku	21	Cairo
10	Mosul	22	Alexandria
11	Aleppo	23	Medina
12	Beirut	24	Tabriz

U

U-Boat (*Untersee-Boot*) German term for submarine. The U-Boat branch of the navy was organized in four flotillas, usually totalling about 60 vessels at any one time. Some 810 were built during the course of the war of which 210 were lost, either by accident or enemy action.

It is inevitable that when the Germans fully realise the capabilities of this type of submarine.the North Sea and all its ports will be rendered uninhabitable by our big ships, until we have cleaned out their submarines.
  Admiral Fisher on *U-Boats* in *The Submarine Question*, April 1909.

unknown soldier unidentified dead soldier for whom a tomb is erected as a memorial to all other unidentified soldiers killed in war.
  In Britain, the practice began in World War I; the British Unknown Soldier was buried in Westminster Abbey 1920. The USA also has a Tomb of the Unknown Soldier in Arlington, Virginia. France and Belgium are among the other countries to adopt the practice, most subsequent to World War I.

V

Vardar Balkan river, it rises in Serbia, flows NW then SE and empties into the Gulf of Salonika. It was the scene of two battles, both part of the operations surrounding ◊Salonika. The *first battle* took place Oct 1915 when a joint French and British force moved up the Vardar valley from Salonika to assist the Serbs against the Bulgarians. Outnumbered about four to one by the Bulgarians, the Allied forces fell back and retired into Greece 12 Dec.

The *second battle* came Sept 1918 and opened with a strong offensive by the Serbs and French SE of ◊Monastir while British forces were attacking on the ◊Doiran-Struma Front. The French and Serbs drove the Bulgarians up the valley until the Bulgarians signed an Armistice 20 Sept.

Vassich General Peter 1862–1931. Serbian soldier. A colonel 1914, in 1915 he commanded a Serbian force which resisted the Austro-German advance and defeated a Bulgarian attempt at invasion. He commanded an army corps at ◊Monastir 1916 and led the re-constituted ◊Serbian army in the second battle in the ◊Vardar valley Sept–Oct 1918 and played a leading part in the liberation of Serbia.

Vaux-Fossoy, Battle of battle between US and German forces July 1918. Vaux and Fossoy are villages close to ◊Chateau-Thierry and in July 1918 were held by the US 3rd Division. A German attack against Vaux 15 July was held and then driven back by US troops, who succeeded in following up and taking several German positions. Later in the day another German force crossed the river Marne and took Fossoy, but again the US troops counter-attacked and drove the Germans back across the river.

Verdun French fortress town in the *département* of the Meuse, 174 miles E of Paris, scene of bitter fighting for much of the war. It became a first-class fortress after the experience of the Franco-Prussian war 1870, its ring of modern forts being one of the principal French frontier defences. In 1916 the Germans attacked it in great strength; it had great psychological value to the French and the Germans assumed that they would throw large masses of troops into battle rather than lose it. The German plan was not necessarily to capture Verdun but to decimate the French army by constant bombardment and attack. The battle continued for the rest of the year, both sides moving back and forth capturing and re-capturing forts and ground, until the fighting finally died away early Dec 1916. The French lost an estimated 348,300 men, but the German losses were 328,500.

The front then remained relatively stable until the French launched an offensive to regain some of their lost territory Aug 1917. They succeeded in regaining the ◊Mort d'Homme area by 12 Sept and captured about 10,000 prisoners and 100 guns. Although an attack from Verdun northwards would have liberated useful territory and threatened the German lines of communication throughout the war, German defences in this sector were extremely strong and it was not until Sept 1918, after the reduction of the ◊St Mihiel salient, that a successful attack was launched as part of the general Allied offensive.

Versailles Council Allied military co-ordinating committee. After the Italian defeat at ◊Caporetto Oct 1917 ◊Lloyd George led a movement to set up a supreme Allied council to co-ordinate the military effort. A leading soldier from each Allied country sat on the council, although most soldiers were critical of the idea of command by committee and General ◊Robertson resigned from his position as British Chief of Staff in protest. In fact it was largely a piece of political mischief by Lloyd George who detested both ◊Haig and Robertson and hoped to isolate them and reduce their authority. In the event, the ◊German Spring Offensive 1918 and the appointment of Marshal ◊Foch as Allied supreme commander made the council redundant and it had no further effect on the war.

Versailles, Treaty of peace treaty between the Allies and Germany ending World War I, signed 28 June 1919. Germany surrendered Alsace-Lorraine to France, and large areas in the east to Poland, and made smaller cessions to Czechoslovakia, Lithuania, Belgium, and

Denmark. The Rhineland was demilitarized, German rearmament was restricted, and Germany agreed to pay reparations for war damage. The treaty was never ratified by the USA, which made a separate peace with Germany and Austria 1921. It also established the League of Nations.

Vickers British engineering company, prominent in the manufacture of munitions. In addition to naval and land artillery, the company gave its name to the 'Vickers gun', a modified form of the ◊Maxim machine gun, adopted by the British army 1912, as well as to a series of aircraft.

The Vickers F.B.5, generally known as the 'Vickers gun-bus', was a pusher biplane (with the engine behind the pilot so that the propeller pushed rather than pulled the machine), with the observer seated in the front with a Vickers machine gun. First flown 1913 it was one of the earliest combat aircraft in the world, though due to a series of modifications and changes it did not actually go into action until July 1915. Although slow, it proved an efficient fighting scout machine until confronted with improved German aircraft with synchronized guns. The Vickers Vimy was a twin-engined heavy bomber designed for the Independent Air Force element of the ◊Royal Air Force, with a great enough range to attack Berlin, but it was too late for the war. It went on to acquire fame as the first aircraft to fly the Atlantic Ocean non-stop June 1919 and fly from Britain to Australia Nov 1919.

Vilar Perosa Italian machine gun. Specially designed for use by mountain troops, it consisted of two small and simple machine guns firing 9 mm pistol ammunition attached to a frame which the soldier carried on his chest, secured by a strap around his neck. It had a very high rate of fire and proved somewhat impractical, so the guns were then removed from the frame and fitted individually into conventional stocks to become sub-machine guns.

Vimy Ridge hill in N France, taken by Canadian troops during the battle of ◊Arras, April 1917, at the cost of 11,285 lives. It is a spur of the ridge of Notre Dame de Lorette, 8 km/5 mi NE of Arras.

Vindictive, HMS British cruiser armed with ten 6 inch guns, 5,700 tons displacement. By 1918 the ship was obsolete and was refitted with boarding gangways and used to raid the Belgian port of ◊Zeebrugge 23 April. After this raid, which resulted in some damage to the upper works of the ship, it was filled with several hundred tons of concrete and used as a blockship in the raid on ◊Ostend 10 May 1918, where it was sunk in an attempt to block the harbour entrance. It lay there until it was raised and presented to Belgium 1920.

Virton Belgian town in the SW of the country, close to the French border about 65 km/40 mi NW of Metz; site of a French defeat by the Germans Aug 1914. The French thought the Germans only had 14 corps in Belgium at this early stage of the war and so the 3rd and 4th French armies advanced to the town 21 Aug on a 97 km/60 mi front from the French border. In fact the Germans had 27 corps in the area, most of which were marching across the French front from Luxembourg to Belgium. In order to avoid alerting the Germans to their advance, the French were forbidden by GHQ to send out scouts and were ordered to move only at night, through hilly and forested country. Consequently when they met the German forces it was in small individual parties which invariably got the worst of the exchange. The French continued to advance as the Germans poured in on their right flank trying to reach their rear, leading to heavy French losses with no corresponding gains.

A general retreat began 22 Aug as General ◊Langle de Cary's 4th Army fell back on Sedan and the Meuse, placing the whole French front in danger through his failure to hold the Germans. The 3rd French Army was also in difficulties, having run into a strong German force with several artillery units, which the French were unable to counteract since their own artillery was still struggling through the forests. However, their commander, General ◊Ruffey, managed to hold his troops together, pulled back a short distance, and called for his reserves so as to mount a full attack. At this point Marshal ◊Joffre withdrew Ruffey's reserve troops to use elsewhere and ordered the 3rd Army to fall back into line with the 4th. Ruffey, who had been the only French general to show any spirit against the Germans in this battle, was relieved of his command and held no important post for the remainder of the war.

Vittorio Veneto, Battle of official Italian name for their victory over the Austrians, Oct–Nov 1918, which heralded Austria's final defeat. Also called the third battle of the ◊Piave.

Voisin French aircraft. Voisin made the first practicable aircraft in Europe and early 1914 developed a two-seat pusher biplane (with the engine behind the pilot so that the propeller pushed rather than pulled the machine) with a short fuselage and the tail unit carried on an open framework. It was a rather unusual design in that the pilot sat at the front, with the observer standing behind him and firing the machine gun over his head. This basic design, with periodic improvements, was turned out in large numbers for the French air service, and a Voisin III shot down the first enemy aircraft to fall in combat 5 Oct 1914. Principally used as bombers, later models carrying up to 300 kg/660 lb of bombs, they were also used in reconnaissance and training roles and many were built in Britain under licence.

W

war graves graves of soldiers who fell during the war, buried in the war zones. Vast cemeteries were established after the war by the countries which fought in the various theatres, and in France and Belgium, where most war graves lie, the land was presented to the countries whose men are buried there. Each nation established its own Graves Commission to supervise the construction, interment, and maintenance of the cemeteries, which has continued to the present day. It is noteworthy that, without formal agreement, the warring armies avoided damaging these cemeteries during World War II.

Warsaw capital city of Poland, on the river Vistula. The Germans attacked Warsaw Sept 1914 in order to relieve Russian pressure on the Austrians in Galicia, and hoping to take the city and conquer Poland up to the line of the Vistula. Five armies, totalling 1.5 million men, advanced under ◊Hindenburg, four against Warsaw and one against Ivangorod (now Deblin). By 15 Oct the Germans were outside Warsaw but a powerful Russian force from the Niemen swung across the Vistula north of Warsaw and struck the German flank and rear in the *first battle of Warsaw* 15–21 Oct, compelling them to withdraw.

The Germans made a second attempt to take the city to parry a Russian thrust against Cracow Nov 1914. Hindenburg set out again, this time with 2 million men, striking south from Thorn in E Prussia (now Torun, Poland), in the *second battle* 7–13 Dec. The attack was diverted from Warsaw by the need to deal with various Russian manoeuvres. A third attempt on the city was made Jan 1915. This was foiled by the Russians holding off the Germans at the battle of ◊Bolimov. Eventually the Russians decided that holding on to Russian Poland was too expensive and they conducted a skilled fighting retreat, holding the Germans on a line east of Warsaw for long enough to allow the city to be cleared of all military stores and personnel. The Vistula bridges were then blown and the city abandoned; the Germans finally captured it 5 Aug 1915.

Western Front battle zone in World War I between Germany and the Allies, primarily France and Britain, extending as lines of trenches from Nieuport on the Belgian coast through Ypres, Arras, Albert, Soissons, and Rheims to Verdun, constructed by both Germany and the Allies.

For over three years neither side advanced far from their defensive positions. During the period of trench warfare there were a number of significant changes. Poison ◊gas was used by Germany at Ypres April 1915 and ◊tanks were employed by Britain on the River Somme Sept 1916. The German spring offensive of 1918 enabled the troops to reach the Marne River. By summer the Allies were advancing all along the front and the Germans were driven back into Belgium.

Wester-Wemyss Admiral Rosslyn Erskine Wemyss, First Baron (more commonly known as Sir Rosslyn Wemyss) 1864–1933. British sailor. He joined the navy 1877 and by 1912–13 was commander of the 2nd Battle Squadron. He commanded the naval squadron at ◊Gallipoli 1916 and provided naval support for the subsequent evacuation. He became First Sea Lord 1917, a post he held until 1919 when he was raised to the peerage. He became admiral of the fleet 1920.

Weygand General Maxime 1867–1965. French soldier. He joined the artillery 1887 and was appointed Chief of Staff to Marshal ◊Foch 1914. Took part in most of the major French operations on the Western Front and was appointed French representative on the ◊Versailles Council 1917. He rejoined Foch March 1918 and his work in the critical battles of 1918 was highly regarded.

He had a distinguished career following the end of the war, becoming military adviser to the Polish Army 1920, and rising to become commander in chief of the French Army before retiring 1935. He was recalled to serve during World War II but was captured by the Germans 1940.

Whippet tank British light tank, officially known as the 'Medium Mark A'. It differed from the other, lozenge-shaped, British tanks in having a low-set track, engine at the front, and an armoured

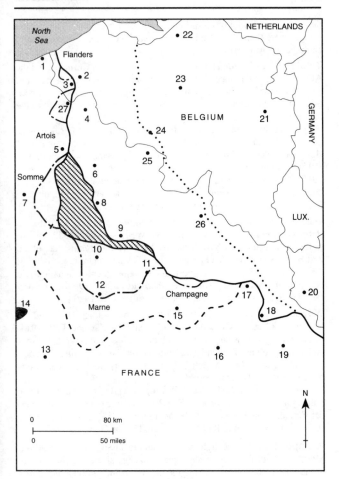

THE WESTERN FRONT 1914–18

Key

– – –   Maximum German advance Sept. 1914

———   Front line 1915–17

——--   Maximum German advance Spring 1918

· · · · ·   Armistice line Nov. 11 1918

▨▨▨   German-held territory evacuated during retreat to 'Hindenburg' line March 1917

Cities/towns

1	Dunkirk	14	Paris
2	Passchendaele	15	Châlons-s. Marne
3	Ypres	16	St Dizier
4	Lille	17	Verdun
5	Arras	18	St Mihiel
6	Cambrai	19	Toul
7	Amiens	20	Metz
8	St Quentin	21	Liège
9	Laon	22	Antwerp
10	Soissons	23	Brussels
11	Reims	24	Mons
12	Château Thierry	25	Maubeuge
13	Melun	26	Mézières
		27	Armentières

compartment at the rear for the crew of three. Armed with three or four machine guns, it had a top speed of 12.5 kph/8 mph and was intended as a reconnaissance and pursuit machine to fill the role of cavalry in a break-through. Production began late 1917 and numbers were used on the Western Front and in Mesopotamia.

whizzbang British soldier's name for shells fired by German 77 mm field guns, since their velocity was greater than the speed of sound so that the victim heard the 'whizz' of the shell before he heard the 'bang' of the gun and hence had no warning.

Wilhelm Frederick, Crown Prince 1882–1951. Eldest son of Kaiser ◊Wilhelm. In 1914 he was given nominal command of a group of armies on the Western Front, but did not distinguish himself, the actual command being conducted by officers of the General Staff. In 1918 he accompanied his father into exile in Holland and retired into private life.

Wilhelm Kaiser 1859–1941. German emperor and King of Prussia 1888–1918. In 1890 he dismissed Chancellor Bismarck and took over the direction of German foreign policy, determined to find Germany its 'place in the sun', seeking colonies and enlarging the army and navy.

He declared war on Russia in response to Russian mobilization 1 Aug 1914, France 3 Aug, and invaded Belgium 4 Aug, thus bringing Britain into the war. During the war he toured the various fronts as nominal commander in chief but left the direction of the war to ◊Hindenburg and ◊Ludendorff. He failed to see Germany's collapse was imminent in 1918 and only finally abdicated 9 Nov, going into exile in Holland. The Allies declared him a war criminal and demanded his extradition 1920 but the Dutch refused and he remained there until his death.

Wilson Sir Henry Hughes 1864–1922. British soldier. He joined the army 1884, serving in Burma and the South African war 1899–1902. Commandant of the Staff College 1907–10 and then director of military operations 1910–14, he went to France 1914 on the staff of Sir John ◊French. His performance during the retreat from ◊Mons was not inspiring and he was posted out of harm's way as liaison officer to the French GHQ. He was given command of a corps Dec 1915–Nov 1916 and then returned to his liaison role. He fell foul of General ◊Pétain and was summarily dismissed, returning to Britain to take over the Eastern Command of the Home Forces. He was then sent on a mission to Russia 1916 but on returning home was appointed to the ◊Versailles Council by Lloyd George who thereby hoped to gain supreme command of the war. He moved from this post to take over as Chief of the Imperial General Staff in place of General ◊Robertson. Rewarded for his war service by a baronetcy, promotion to field marshal, and a grant of £10,000 he retired 1922. He then involved himself in Irish politics and was murdered by two Sinn Fein gunmen in London June 1922.

The world must be made safe for democracy.
Woodrow ***Wilson***, address to Congress 2 Apr 1917.

Wilson Thomas Woodrow 1856–1924. 28th president of the USA 1913–21, a Democrat. He strove to keep the US neutral during World War I, but the unrestricted German U-boat campaign, sensationalized by the sinking of the British liner Lusitania (with 128 US citizens lost), forced him to declare war 1917. In Jan 1918 he issued his ◊'Fourteen Points' as a basis for a just peace settlement. At the peace conference in Paris he secured the inclusion of the League of Nations in individual peace treaties, but his refusal to compromise on the text of the League of Nations proposal contributed to Congress's refusal to ratify the treaties. In 1919 Wilson suffered a stroke during a nationwide campaign to gain support for the League and retired from public life. He was awarded the Nobel Peace Prize 1919.

women's services organized bodies of women forming part of military or other forces. Prior to 1914 the only place for women in war was nursing, but the shortage of manpower in every combatant nation led to the introduction of women, not only in industry but in the armed forces. However, their participation was strictly in non-combatant roles such as clerical work, cooking, store-keeping, driving motor vehicles and ambulances, and as telephone operators and telegraphists. These organizations were all disbanded by 1920, but were hurriedly revived at the outbreak of World War II 1939.

Woolwich arsenal principal British government arsenal, on the river Thames E of London. Established in the 17th century it was composed of three main units: the Royal Gun Factory; the Royal Carriage Department (making gun carriages and mountings); and the Royal Laboratory (making ammunition). Before 1914 it was the principal munitions manufacturing plant in the country, though certain work was contracted out to engineering companies such as ◊Vickers. However, the demands of wartime meant that more government factories had to be set up and more work placed out to civil firms, though Woolwich always retained its place as the senior establishment and was responsible for the design and development of new weapons. At the outbreak of war it employed about 14,000 people; at the Armistice 97,000.

Woyrsch General Remus von 1847–1925. German soldier. He joined the army 1866 and fought in the Franco-Prussian War 1870–71. In 1914 he was one of Hindenburg's staff during the first attacks on Russia, and in 1915 commanded various formations in SW Poland, as far as the Vistula. Operating with ◊Kovess, he captured ◊Ivangorod 4 Aug 1915. In 1916 he commanded the German 9th Army on the Eastern Front before being retired on reaching the age of 70.

Wrangel General Peter Nikolaievich, Baron von 1878–1928. Russian general. Educated at the School of Military Engineering, he served in the Russo-Japanese War and then transferred to the cavalry. Promoted to general, he commanded a division of Cossacks during the war, but on the abdication of the Tsar he joined forces with Alexieff, and when the Bolsheviks took power he sided with ◊Denikin. In 1920, after succeeding Denikin as commander in chief of the White Army, he was defeated by the Bolsheviks in the Crimea, was evacuated with the remainder of his troops by the British, and then vanished from the scene. Later he became a mining engineer in Brussels.

Württemberg Duke Albrecht von 1865–. German soldier, commander in chief of the German 3rd Army, operating in the Ardennes and Luxembourg, 1914–17. His forces advanced to the Plain of Chalons, moved back in the general retreat after the Battle of the ◊Marne, and later captured Dixmude in Belgium. In 1917 he was moved to command in the Vosges region and served there for the remainder of the war.

Son of the Duke of Württemberg and Archduchess Theresa of Austria, he was commissioned into the German cavalry 1883, and became a general 1908.

X

xylyl bromide lachrymatory (tear) gas, first used by the Germans at ◊Bolimov 31 Jan 1915 under the name '◊T-Stoff'. It was highly effective and relatively non-lethal, but was found to corrode its containers and was not very effective at low temperatures. It was also readily absorbed by the charcoal used in gas-mask canisters and thus by 1917 had been replaced by more powerful agents. About 500 tons were used in artillery shells by the Germans and although this caused no serious casualties, it demonstrated the tactical possibilities of gas shells and paved the way for more effective chemical agents.

Y

Yankovich Bosa. Serbian soldier. He played an important part in the Balkan Wars 1912–13, commanding the 3rd Serbian Army. In 1914 he repelled the Austrian invasion attempt and was prominent in rearguard actions during the great retreat of the ◊Serbian Army 1915. In 1918 he led a combined Serbian and Montenegrin army with distinction in ◊Salonika.

York Alvin Cullum 1887–1964. US war hero. Although a conscientious objector, York was drafted as a private in the 82nd Infantry Division in World War I and promoted to the rank of sergeant. At the Battle of the ◊Argonne Forest 8 Oct 1918, York led a charge against a German position in which he and his comrades captured 132 prisoners and 35 machine guns. A film biography, *Sergeant York*, appeared 1940. He was awarded the Congressional Medal of Honour and the French *Croix de Guerre*.

Ypres Belgian town in W Flanders, 40 km/25 mi S of Ostend, site of three major battles 1914–17 between German and Allied forces.

The *first battle* took place Oct–Nov 1914 when a British offensive aimed at securing the Channel ports of Dunkirk and Ostend clashed with a German offensive aimed at taking those ports. The subsequent fighting was extremely heavy and ended with the Germans gaining the ◊Messines Ridge and other commanding ground but with the British and French holding a salient around Ypres extending into the German line. German losses were estimated at 150,000 men, British and French at about the same number.

The *second battle* April–May 1915 opened with a German chlorine gas attack; this made a huge gap in the Allied lines but the Germans were unprepared for this success and were unable to exploit it before the Allies rushed in reserves. More gas attacks followed, and the

British were driven to shorten their line, so making the Ypres Salient a smaller incursion into the German line.

The *third battle* (also known as Passchendaele) took place July–Nov 1917. An allied offensive, including British, Canadian, and Australian troops, was launched under British commander in chief Douglas Haig, in an attempt to capture ports on the Belgian coast held by Germans. The long and bitter battle, fought in appalling conditions of driving rain and waterlogged ground, achieved an advance of only 8 km/5 mi of territory that was of no strategic significance, but the Allies alone lost more than 300,000 casualties.

The *fourth battle* (also known as the Battle of the Lys) took place 9–27 April 1918 and formed the second of the major attacks in the German Spring Offensive. Preceded by a heavy artillery bombardment, the German thrust cut through the Portuguese lines in front of Neuve Chapelle and thus created a gap in the British lines through which a mass of German infantry was able to pour, capturing some 7,000 British troops and 100 guns. The German attack was slowed and Haig issued his famous order 'There is no other course than to fight it out with our backs against the wall'. The German advance was finally halted on a line roughly between Ypres and Hazebrouck, where they remained until the Allied autumn offensive began.

Yser, Battle of the battle between Allied and German forces 15–31 Oct 1914 as the last part of the ♢race to the sea. This battle saw the successful defence of the river Yser from Nieuport to Dixmude by a mixed Belgian and French force against the 4th German army.

Allied troops took up positions on a railway embankment and, with support from British ♢monitors shelling German positions from the sea, managed to stave off successive German attacks. The Germans brought up heavy artillery and the Belgians, running short of ammunition, decided to open the sluices at Nieuport and let the sea flood the area in front of their position, which lay below sea level. Several hundred German troops were drowned, but the Germans managed to capture Dixmude, though without penetrating the rest of the line, which stayed more or less firm for the remainder of the war.

Yudenich General Nikolai Nikolaevich 1862–1933. Russian soldier. He joined the army 1879 and saw service in the Russo-Japanese war

1904–05. In 1914 he was Chief of Staff and de facto commander of the Army of the Caucasus (the Grand Duke Nicholas was in nominal command) and defeated the Turkish offensive in the Caucasus led by ◊Enver Pasha 1915. In 1916 he captured ◊Erzerum and Trebizond and conquered Turkish Armenia. He turned up again in Finland 1919 and commanded White Russian forces in an offensive against the Bolsheviks near Petrograd (now St Petersburg) but was defeated and went into retirement.

Z

Zeebrugge Belgian coastal town in the province of West Flanders. Occupied by the Germans 1914, it became a major submarine and torpedo-boat base. It was frequently bombarded by British warships and bombed from the air but the Germans built large concrete shelters which were impervious to the bombs of the time for their submarines.

It was finally put out of action by a British attack 23 April 1918. A party of Royal Marines was landed from HMS Vindictive on the 'mole' or breakwater, to cause what damage they could, while a submarine packed with explosives went beneath the bridge connecting the mole with the shore and exploded, cutting off the defenders on the mole from any reinforcement. All this was a diversion to attract the attention of the German defences, and while they were diverted, three blockships, obsolete cruisers filled with concrete, were sailed into the harbour and sunk in the channel so as to prevent any German vessels entering or leaving. The Vindictive then recovered the landing parties and sailed back to England, leaving Zeebrugge sealed up for the rest of the war.

Zeppelin Count Ferdinand von 1838–1917. German ◊airship pioneer. On retiring from the army 1891, he devoted himself to the study of aeronautics, and his first airship was built and tested 1900. He also helped to pioneer large multi-engine bomber planes (see ◊Staaken).

By 1906 he had developed a practical airship and the German government then subsidised him with a National Zeppelin Fund. At the outbreak of war the German Navy owned a number of Zeppelin airships and ordered more; the German Army at first used Schutte-Lanze airships but then adopted the Zeppelin design, and both forces used them for air raids on Britain and France 1915–16. As the Allied air defence organization improved, the large size and slow speed of the Zeppelin made it a relatively easy target, and their use for bombing purposes ended in late 1917. They remained in use for supply purposes; in Nov 1917 Zeppelin L57 flew from Jamboli in Bulgaria to Dakla Oasis in W Egypt and back – 2,400 miles – in 24 hours.

Zimmerman telegram ciphered telegram sent by Alfred Zimmermann, German foreign secretary, to von Eckhardt, German ambassador to Mexico. In it he proposed that Eckhardt discuss with Mexico the recovery of their 'lost' territories of Texas, New Mexico, and Arizona in the event of US-German hostilities. He also made remarks on unrestricted submarine warfare against the USA and the possibility of inveigling Japan into an alliance with Mexico. The message was intercepted and deciphered by the British naval intelligence service of ◊Room 40, and a copy was passed to the US Ambassador, who in turn sent it to the US State Department. President ◊Wilson permitted it to be published 1 March 1917 and its contents caused a public outcry and played a considerable part in the US decision to declare war 6 April 1917. Zimmermann 'resigned' shortly afterward.

Zion Mule Corps Jewish military unit of the British Army. It was formed in Egypt from Zionist refugees from Palestine by a Lt Jablonsky, a Russian journalist, and commanded by a British officer Lt Col Patterson. It served with distinction in ◊Gallipoli 1915, carrying rations and ammunition to the forward troops, and after the evacuation of the peninsula the corps was merged with the ◊Jewish regiment 1917.

Appendix

Military Strengths: Divisions at the Front 1914–18

	1914 Aug	Dec	1915 May	1916 Feb	Aug	July
Belgium		6	6	6	6	6
Britain		20	67	77	79	81
France		74	74	81	99	102
Greece		3	3	4	7	10
Italy				36	38	47
Portugal						
Rumania					21	
Russia		108	108	112	136	142
Serbia		12	12	12	6	6
USA						
Allied total		220	267	324	364	405
Austria		49	57	64	60	70
Bulgaria					12	12
Germany		94	117	149	159	169
Turkey		37	38	52	53	
Central Powers total		143	212	248	283	304

	1917 Oct	Mar	1918 July	Oct	Nov
Belgium	6	12	12	12	12
Britain	87	85	85	85	85
France	116	114	114	114	114
Greece	3	4	7	10	10
Italy	66	53	56	58	58
Portugal	1	2			
Rumania					
Russia	202				
Serbia	6	6	6	6	6
USA	3	5	25	32	42
Allied total	505-	281	305	324	329
Austria	78	78	72	74	66
Bulgaria	12	12	12		
Germany	234	234	235	214	210
Turkey	45	41	37	37	17
Central Powers total	369	365	356	325	278

* Divisions reduced in size

Principal actions of World War I

1914
Western Front

16 Aug	Liège
23 Aug	Mons
5–10 Sept	first battle of the Marne
14–20 Sept	Aisne
2 Oct	Arras
10 Oct	La Bassée
12 Oct	first battle of Messines
15 Oct	Yser
19 Oct–17 Nov	first battle of Ypres
16 Dec	Givenchy
20 Dec	first battle of Champagne

Eastern Front

7 Aug	Russian invasion of East Prussia
18 Aug	Russian invasion of Galicia
20 Aug	Gumbinnen
23 Aug	Lemberg
26–31 Aug	Tannenberg
28 Aug–8 Sept	Niemen
3–11 Sept	Rava Russka
15–21 Oct	first battle of Warsaw
11–25 Nov	Lodz
7–13 Dec	second battle of Warsaw

Balkan Front

12 Aug	Austrian invasion of Serbia
8 Sept	Drina

Mesopotamian Front

7 Nov	British landing in Mesopotamia

Sea

5 Aug	first German loss: minelayer *Königin Louise*
6 Aug	first Allied loss: HMS *Amphion*
28 Aug	Heligoland Bight

22 Sept	HMS *Aboukir, Hogue* & *Cressy* sunk by *U-9*
1 Nov	Coronel
8 Dec	Falkland islands
16 Dec	bombardment of the Hartlepools

1915
Western Front

10–13 Mar	Neuve Chapelle
22 Apr-25 May	second battle of Ypres
26 Jun-4 July	Argonne
25 Sept–6 Nov	second battle of Champagne
25 Sept–8 Oct	Loos

Eastern Front

31 Jan	Bolimov
2 May	Gorlitz–Tarnow Offensive
5 Aug	third battle of Warsaw and capture of the city
25 Aug	Brest-Litovsk
19 Sept	Vilna

Italian Front

23 June	first battle of Isonzo
18 July	second battle of Isonzo
18 Oct	third battle of Isonzo
10 Nov	fourth battle of Isonzo

Balkan Front

6 Oct	Austro–German invasion of Serbia
11 Oct	Bulgarian invasion of Serbia

Dardanelles

19 Feb	first Allied naval bombardment
25 Feb	second Allied naval bombardment
18 Mar	Allied naval attack
25 Apr	first Allied landings